A FATE WORSE THAN HOLLYWOOD

A Fate
Worse than
Hollywood

A MEMOIR

DAVID AMBROSE

Z

CHAPTER 1

The family never entirely came to terms with Uncle Harry's homosexuality. Nor for that matter, I suspect, did Harry himself.

He was one of four brothers all born within a span of ten years. My father, Eddie, born in 1905, and Harry, born in 1907, were the middle two. The eldest was Horace, a cobbler who later rose in the world to become a chiropodist. The youngest was Tom, a self-employed plasterer with his own little firm that kept him in modest comfort and left him time enough for his ruling passions of golf and home-brewed beer.

I don't remember when I first became aware of subtle undercurrents suggesting that Uncle Harry had been recognised as "different" all his life. I suspect it was an unacknowledged truth that had been absorbed into the family's collective unconscious long before my time. "Eeee," or "By 'eck," I would hear with the frequency of some kind of mantra, "our 'Arry should've been born a lass."

When eventually I inquired about the significance of this observation, my father said only, "Well, when us lads were all out playing football, he'd be indoors, knitting, and dressing up his dolls".

It was said without any obvious disapproval or hint of a sneer, more in a tone of innocent incomprehension, though I came to suspect in time that denial played a part in the family's (there were two sisters as well) general attitude.

Mind you, it has to be said that Harry himself went to considerable lengths to avoid the risk of any breath of scandal attaching to his or the family's name. With good reason, of course: in those days not only was homosexuality a criminal offence punishable by imprisonment, it represented scandal and disgrace on a scale unimaginable to the lower-middle and "respectable" working classes of small-town and rural Lancashire. It was discussed, if at all, only between consenting male adults in hushed voices at a safe distance from the womenfolk and children. In fact women for the most part had no idea that such a thing existed. Noël Coward and his ilk were simply "gay" in the old-fashioned sense of the word, "confirmed bachelors" because they hadn't had the luck to find the right girl yet. Occasional press reports of celebrity arrests in public lavatories or some dark corner of St James's Park were phrased in such a way as not to alarm the determinedly pure of heart. "Indecent behaviour" was, after all, a term vague enough to cover a myriad of social solecisms that did not necessarily threaten the very fabric of society.

So Uncle Harry married. He married my mother's sister, who was twelve years older than he was. Marion was a gentle, kindly and naive soul, verging on the truly dim. I cannot be entirely sure, since I never explicitly questioned her on the subject, but I doubt whether the dear thing had even the most rudimentary idea of what sexual relations actually involved. Spoilt by her father, an alcoholic rent collector who doted on her, she had grown up almost preternaturally insulated from the knocks and hardships of an impoverished childhood.

Even though, like my mother, she had been pulled out of school and sent to work in the local cotton mill at the age of twelve, the world seemed to glide past her leaving absolutely no impression. It was as though she had made some unconscious pact with fate, by which if she avoided any engagement with life, then life promised to leave her alone and undisturbed.

Certainly Harry left her alone and undisturbed. They shared

a bedroom and indeed a double bed, though I am reasonably certain that nothing of a physical nature ever occurred in it – at least not between them. Harry and cousin Jimmy, however, was a different matter.

Harry had been apprenticed in his teens to a firm of carpenters in Leyland, where the buses used to come from, eventually becoming a master carpenter, or "joiner" as the trade was more commonly known. Having been thwarted in his ambition to be promoted foreman of the firm, he decided to set up on his own, as his younger brother Tom the plasterer had done, also in Leyland. Unlike Tom, who had a number of men working for him, Harry only had the one, Alan, a cocky lad with a breezy manner who I suspect had got Harry's number early on. Nothing untoward ever happened between them, of that I am fairly sure. But Alan sensed instinctively that his employer had "vulnerabilities", and never took him seriously as a boss. Harry, conversely, never quite dared assert himself too firmly, sensing he was on thin ice somewhere and forever on the back foot, having to content himself with complaining to Marion and anyone else who would listen about "that lad with his back-talk and cheek".

Amongst those who lent a sympathetic ear was Marion's and my mother's cousin Jimmy, from the Isle of Man. Jimmy lived with his widowed mother outside Onchan, where he was an assistant-manager of the local pharmacy. He was a soft-fleshed little man with a face oddly skewed to one side, rather like a ball of plasticine that someone had stepped on, not hard, but just enough to distort it slightly. The effect was most alarming, I found at the age of three or four, when he broke into a twinkling smile without any warning.

In stark contrast to his non-macho appearance, Jimmy rode a large and powerful motorbike. It was a Douglas, a luxury model for its time, with an engine that generated a rich, mellifluous purr in contrast to the noisy rasp of most others. Jimmy would frequently come over on the Isle of Man ferry, with his bike, and stay with Harry and Marion in their two-up-two-down terraced house opposite the gasworks. At some point during each stay, the two men would ride the seven miles or so from Leyland to our cottage in the country to visit cousin Annie (Mum). On these occasions I would be treated to a brief whirl through the surrounding lanes, perched on the pillion seat with arms clamped around cousin Jimmy's comfortable midriff, then cups of tea would be drunk back at home, and the two men would depart. No particular comment was ever made about their friendship, beyond the observation that the two of them appeared to be "palling on" increasingly, with Harry spending most of his free time – weekends, bank holidays and such – either visiting Jimmy on the island, or the pair of them would take the bike up to Morecambe or Heysham or the Yorkshire Dales, overnighting at some bed and breakfast, while Marion remained quietly and apparently contentedly at home. Nothing was said, no comments were made; it was not the family's habit to go looking for fire where there was no smoke. But eventually a few wisps began curling skywards, and the obvious conclusions became hard to ignore.

Marion paid a visit once a week to her sister, taking the bus outside her door in Leyland and alighting in the country just a few steps from our gate. She would stay for a cup of tea, biscuits or a slice of sponge cake, then go out and wait for the returning bus back to Leyland about ninety minutes later. These visits were something of a lifeline for me, because she brought me every time and without fail the latest issues of two comics I was hooked on, *The Dandy* and the *Eagle*. There was no way I would have got them otherwise, because there were no shops within reach of where we lived, and my parents wouldn't have bought them for me because they regarded comics as a generally bad influence with their brash humour and crude adventure. However, the *Eagle*, created as it was by an ordained vicar of the Church of England, was considered at least partially respectable, which was a good thing, because there was practically no other reading matter in the house.

As usual on Marion's arrival, I pounced on my comics and stretched out on the floor in a corner of the room, leaving the grown-ups' conversation as mere background noise. Immersed as I was in the adventures of Dan Dare and Digby, I cannot recall what it was on one particular occasion that made me prick up my ears and start listening more closely. I think Marion was talking about something she'd been unable to find because her belongings had got a bit scattered since she'd moved into the spare room.

Spare room?

"Well, it's better for the men to have the big bed for themselves. I don't mind the little room, there's plenty of space for me."

Silence, broken by the sound of pouring tea.

"Was that your idea, or Harry's?"

"Harry's. But only when Jimmy's here."

Another silence. Tea was sipped, the conversation meandered on through other topics, and I returned to Dan Dare's struggles with the Mekon, thinking no more of this exchange until later when Dad was home. Nothing was said at first, until after several further cups of tea (we were a virtually teetotal household) Mum dropped her voice and adopted a tone that she thought, wrongly, would discourage young ears from paying attention, and told him what her sister had said.

I don't remember my father's response exactly, but it was something like, "They what?!", followed by a long pause, and then: "By the left! I hope she doesn't go round telling everybody!"

Sensing this was not a moment at which a request for further clarification would be welcomed, I pretended I'd heard nothing and let the matter pass. Which was perhaps why, when Uncle Tom dropped in later on, Dad didn't even bother to make sure that I was out of earshot before saying, in confidential tones, "D'you know what Marion told Annie about our Harry and Jimmy?"

As Dad recounted the tale, Tom's eyes closed like a man fighting a sudden migraine. "Bloody Hell, Eddie, give over will you? I don't want to hear any more."

The subject was dropped. All of which might seem quite civilized – don't ask, don't tell – but it wasn't. It was embarrassment. Dad was phobic about what he considered sexual impropriety of any kind, and as far as "homos" in general were concerned he would have happily officiated at their public flogging. A decade later, when his life as a local worthy on councils and committees of various kinds was crowned with an invitation to sit on the Chorley magistrates' bench, he had to be taken aside on his first day by the court secretary, a qualified solicitor, and have it firmly explained to him that corporal punishment was no longer on the statute books for men caught importuning in a public lavatory.

Fifteen years on, the law would be changed. Homosexual acts between consenting adults aged twenty-one or over, and strictly in private, would no longer be in breach of the criminal law. However, as Dirk Bogarde said to me one day in 1967, as the Bill was going through parliament, it would be at least another twenty years before the bitter prejudice against such things went away.

But later for the name dropping. For the moment…

CHAPTER 2

It is generally acknowledged that the fastest way to empty a room, aside from telling your dreams, is to recount your childhood memories in lengthy detail. So I will try to keep this short.

I hated my childhood. It began as a time of almost penal isolation. I didn't get to know another child my own age until I started at the local village school, a three-mile walk from home, at the age of five-and-a-half. I knew I had cousins, but I never saw them because they didn't live locally and we weren't a particularly close family. There were two children on a farm nearby, but my parents had fallen out with their parents years earlier (I never found out why) and we didn't speak.

We are all the product of one kind of accident or another. In my case it was wartime rubber. My sister Margery, nearly twelve years older than me, recalls vividly the rows, tears and gnashing of teeth she heard in the late summer of 1942 when it was discovered that my mother was pregnant at the age of forty with a second child.

Of course there may have been no rubber involved at all, but what is undoubtedly true is that I was unplanned. Dad was in the RAF at the time, stationed at Barton Hall near Preston, a communications centre for the tracking of aircraft. When he had a spot of leave he could be home in half an hour. Hence me.

I learned later that the main reason why my imminent arrival was greeted with such a marked lack of enthusiasm was because it meant my mother would have to give up the job she had just started and loved. She was married to a man who firmly believed that a woman's place was in the home, and having any kind of employment outside it was at the very least a sign of questionable morals. Only the constant public exhortation that everyone "do their bit" for the war effort had persuaded him to drop his opposition temporarily, allowing Mum to take a job issuing ration books in the Food Office in Chorley. For the first time in her life she was enjoying the companionship of a group of women her own age. As well as feeling useful she was having fun. Pregnancy brought all that to an end.

However, she came to terms with fate, and buckled down to duty. They both did.

And, I have to say, that was mostly how it felt.

The gap between my sister and myself widened with every year that passed. School life occupied her increasingly, blighted though it was by endless transport problems. Bus services were patchy, which made after-school activities a problem, as they would be for me years later. We were a one-car family, and Mum didn't drive, endlessly complaining that "Eddie never let me". Eddie himself (Dad) was rarely available to act as chauffeur. For years, Mum, Margery and I were obliged to walk miles every week, often carrying heavy school or shopping bags.

•

My early days at our isolated cottage were spent riding endlessly around the small garden on a tricycle, or perched for hours in the branches of an old sycamore tree that looked out over the fields behind our house. I don't know what I thought about during those long hours. I suspect I didn't think about very much at all, but somehow hypnotised myself into a trancelike state to make the time go by a little faster.

Father described me, to anyone who inquired about this slightly odd habit, as being "happy as the day is long up his tree". Of course it suited him to believe that: it meant I didn't have to be thought about. If ever I did actually complain within his hearing that I was bored and had nothing to do, all I got in reply was, "Will you stop your moaning! When I was your age we made our own fun."

Yeah, Dad. You and your brothers (well, not Harry maybe) and your bunch of mates, and a football. Football's not much fun when you're a team of one.

Despite the fact that "quality parenting" by fathers hadn't really caught on in a big way back then in rural Lancashire, it would have been nice to have had a little fun with him occasionally. The fact is I don't recall playing a game of any sort with him, ever. There were no friendly chats, no sense of companionship, however fleeting, no interest in how I might be feeling, what I might be thinking, what I might like to do. Nothing. I do remember that one late summer afternoon when I was five or so he took me fishing down to the old canal, but only once, and that was at my mother's suggestion to get me out from under her feet because she was stuck home alone with me all day.

My reaction to this grinding tedium was one that still vaguely troubles me even now. My parents kept a dozen or so hens, and I remember on more than one occasion killing by slow and deliberate drowning, several new-born chicks. The memory of that sadistic cruelty still makes me shudder.

I remember that the reaction of my parents was bafflement rather than anger. They didn't know it, but such behaviour, I later learned, is one of the classic signs of an emerging psychopathic personality.

Why did I do it? Was I really going round the bend? I think perhaps I was, wringing the life out of those helpless little creatures because I didn't know how else to get at it.

I was punished for my crimes by nothing worse than a smack on the back of the knees and being sent to bed early, and on another occasion by being banned from eating chicken for a week. I don't remember how many times it happened. I hope not many. It didn't occur to anyone that such behaviour by an inarticulate child of three or four must be, at least in part, a distress signal of a rather dramatic kind.

•

My one lifeline out of those lonely days was the radio. I used to sit huddled with an old set under the stairs. My parents had a newer set in the living room in those pre-television days, but they rarely listened to it.

I found myself transported to the magic world of *Childrens' Hour*, never missing an episode of *Toytown* or *Jennings at School*. The sepulchral voice of Valentine Dyall intoning creepy tales as "The Man in Black" gave me sleepless nights, and the stand-up comics on *Workers' Playtime* had me cackling with laughter. Mum said I used to pick up songs and catchphrases from the radio even before I could talk properly.

Odd though it may sound, I discovered movies on the radio before ever seeing one. There was a weekly program on the BBC Home Service about new releases in the cinema, with star interviews and general gossip. They would play brief excerpts from the soundtrack of whatever film was under discussion, and I could tell at once that we weren't dealing with your average radio drama here. There was a curious sense of space in what I was hearing. Something more was going on than words alone. I could sense movement, hear footsteps, detect faint sounds in the distance, and sometimes even the startlingly close rustle of clothing as someone turned before speaking. When I finally saw a film (I must have been eight or so) I remember thinking: "Oh, *that's* why they sound the way they do."

To me the radio was a door to a great unknown "out there". I didn't know what it was or where it was, but I wanted desperately to be part of it.

·

As already mentioned, walking played a large role in our lives back then. Not Dad's: he had the car. But aside from all the necessary miles tramped on a daily and weekly basis, Mum embarked once a year on a voluntary walk-a-thon for the Royal National Lifeboat Institution. She covered miles to collect donations from every home in Brindle village itself and all outlying homes, handing out pins with little paper cut-outs of a lifeboat on them. Until I went to school I would have to go along with her because there was nowhere to leave me, sometimes peddling on my tricycle because the walk was too exhausting.

While Mum's devotion to this worthy cause was undoubtedly sincere, she also considered it a cut above other charitable organisations in terms of status and respectability. Since its inception in 1824 its Patron had always been the reigning monarch of the day, and its hierarchy in general consisted of what Mum considered to be "a better class of person". So it was a source of huge pride when a letter came from RNLI headquarters "down south" saying that one of its high-ups would be touring the region and would like to visit Mum to express the institution's thanks for her support over the years.

Shortly after I had turned five, it was solemnly explained to me that a person of great importance and distinction would be coming to our humble home for tea the following day. This of course was not just afternoon tea, but tea as it was understood in the north – high tea at five o'clock, which, along with "dinner" at midday, was one of the two main meals of the day.

Everything had to be perfect for this grand occasion: the table properly laid, the boiled ham of the best quality, the salad fresh and the bottle of Heinz dressing alongside it new and unopened. My sister, who would have been sixteen or seventeen at the time, wasn't present, but I was washed and scrubbed up to perfection, dressed in my Sunday best short pants and shirt, and given stern warnings to be on my best behaviour and not speak unless spoken to.

It was a day that left a deep impression on me, which is why I have such a clear memory of being seated at the table on two cushions to bring me up to the right height. I can still see the fold lines standing up like ridges in the starched white tablecloth, and the careful symmetry with which everything had been set out on it. The VIP visitor himself was a genial old codger, Captain or Commander something, in a fine-looking tweed jacket, with a mustard waistcoat and a splendid grey moustache. Being a proper gent, he acknowledged my presence by asking the obvious questions that one asks a five-year-old, then devoted himself to polite conversation with my parents as tea proceeded. Suddenly I realized I was being addressed by my father, in his best voice.

"David, would you pass the cruet?"

The what? Crew? It? I hadn't a clue what he was talking about. Nevertheless, I had been spoken to and therefore must reply.

"What's a cruet?" I piped up, feeling no self-consciousness at my ignorance but anxious to learn and comply with the request.

My father's face darkened with ill-concealed fury.

"Salt and pepper," he snapped under his breath.

Oh, well, that was easy. Why didn't he say so in the first place? I reached out for the small pewter holder that carried both condiments and passed them over, imagining that would be the end of the matter. But I was to be sharply disabused once our distinguished visitor had left.

"How could you show us up like that?"

What?

"I've never been so embarrassed!"

I looked from one parent to the other, baffled by their anger.

"If you don't know the name of something, just say 'I'm sorry, I can't see it'. You don't just come out with 'What's a cruet?' like an ignoramus!"

That was Dad giving me pointers on social comportment, backed up by Mum with a reprise of, "Showing us up like that. I didn't know where to look."

It seemed I'd ruined their afternoon and brought the whole event crashing down in ignominy. That certainly wasn't the impression I'd got from the distinguished visitor. So far as I could tell he hadn't even noticed my blunder, but just continued with the conversation as though nothing had happened. But perhaps, I thought, that was what a better class of person did in such circumstances.

My humiliation complete, I was sent to bed early and in tears. As I lay sleepless, with daylight still pouring in through the thin curtains over my window, I pondered the unfairness of life.

But I had learned a lesson. I could see clearly, even at that early age, how preferable it was to be the distinguished visitor in life rather than his anxious and self-humbling hosts.

Not only had I made my parents ashamed of me: *I* was ashamed of *them*.

CHAPTER 3

"They fuck you up, your mum and dad," Philip Larkin proclaims in his most quoted poem, then reminds us tellingly: "But they were fucked up in their turn..."

Dad left school at eleven. The minimum leaving age at that time, 1916, was twelve, but he ducked out a few months early to work on a farm, heaving sacks of potatoes and shovelling manure. He attributed his shortness of stature – five feet four inches, but with the chest measurement, he boasted, of a six-footer – to the fact that such heavy work at so early an age had stunted his growth. He firmly rejected any suggestion that smoking since childhood had anything to do with it; indeed, his brothers all smoked, and even though they'd all started work at about the same age, they were all a little taller.

After a few years of farm labouring, he decided to better himself by learning a trade, and enrolled as an apprentice upholsterer at Leyland Motors. This required a pre-dawn seven-mile walk every morning, and the same back home in the evening. In time he became the proud owner of a powerful BSA motorbike, recounting in later years how he was the only one of a group of biking chums to have survived into his thirties, the rest of the "mad buggers" having died in accidents.

The upholstery business turned out to be a dead end after Leyland Motors switched to more mechanised methods of manufacturing their bus seats, and Dad set about looking for another line of work.

Married by then, and pushed by an aspirational element in my mother's personality, he eventually got a white-collar job selling life insurance for the Pearl Assurance Company. He would stay with them for the rest of his working life, becoming over the years a town councillor, a county councillor, a Freemason, a Rotarian, and a magistrate, finishing up – a proud achievement – as Chairman of the Chorley Bench. Not bad for a man whose education had extended no further than learning how to read and write. But he had a quick mind, though not a very subtle one, and could calculate figures in his head with amazing facility. He claimed that the "University of Life" was superior to book learning, though he did tell me much later that if he'd had an education like mine, and which he considered me to have wasted, nothing would have stopped him from becoming a barrister, QC, and ultimately judge.

My mother came from an even more impoverished background. Her mother, orphaned at the age of seven, had been brought up by a succession of aunts and uncles too poor to afford the one penny a week it would have cost to send her to school in mid-Victorian times. Consequently, she was illiterate all her life, able to sign official forms only with an "X". She died when I was six, but I remember her well, a sweet and endlessly patient old lady who was anxious to be no trouble to anyone.

Her married life had been a nightmare. Her husband's family had once had a little money in property, so at least he had the benefit of a decent education and, amongst other things, was a gifted artist. But by the time he "knocked up" the illiterate servant girl and was forced into marriage, the money had disappeared and he had taken to drink.

A relative got him the job of rent collector for a few terraced houses that had once, in better days, been owned by his family. Regrettably, he developed a habit of collecting rents all morning, then going to the pub where he would spend the lot on getting blind drunk. Many was the time that his unfortunate wife was forced to scuttle around borrowing money from the neighbours to cover his debts and keep him out of jail. She would repay these loans in the only way she could: taking in extra washing and doing menial chores for these same neighbours until they felt they had been sufficiently repaid.

My mother doted on her older brother, Tom, claiming he had helped her through a painful childhood with concern and care. Whether he volunteered for World War One or was conscripted I don't know, but he was gassed in the trenches in France, returning home a husk of his former self, to die within weeks. Before the year was out my mother had also lost her father to cirrhosis, and her older sister Alice to peritonitis after suffering an improperly treated burst appendix.

Out of all this was born in my mother a fierce independence, a rigid sobriety, and a belief that you make your own way in life and don't pray for manna from heaven or demand hand-outs from the state. She rejected socialism on a visceral level. "They think the world owes them a living." "What belongs to everybody belongs to nobody." "If you're that keen on it, go and live in Russia."

How I would have coped with a start in life like theirs I find hard to imagine. I feel guilty for criticising them, yet I do.

Why?

They did their best for us, my sister and myself. But why did it feel more like duty than love? An obligation met, not a joy fulfilled?

Money I suppose was part of it. I lost count of the times, alone in the back of the car as we drove somewhere, I listened to Mum wondering how Tess and Albert (my godparents) could afford yet another exotic holiday so soon after the last one. "Because they've got no kids," came back Dad's weary reply, and one always felt a "bloody" was implied.

17

By the time I was ten, my sister had qualified in piano and voice at the Northern School of Music in Manchester, and had started teaching at a brand-new county secondary school near Preston. She had also got married at the age of twenty-one to a pleasant young man called Malcolm, whose background was gratifyingly posher than hers. His family owned a cotton mill near Blackburn, and even though the industry was in terminal decline by then and they were comfortably off rather than wealthy, they remained several rungs higher up the social ladder than we were. One afternoon barely a couple of years later, my sister drove over to see Mum for a "special talk". I was around, at my habitual loose end and largely invisible, so I heard all of it. Margery announced that she was going to have a baby. I got the impression she would have liked congratulations, reassurance, and possibly some advice. But she got none of those things.

Mum hit the roof. "How could you be such a fool? You're young, you have your whole life in front of you. Why d'you want to saddle yourself with children?"

Within minutes they were both in angry tears, my sister protesting, "I thought you'd be happy for me."

"You've had every chance, and you've thrown it all away!"

Harsh words were exchanged, not least of which was my sister's charge that the main reason she got married so young was to get away from home.

The sad thing was, it was true. The atmosphere in that house was narrow, stifling and joyless. It was impossible to get through a meal without Mother indignantly listing the price of every ingredient on the table. Worst of all was her habit of serving full plates to the rest of us, then herself ostentatiously munching a single slice of toast because "with the price of everything there isn't enough for me".

It was utter nonsense. True, my parents had been very poor in the past, but by the early fifties, thanks to an inheritance (two thousand pounds – about sixty thousand now) from a maiden aunt whom Dad had been sedulously courting for years, they had built a new house on a piece of land attached to the crumbling old cottage they'd had since their marriage. We still lived in the middle of nowhere, but now with central heating and all "mod cons" thrown in. There wasn't much money to spare, but we weren't poor.

It's not hard, with hindsight, to see how these strident shows of self-denial on my mother's part were in reality some sort of crude appeal for the affection she felt she had been denied all her life. Sadly, what they achieved was the opposite. Her husband resented the inference that he was an inadequate provider, which was neither true nor fair, and I felt demeaned by the suggestion that I came from a family that couldn't feed itself.

Mum was an angry woman, frustrated on every front. She hated living in the country and being denied easy access to friends and community life. In fact when she married she had agreed to give life in Brindle a trial for eighteen months; then either she would agree to stay on, or her husband would agree to move somewhere a little more lively. In the event, she never agreed to stay on, and he never kept his promise to move. As the years went by and Dad became increasingly involved in his meetings and committees and masonic lodges, she found herself alone at home up to three, four, sometimes five nights a week.

After Dad suffered a heart attack at forty-nine, when I was eleven, he cut down on his activities somewhat and began to spend more evenings at home, though it didn't seem to enrich their relationship in any significant way. The closest they came to some kind of intimacy was in their ability to reinforce each other's perpetual sense of grievance against a world in which they both felt at an unfair disadvantage. It became a nightly ritual that they would sit hunched in their chairs over a dying fire, grumbling about some imagined slight or subtle insult from someone with, they felt, pretensions to a higher social station than theirs. "Oh, she thinks she's Lady Muck, that one. As for him, his family were nobodies."

In their later years, thanks to a decent pension from the Pearl Assurance Company, they began to enjoy some of the modest luxuries they'd been denied when younger. They began taking annual coach trips to Europe with the Rotary Club of Chorley. Dad had served a year as president, and Mum a term as president of the women's section, the Inner Wheel. (It was my job in my early teens to write her speeches for any formal occasion she had to chair.) Switzerland became a favourite holiday destination ("It's very clean"), with Lugano in particular winning their affection. Dad's idea of bliss was spending the day on one of the elegant old steam ships pottering around the lake, while Mother strolled off to explore the town with a couple of friends.

These were in many ways the best years of their lives, briefly snatched before the depredations of old age set in, which for both of them would be acutely painful. Mother, a victim of Alzheimer's from her mid-seventies (like her mother and sister) would be confined to a nursing home until her death at ninety. Dad never visited her by himself, claiming, unconvincingly I thought, that it would be too painful. He wouldn't even go with me when I took the train up from London to visit them, though he did go once or twice with my sister.

He died several years before Mum, having fallen victim to circulatory problems which cost him his left leg from the knee down and confined him to a wheelchair in sheltered housing.

They were buried separately, he in Brindle church, she some ten miles away in her home town of Euxton, having made it clear to my sister and myself years earlier that she did not wish to be buried in Brindle. She never forgave her husband for the life sentence he had made her serve there.

Sad people, miserable lives. Despite the hardships they'd lived through, it didn't have to be that way. Or so I always felt.

I loved them, of course. How could I not? They were my parents. I just wish I could have liked them a little more.

CHAPTER 4

Though thwarted of a proper education, Mum was still able to quote chunks of Shakespeare, Tennyson and Wordsworth remembered from her all-too-brief schooldays. She was adamant that my sister and I should not suffer the same fate. It was to be grammar schools for us, those now frowned-upon establishments which gave the brightest and most ambitious of the poorer classes the opportunity to "better themselves".

My first school, Brindle St. James', was a Church of England establishment in the village. There were something between twenty and thirty kids in the school, taught by a staff of two. Being unused to company of my own age, I was unsure of myself at first, and because of that got beaten up a few times. However, I got the hang of things before too long, and made a handful of friends. I also discovered that girls were interestingly different and nice to be around, and I regretted that they mostly played their own games during break while we boys played ours. One thing that fascinated me was the heady, slightly sweet fragrance that wafted off them whenever I got sufficiently within range. It was, I discovered later, the smell of soap and fabric softener, and to this day I cannot pass a tumble dryer without flashing back to those times, and my hopeless unrequited love for Mabel Bracegirdle, who barely knew I existed.

At the age of eight Mum put me in for an exam I hoped to fail, but which I didn't, and consequently was given a place at a prep school attached to Queen Elizabeth's Grammar School in Blackburn. I hated the experience. It was a ten-mile bus journey and a two-mile walk every morning and evening. Because I was in town all day I lost all my friends from the village school, and because I lived out in the middle of nowhere I made few new friends in town. But I did academically well, and passed the eleven-plus with no problem, and so progressed into the main school itself.

Having had enough of exams for the time being, I drifted for the next couple of years, and wound up dropping from the "A" stream to "C", with only "D" left to go. Bottom of the heap.

Mum's distress manifested itself in a dramatic way. "You'll never amount to anything," she shouted at me in the garden one morning, "because you're weak, just like your uncle Harry." I didn't know what to make of that, so just stood there and took it as she went on. "We'll just have to sell up and buy you a business, a paper shop or something."

In other words, something that even a loser like me couldn't make a mess of.

That did it. Next year I was back in the "A" stream. I was beginning to realise that I possessed a life-saving ability to get through exams when I absolutely had to. If the subject interested me, I could even do very well. If it didn't, but I had to have it for whatever reason, I would usually manage to scrape a pass mark.

It was about then that I began a radical overhaul of myself on several levels. First, I decided the northern accent had to go. I began re-molding my vowels on the received English I heard on radio and television, stumbling past clangers like "pat the booter on the table" until eventually I began to sound more like a character in *Jennings at School* than a northern grammar-school kid. How I got away with it without being ridiculed to death I don't know, though it may have had something to do with my decision to start a serious weight training program at about the same time. Word got around that I was not a soft target.

But what was I trying to re-mould myself into? And why? What was wrong with being a northern grammar-school boy with a few brains who hoped go to college some day? What was the phoney upper-class accent all about? Useful, I supposed, for someone planning on becoming a barrister, something I vaguely mumbled about when asked about a future career. But in truth I was increasingly drawn to the world of theatre and film, where the era of working-class heroes like Albert Finney and Tom Courtenay was already under way. Why was I poncing around like some Rank Charm School product of the forties, copying the plummy tones of Eric Portman or Rex Harrison as they wafted through their elegant drawing rooms in dinner jackets, pouring drinks for Margaret Leighton? Who did I think I was?

I think I wanted to be the opposite of who I was afraid I was.

•

A couple of years later, when I had just turned fifteen, something unexpected happened. My class, 5A, was set the task for English homework of writing a short story for the school magazine. The one judged best by our English master, Tom Crehan, would be printed. I was not a voracious reader compared with some of my contemporaries, several of whom had already ploughed through shelves of major classics even though they weren't studying English. Outside of set books I had fairly popular tastes, and at that time I had been reading H.E. Bates's "Uncle Silas" stories about country life. Using my own memories of childhood at Brindle school, I knocked up a rather derivative Bates-like story about an enterprising ten-year-old who plays truant to go fishing, then bribes his irate schoolmaster with a fresh trout to escape punishment, and thereafter strikes a deal to do the same on a fortnightly basis. I wrote it in half an evening and no longer have a copy of it, but something about it must have worked, because a few days later Mr Crehan called me up to his desk for a quiet word. He had my story in front of him.

"Did you write this yourself?" he asked.

"Yes, sir," I said, rather taken aback by the implication that I'd needed help.

"Did you think it up, or get it from somewhere?"

So now I was a suspected plagiarist? I told him that I'd made it up, though I admitted that I'd been reading the "Uncle Silas" stories which had served as a kind of starting point. However, Mr Crehan knew those stories too, and could see that there was only a marginal overlap between them and what I'd written. He pursed his lips, running his eyes over my story once again, and an amused smile began to play across his face. Then he dropped his bombshell.

"D'you know," he said, quite casually, as though idly speculating on nothing more important than whether it may or may not rain later on, "you could be a writer."

He saw the blank look of shock on my face and shrugged.

"It's a possibility. That's all I'm saying."

I returned to my desk in stunned silence as I glimpsed a future that I had so far not even dared imagine for myself. True, I had started writing short plays for a puppet theatre I had built out of plywood when I was eight or nine. I had discovered that I enjoyed watching plays more than anything else on television, and by the time I was thirteen my most prized possession was a charming letter from someone in the drama department of BBC Leeds (on official writing paper, no less) thanking me for submitting my first radio play, but regretting that it was not exactly what they were looking for at that time. Over the next couple of years I sent in several more, with the same result, and was beginning to suspect the whole writing thing might turn out to be a losing proposition.

But now, quite suddenly, the prospect of actually becoming a grown-up, professional, full-time writer seemed to me to be an actual possibility. A dream! It meant being my own master with no boss to answer to, something that even then I was becoming increasingly aware was important to me. It meant being able to use my imagination, of which I suspected I had a sizeable endowment, as a source of income instead of mere day-dreaming. It meant a kind of life that people like me just didn't, or daren't, aspire to. A life of freedom, independence and (let's face it) with a certain amount of glamour attached.

•

Tom Crehan followed up this generous encouragement with an even more generous amount of spare-time tutoring. I had always understood that writers should write about what they knew, and Tom agreed this was a good rule of thumb. However, the catch was that it required you to actually know something.

"At your age you don't have a bloody thing worth saying about life, so you'd better just start out by learning how to tell a story – how they're constructed, how to handle dialogue, how different writers have done it."

I was given a reading list from Maupassant, through Katherine Mansfield, "Saki", Somerset Maugham – all the way down to women's magazines, which featured a lot of fiction in those days. It might be pulp, Tom said, but it was not to be sneered at. This was real professionalism and I could learn from it. Then, he said, if I wrote some stories of my own, he would look at them.

During many midday breaks I stood by his cubby-hole under the stairs in the sixth-form building, listening to his comments on my latest efforts. They were mostly practical: when not to over-describe or under-describe; how to pace things to get the effect wanted; how dialogue could bring key elements to the foreground of the narrative. He neither particularly encouraged nor discouraged me. The test, I suspected, was whether I persevered or not. I did, and after a while, under Tom's direction, began submitting stories to various magazines, from *Argosy* to *Woman's Own*. I wasn't terribly surprised they were rejected, but it was still a disappointment. Tom was philosophical, and said at least I was being read.

Tom Crehan was one of those teachers you remember for the rest of your life. He must have been in his mid-forties, with a thatch of grey hair that was always casual to the point of dishevelled, but, curiously, never untidy. He was a little above average height, walking invariably with a preoccupied air and a slight stoop to one side, as though in conversation with an agreeable though invisible companion. I don't think I ever saw him crossing from one part of the school to another without a sizeable clutch of books under his arm, not just school books for marking, but all kinds of apparently irrelevant things. Although his job was teaching English, he would frequently bring in vast art books in order to illustrate some point about the Renaissance or any other period of history that he considered we might benefit from knowing about. One day he turned up with a huge volume of paintings by Breugel the elder, printed by some new process which, he enthused, reproduced the colours more richly than had been previously possible. He talked at length about the period and society depicted, not omitting to point out, in his gently Scots-accented voice, that if we searched very carefully among the details of the canvas, especially the corners, we would find not infrequently some chap with his trousers round his ankles taking a crap.

At other times he would turn up with the school gramophone

and play recordings of things that had nothing to do with the syllabus but which he thought we should be educated to enjoy. I remember, for example, how we all sat enchanted by the sound of Dylan Thomas reading *A Child's Christmas in Wales*. One English lesson was spent in helpless laughter over the poetry of William MacGonagall ("And the cry rang out all o'er the town, Good heavens! The Tay Bridge has blown down").

He made comparisons between plays and poetry and transcendent passages from Wagner or Beethoven's late quartets, playing us passages to illustrate his point, often with the warning that we were far too callow to appreciate them fully, but we might like to file them away for future reference.

Tom had a theory about getting us through our exams. Any fool, according to him, could pass quite respectably just by memorizing the bunch of notes he would dictate to us over a period of three weeks before the exams took place. He knew what the examiners wanted, and he could cover all those bases. At the same time, he said, those of us with a bit of flair, the ones who might be capable of doing really well, the "high flyers" as he put it in his slightly Jean Brodie-ish way, would benefit hugely from all the "irrelevant" stuff we'd been doing. Candidates who could make connections beyond their set texts, shining light on them from a broader culture, would benefit heavily. And he wasn't wrong. He got results.

Unlike some of his colleagues, Tom rarely had to worry about keeping order in class, because everybody was having too good a time to spoil things by behaving badly. But his patience was tested to its limit one day, with dramatic results.

Trevor was a good kid. The worst one could say of him was that he was boisterous to the point of being a bit overwhelming at times. He had been playing the fool throughout the class, ignoring Tom's repeated and reasonable requests to sit down and shut up, for God's sake. When Trevor started up his foolery yet again, Tom snapped, and slugged him.

Trevor was a big kid, well on his way to six feet even then at age fifteen (he later became a senior police officer in Manchester), but he went down like a log, banging his head against a steel desk leg on the way. There was a total silence, one of those moments when you aren't quite sure what just happened, but you know it could be bad. Tom vaulted anxiously between desks, clumsily Tarzan-like, to reach the boy and check for injuries.

It was not serious, just a bit of a gash and a bump that would be visible for several days. Trevor recovered quickly, and to everyone's relief returned to sit in silence at his desk, holding a handkerchief to his head. There was a certain embarrassment all round: from Tom because he knew he had overstepped the limits of permissible conduct by a yard or more and risked causing the boy serious injury; and from the rest of us because we knew that Trevor had been behaving like a prat, and we didn't want Tom getting into trouble because of him.

To his credit, Trevor absorbed the general feeling, and assured Tom that he didn't need to go to see the school marshal (male matron) for a check-over. It was understood between all of us that this was a private matter and should remain within the class. Which it did, the only price Tom having to pay for our discretion being to accept with resigned good nature the appellation of "Floyd" Crehan for the next week or two, a reference to the current world heavyweight champion Floyd Patterson.

Around eighteen months later Tom was appointed headmaster of another grammar school across the Pennines in Yorkshire. Heartbroken to see him go, we had a whip-round to buy him a rather nice calfskin wallet as a parting gift. I was deputed to make the presentation, along with a short speech to say how much we were going to miss him.

Tom was genuinely touched, and spent an hour talking to us in an easy, freewheeling way about our futures, the challenges life might throw at us, and the way each of us with our different personalities might respond. He talked about his concerns as a teacher that the power to influence young minds was something to be used with care. Tom had never concealed his own opions from us, whether on politics, religion or anything else, often expressed in un-schoolmasterly salty language, but had never sought to pressure us into agreement with him. On the contrary, we assured him, he'd helped us more than anyone we'd known to think for ourselves.

It was a touching, precious moment we would all remember for the rest of our lives. Trevor was in tears.

None of us was far from.

CHAPTER 5

At school I wound up as head boy, editor of the magazine, and the drama society's leading actor with my pick of parts. In 1960 a travel scholarship, awarded by a local brewery, took me to America for three memorable months. In Boston I saw the great Erroll Garner in concert, which was the beginning of a lifelong passion for piano jazz. In New York I saw the wonderful Anne Bancroft in *The Miracle Worker* on Broadway, then bluffed my way backstage to meet her, and was rewarded for my brass neck with a glass of champagne and a charming chat. In 1961 I won a place at Oxford to read law.

I arrived there in the autumn of 1962 armed with a posh accent but a still unsure sense of my place in the world. An Old Etonian I met that first day told me, years later, how impressed he'd been by this figure in an obviously brand-new tweed suit striding confidently across the college lawn to his rooms. Whether or not this was haute politesse for "overdressed grammar-school prat" I was never sure, although the element of doubt proved no obstacle to a lasting friendship.

My parents had driven me down. I would have been perfectly happy to take the train, but I could see they wanted to get at least a sense of this fabled place I was about to become a part of. Although they never said so, they were proud I was the first member of the family, or its circle of friends, to go to university. And not just any university, but Oxford. Top of the heap! This was "getting on" in a major way. As a local Brindle farmer had put it to me when he heard the news, "Oxford? By 'eck, tha're med fer life now!"

I knew the town hardly better than my parents, having been there only twice, and briefly at that: once to take the written exam, and once for a follow-up interview. I remember we walked through my college grounds (Merton) and a few of the streets surrounding it. I could tell that my parents felt somewhat over-whelmed by the place, its ancientness, its sense of history, above all by the authority that seemed to percolate out from its stone walls and mullion windows. We had tea in the High Street, but they didn't stay long, and we parted with the usual stiff formali-ties: a kiss to Mother's cheek and a handshake with Father. Then they headed back up north to Lancashire, planning to stay some-where overnight en route.

It was their first and only visit to Oxford. Three years later, having drawn their own conclusions about the insidious effect of higher education on previously respectable young men, it did not even occur to them to be present for my graduation. Mind you, I can't blame them for that. I didn't bother to show up for it myself. I was leaving with an indifferent degree in law, which I had discovered was perfectly good enough; I would pass bar finals in six months' time, and I would enter a prime set of chambers in the Inner Temple because I had been awarded something called a Duke of Edinburgh Award on the strength of a mock trial I'd taken part in before a high court judge.

How I backed into that trial I cannot recall. Conceivably, because I had become a regular paper speaker at the Oxford Union: that is to say, an undergraduate whose name appears on the paper announcing the debate, usually speaking alongside some high-profile guest from politics, academia or the arts. At different times I found myself sharing the bill with cabinet min-isters from Left and Right, from Enoch Powell and Quintin Hogg to Richard Crossman and the General Secretary of the TUC. It was an interesting and often daunting experience, run according to the rules of parliamentary debate. The drama of it all was heightened by the element of formal dress, with the four elected officers (president, librarian, treasurer and secretary) in white tie and tails, and the guests and paper speakers in black tie. My dad's old dinner suit, given a nip and tuck and a bit of an extension in the leg, had proved remarkably serviceable. The debates were mostly well attended, and there were some sharp minds out there, often with even sharper axes to grind, who would take a delight in picking you up on any inconsistency, questionable claim or ambiguity. You had to master your brief and learn to think on your feet. And if you could be funny occasionally, that was a great help too, especially for the once-a-year "humorous" debate, where at different times I warmed up for Terry-Thomas, James Robertson Justice and Fenella Fielding.

So when someone proposed a mock trial in the Alice Garden at Christ Church, I imagined some kind of Mad Hatter's tea party, and said yes for the hell of it. In truth, it was hardly a serious affair, though it was conducted under some simulation of trial conditions. The judge was an actual high court judge, perched incongruously on a tennis umpire's ladder, with the jury and the rest of us arranged amongst the rose bushes. Prosecution and defence counsels were briefed on the "facts" of the case and instructed on the rules of evidence. I was shown considerable leniency by the judge as I spun a succession of wild theories about how a kitchen shelf might have collapsed of its own accord, and not necessarily been sabotaged, as a result of which the prosecution failed and the White Rabbit was spared the noose.

It turned out that this "award" I was to receive for having won the case (I'd imagined a plaque or perhaps even a book token) was in fact a kind of scholarship, a subsidised entrée to a distinguished set of chambers in the Inner Temple (one of the four Inns of Court in central London) which guaranteed a flying start to a career at the bar. Not a thing to be lightly walked away from.

However, parallel with all this I had also been doing things in the theatre. In the first term I had auditioned for the Merton College players, and had played the central and showy role of the Devil in Max Frisch's "Afterpiece" to *The Fire Raisers*. We won the OUDS prize for best production. I was the recipient of a lecture by Sheridan Morley, who had cast me in the role, to the effect that I should forget all this Union politics nonsense and concentrate on acting.

The following year I wrote the play that my college society performed. I was not in it, but the leading woman was Maria Aitken, whose brother Jonathan I knew in my other world of the Union. He had told me his "kid sister" was coming up the following term and wanted to act, so I said she should come and audition.

We won again. Mine was the only new play on show, the rest as usual being culled from the repertoire of classic one-act plays ancient and modern. One of the judges was a leading Oxford actor called Michael Johnson, who went on to become Michael York. I got another pep talk from him about sticking with the writing.

Before I was through I'd written two more one-act plays which were being performed now not just in Oxford but one or two other universities and drama groups; I'd appeared in a couple of Shakespeare productions, and co-directed (with a professional director) a production of *Baal* by Bertolt Brecht.

Finally, in a Union "arts" debate I had spoken passionately against the motion "That the Purpose of Art is to Teach". The guest speaker on my side was John Mortimer, then at the height of his career as a barrister, playwright and broadcaster. Afterwards, he told me how much he'd liked what I had said, and invited me to call and see him when I was next in London. He gave me his home number.

When I phoned about a week later, he said come for tea. I was excited and full of anticipation as I stood at the door of a large Victorian house in Swiss Cottage. I wasn't sure what to expect, but I knew what I was hoping for: a welcome into the glittering world of famous London liberal-intellectuals. This could be, I suspected, one of those formative moments in a young man's life; before I knew it I could be dining with the Oliviers and clinking champagne flutes with the likes of Diana Rigg and Maggie Smith.

John opened the door and was, as always, charm itself. He was married at that time to the novelist Penelope Mortimer, whose best-selling *The Pumpkin Eater* had been turned into an acclaimed film with Peter Finch and Anne Bancroft the previous year. I was taken into a spacious room that displayed the comfortable yet somehow elegant untidiness that I took to be the hallmark of sophisticated living. His wife was seated before a coal fire, smoking a cigarette, and dressed, or more accurately draped, in some fine grey material that gave the impression of a classical statue carved out of marble rather than a human being. She extended a limp handshake and regarded me from beneath hooded eyes above high cheekbones in a long, pale aquiline face. Evidently John had already explained who I was and what I was doing there, and I could see at once that Mrs Mortimer was far from pleased.

As he poured tea, she lit another cigarette and talked past me about people they had to remember to call and other (mainly social) things to take care of. It was clear to me at once that my presence was an awkward and unwelcome intrusion, and she was obviously annoyed with her husband for not putting me off. Or maybe she was angry with him for some other reason.

Although they were one of the chic-est couples in London at that time, without whom no fashionable gathering was complete, it emerged later that they had been suffering marital problems for many years. Shortly before this abortive tea party, I later learned along with the rest of the world, John had fathered a child with the actress Wendy Craig. Penelope too, it was said, had several affairs. However, as it was another seven years before they finally divorced (in 1971), I cannot believe that whatever hostility was in the air that day proved to be any kind of crisis point. Maybe they were just always like that.

I hoped things would mellow slightly when Caroline, one of Penelope's four daughters by a previous marriage, showed up. Barely a year older than me, and an attractive brunette, Caroline Mortimer was already a successful actress, and had just spent the day filming with the American actor William Sylvester, whom she described, in response to her mother's inquiry, as being "all right, but a bit beery", and having trouble remembering his lines after lunch.

Although I felt curiously privileged to be a party to this kind of insider gossip, I was no doubt flattering myself foolishly. The fact was the whole conversation was simply taking place as though I wasn't there. John made a couple more attempts to include me in the loop, but it was no good; he seemed oddly distracted, as though his mind was elsewhere, and I decided that as soon as I had finished my second cup of tea I would make my excuses and leave. It transpired, as further details emerged from these familial exchanges on which I was being permitted to eavesdrop, that he had been rather shaken up by an incident that morning. Apparently, a rumour had flown around London that he had dropped dead on the platform of White City Tube station outside the BBC Television Centre. The rumour had been quashed by lunchtime, the unfortunate John Mortimer in question having been identified as a BBC electrician. However, rational and sceptical though John was, I got the impression that he had been thoroughly spooked by the incident. Whether that accounted for the state of mind in which I'd found him, or the strange atmosphere in the house, I don't know. He saw me out, charming and solicitous as ever, and said we should stay in touch.

We didn't, of course, though I would see him on and off for the next forty years, usually at someone else's house, or in a restaurant or at the theatre, and more latterly at the Garrick. He was invariably friendly and obviously happy in his second marriage (to another Penelope), and was very complimentary one day in the mid-eighties about a collection of short stories I'd written about Hollywood. We never spoke of that oddly embarrassing afternoon in Swiss Cottage. I don't even know if he remembered it.

•

Along with those already noted, the other two major distractions from academic work in Oxford were friendships and sex. Although the two things were not by definition mutually exclusive, in practice they tended to be. The colleges in those days were still segregated by gender, and there were strict rules about the times it was permissible to have a member of the opposite sex in one's rooms. As a result, the great majority of carnal couplings took place in the interval between lunch and dinner, which I would later discover has always been by general consent considered the best time for such things. But this was the early sixties, the beginning rather than the culmination of the freedoms realized in that decade.

Nevertheless, attitudes were changing – though not, as I was to find out to my cost, in Brindle.

Sally was at one of the many crammer-cum-finishing schools dotted in and around Oxford. These establishments, along with a number of secretarial colleges, were a wonderful source of girls in addition to the female undergraduates, who were still in a minority in the university and on the whole rather more preoccupied with their studies than these (with any luck) flightier girls needed to be. By the end of my second term Sally and I were a major item, and my "oak" would be "sported" for an hour or two on as many afternoons a week as we could manage to get together. To clarify: the "oak" was the outer door of the two doors with which all undergraduate rooms in college were equipped. When the oak was sported (closed), this was a sign that the room's occupant was not to be disturbed under any circumstances short of fire or natural catastrophe. Historically, the sported oak meant "student hard at work", which in a sense was still true, though not in quite the manner intended.

During the Easter "vac", as we airily called the vacations which made up half the year, and which were theoretically for catching up on essential academic reading, I was invited to stay with Sally's family for a week. They lived in a sprawling, ivy-clad house in one of the most fashionable parts of upmarket Buckinghamshire. It was a world of Jaguars and drinks parties, braying voices and middle-class entitlement. Sally was an only child, indulged though not spoilt. Her father was on the board of a pharmaceutical conglomerate which had taken over the family business he had inherited from his father. Her mother was a charming hostess, and a keen golfer. They were easy-going parents who welcomed me into their home, wanting to know nothing about my background other than that I was an Oxford undergraduate studying law. My acquired accent, long since honed to more or less perfection with all northern edges ironed out, made me one of them, at least sufficiently to pass muster. Amongst the scions of neighbouring families with whom Sally had grown up I was something of a misfit, but they accepted me willingly enough. I may have known nothing about rugby, couldn't ride a horse or play tennis, had never learned to ski or summered in the south of France, but

I had pulled the girl that many of them had fancied for themselves. I told myself smugly that, everything considered, I was getting on rather well in the world.

And Sally and I were having terrific sex every moment we could manage. The parents had given us separate rooms, which was a nod to propriety that neither of us questioned. However, there was plenty of surreptitious movement in the night, and whether the parents suspected, heard or even saw any of it remains a matter of conjecture. Their good nature never wavered, even when the paternal grandmother, who suffered from mild dementia and lived with a nurse in a self-contained wing of the house, reported that one of the bathroom doors had been locked all afternoon and strange noises had been coming from within, as though someone was ill and in pain. Parental eyes were discreetly averted to avoid further embarrassment to the two beetroot faces at the table.

CHAPTER 6

It was somehow taken for granted that a visit to Brindle was inevitable. Sally was naturally curious to meet my parents, and Mother was joyful at the news that I was seeing a young lady from a good background on a regular basis, and to whose home I had already been invited. To Mother, this was almost an engagement.

Although I had misgivings about the whole enterprise, I didn't want my parents to get the impression that I thought them "not good enough" to meet my girlfriend. That was not the case, and it was not what I felt. My main concern was that, whereas Sally's family merely accepted in a common-sense way that their daughter had a boyfriend, my parents came from a world where you married the first person you "walked out with" seriously; and, by the way, "walking" was all you got up to before the wedding vows were exchanged and rings placed on fingers. So there was ample room here for some Feydeau-esque misunderstandings, and they duly happened.

Sally and I arrived at Preston railway station one autumn afternoon during the next "vac". Dad was there to meet us, flashing his best smile and shaking hands as though he really meant it. We made small talk on the way home, where Mother was waiting at the door. She gushed a welcome, and as we arranged suitcases in our respective rooms upstairs she confided, "Ooh, David, what a *lovely* girl!"

I was relieved by that response. I'd been aware for many years of Mother's obsession with "nice" girls as opposed to the kind most young men of my age preferred. Sally was in fact very nice, very nice indeed; but not in the way Mother meant. Try as she might, Sally would never have succeeded in looking anything other than sexy. Mess up the expensively styled hair, take away the fashionable and always colourful clothes, wipe off the perfectly applied make-up, and Sally could never pass for the vicar's daughter in a knitted hat. But she seemed to have met with approval. Eyebrows had not been raised, and that was a relief.

I do not recall the details of that evening, or of the next day or two. The worst thing about our house was that there was nothing to do in it, ever, and not enough room to be alone and do nothing comfortably. Televison could be watched in a small dining room with only two armchairs, guests having to perch on one of four straight-backed, armless dining chairs. The front room was bigger and more comfortable. At least there was a three-piece suite and a couple of other serviceable chairs. But there was no television in that room, so conversation was obligatory, tending quite soon to wear a little threadbare, and sustained only by offers of second or even third cups of tea and another piece of cake.

Luckily I had a second-hand Morris Minor. Dad had bought it for a hundred pounds, calculating that the running costs would be less than the price of rail tickets back and forth to Oxford throughout the year. Plus, of course, he had genuinely wanted to make a gift to his son, knowing how thrilled I would be by the independence it gave me. I was surprised, grateful and very touched by the gesture. Our handshake became a truly warm double handclasp for a while.

Because I'd gone down by train to meet Sally in London, I'd left the car in Brindle. We made full use of it now, spending days out visiting any sites of interest and beauty spots we could think of. Sally laughed at my droning on about "this landscape of the Industrial Revolution", but loved the wildness and beauty of the Fells and Forest of Bowland, and was much taken by the seedy charms of Blackpool out of season. Everything was going just fine, until one night a couple of days before we were due to leave.

We came home from a movie in Preston to find the house in darkness, not even the light over the front door was on; which it normally would be if we were coming back late. Inside the house the atmosphere was tangible: utter silence and impenetrable darkness. I found the switch to the landing light which, again, would normally have been left on for us, and, as we climbed the stairs, I saw that the door to my parents' room was firmly shut, whereas usually it was slightly ajar.

I feared the worst. Somehow they had found out. They knew. And their reaction so far suggested none of the understanding or worldly sophistication of which I had half persuaded myself they would be capable when the time came.

Sally and I crept quietly to our separate rooms, she knowing nothing of what was on my mind. In the morning I woke early, about six-thirty, and immediately heard the rattle of teamaking in the kitchen. I pulled on jeans and a jersey and ventured down.

Mother was alone, hair wiry and uncombed, an old dressing gown bunched around her, waves of hostility radiating out almost visibly.

"You're up early," I essayed by way of an ice-breaker.

Silence, broken only by the clank and clatter of porcelain and spoons.

"Is anything wrong?"

"You should know."

"Know what? What d'you mean?"

"I haven't slept a wink all night."

She hugged the fresh-poured mug of tea to herself with an expression of pained self-righteousness.

"Is it me? Is it something I've done?" I said, knowing perfectly well it was.

45

"You and that... that..."

The word escaped her. Or she couldn't bring herself to pronounce it. But it all came out now. They had gone through my drawers after we'd left the house the previous night and found a packet of preservatives.

"You've been doing it with that girl!"

"Why were you going through my drawers?"

"You said you had some films to be developed. Your father was going to take them into Chorley this morning."

To my recollection I had said nothing about films to be developed, but I let it go. Maybe they'd suspected something and gone looking for proof. It didn't much matter. The current situation, for whatever reason it had arisen, was going to have to be dealt with.

"Look," I said, "what's so awful?"

"What's so awful?" she snapped back, as though she'd have liked to smack me in the face. "Your father was in tears. I've never seen him in such a state. He thinks he'll have to resign from the bench because of the disgrace."

This was going a bit far even by their narrow standards of what was and was not "proper". I tried to suggest as gently as possible that this was a serious over-reaction, but she would have none of it.

"We went over to see Malcolm. Your father needed to talk to another man about this. We didn't know what to do."

My brother-in-law Malcolm, I would have hoped, would have talked them down from their hysteria and established a little common sense. But that hadn't happened. My sister told me later how this funereal procession of two had arrived at their door with doom-laden faces. They sat down without taking off their hats and coats and poured out their story.

"Where do they go to do it?" Mother had asked repeatedly. "He'd get thrown out of Oxford for having a woman in his room."

Malcolm, to my sister's amazement, had pursed his lips and

nodded gravely. "You're absolutely right," he said, "it's a very serious matter. I agree with you, he's being very irresponsible. This could ruin his career."

As I mentioned before, Malcolm was a nice man, though neither a bold nor original thinker. My sister would leave him for another man a few years later. Perhaps in the circumstances there was nothing else he could have done, but that night he stoked the fires of moral outrage to the limit.

"Where is Dad?" I asked.

Mother jerked her head towards the kitchen door.

"He's outside."

I found him poking at a small bonfire of dead wood and garden rubbish. He didn't look up or speak as I approached.

"I've just been talking to Mum," I said. "She seems upset."

Still he didn't speak, just went on poking his fire a few moments more, and then came out with a pronouncement.

"I've only got one thing to say. When a country stops looking to its land and its morals, it's on the road to ruin."

A thought, I told myself, to ponder indeed. In its own way, unanswerable.

It was only the second time that Father and I had discussed sex, although perhaps "discussed" is putting it a little too strongly. The first time I was six, or I might have just turned seven. Somehow I had discovered that by lying face down in bed and using my elbows to push myself back and forth, I could produce a surprisingly pleasant sensation in the lower regions of my body. One morning I was doing just that and thinking that life could be very much worse, when Dad's head appeared around my half-open bedroom door. He had shaving cream on his face, a safety razor in one hand and a towel over his shoulder. He must have heard the bed creaking, because my activities were making quite a noise. From the look on his face, despite the half-covering of shaving cream, I knew at once that I was not the recipient of paternal approval. I stopped what I was doing, transfixed by his gaze, as he uttered four heartfelt words.

"You dirty little devil."

With that, he disappeared back along the landing to the bathroom, and the subject of sex was never mentioned between us again. Until that morning by the bonfire.

"Dad," I said awkwardly, hoping we could discuss this in a grown-up, man-to-man sort of way, "aren't you taking this all a bit... well, I mean, it's not that serious, is it?"

"You may not think so," he said grimly, still not meeting my eyes, "but there's right and there's wrong, and that's all there is to it."

I left him poking away at his smouldering ashes and went back inside to tell Sally that we had a problem. She took it very well, showing a good deal more concern for my parents' sensibilities than they did for hers. She dressed quickly and came down with me for breakfast, whereupon my mother turned her back without a word and left the room. We made some toast and a pot of coffee, talked the matter over, and decided the only thing to do was leave.

"You'll have to marry her now," Mother hissed in my ear as I carried our bags out. "You've ruined her for life. Nobody else'll want her."

It seemed pointless to explain that virgins were no longer at a premium in our modern age, and that what was once called a fate worse than death was now considered, in the right circumstances, to be rather fun. Sally and I departed without ceremony in the Morris – thanks again, Dad; at least you allowed me a dignified exit – and drove down to London, where a girlfriend of Sally's had the run of a house in Belgravia while her parents were abroad.

Now that was more like it.

CHAPTER 7

The downside of this bleak little farce that my trip north with Sally had turned into was a widening of the gulf between my parents' lives and my own that became all but unbridgeable. I realized I had been pretending to myself that they were the kind of people I would have liked them to be, instead of the people they were. Was I really expecting a couple of sophisticated London butterflies to burst out from the larvae of my homely Lancashire mum and dad?

Sally and I broke up a few months after the abortive trip north. There was no causal connection between the two events. We were far too young to settle down, and I was certainly too immature. Sally, I had begun to suspect, saw more of a future for the relationship than I did. I, by contrast, was beginning to feel that the best was behind us while the future offered only sameness and eventual staleness. It was, I suppose, looking back, my first experience of the classic confrontation between domesticating female instincts and the commitment-phobic male. We talked. There were some recriminations, a few tears, but we agreed to see "less of each other" for a while, which was a euphemism for "it's over". I remember a long journey in the back of her parents' car from Buckinghamshire to Oxford. Sally was red-eyed and snuffling into a box of tissues, I was looking out of the window, while her admirable parents in the front continued to mind their own business. We were dropped off on a street corner in the centre of town, promising to talk soon, but we didn't.

Even today, I am still asked rather wistfully by old college chums, "Whatever happened to that girl you used to go around with?" Sally was not someone likely to be short of suitors for long. A few months later I heard she had a new boyfriend, a successful businessman a few years older than herself. One day I ran into her by chance. She seemed very happy and said she and the boyfriend were going to live in Canada for a while to see how things worked out. We parted friends. It was the last I ever saw or heard of her. I hope she remembers me with at least some of the affection with which I remember her.

My next visit north, alone, passed off reasonably well, though the atmosphere at home remained cool. Just how far my parents, my mother in particular, had decoupled from my new life in that den of iniquity called Oxford came, however, as a shock. I was seated at the dining-room table one day, flicking through a copy of *The Times* or *Guardian* that I'd picked up somewhere, while my mother assumed her habitual and inelegant posture – chair pulled up close to the fireplace, knees parted to allow the heat to penetrate – reading her *Daily Express*. As I turned a page of my paper, I was pulled up sharply by a large photograph of a girl I knew at one of the women's colleges in Oxford. She was just a friend, but I liked her very much. She was a clever, attractive and serious young woman, studying medicine, and no doubt with a fine career ahead of her. Her body had just been fished out of a river somewhere in Germany. She had been raped and her throat cut.

I must have gasped and said something like, "Good God, I don't believe it!"

"What?" said Mother drily, not lifting her eyes from her own paper.

"A friend of mine, a girl in Oxford. She's been murdered, on holiday in Germany."

Without Moving, mother gave a little sniff and twitched her

paper a fraction. "I'm not surprised," she said in a tone of contemptuous dismissal, "knowing what those Oxford girls are like."

Something closed up in me in that moment, a reflection perhaps of what it was that had closed up in her long since. I found myself speechless, and boiling with rage. Without saying a word, I got up and went for a walk over the fields to the abandoned quarry where I'd whiled away countless empty hours over bygone years. The decoupling from my parents was now complete, I realized, on both sides. Never again would I regard them as people with whom I could share any kind of understanding or anything approaching friendship. It was a relief in many ways. I felt a new-found freedom in the knowledge that I could now stop trying to bridge the gap between us. In future, I would do what filial duty demanded, but no more, because I would be unable to do more and it would be futile to try.

I recalled my mother's repeated lamentation over the years, whenever I had taken issue with her over some question of politics, religion or morality, that it was "a mistake to educate your children; they'll only look down on you".

Well, I told myself that afternoon, if that was the case it was sad, but so be it.

•

I was relieved to be out of the house for much of the rest of my stay. I needed money and, for the second time, got myself a job as a labourer on a gang digging holes to renew water and sewage systems in the centre of Blackburn. About six weeks of that would top up my bank balance enough to return to life at Oxford in the style to which I was becoming accustomed.

The men I was working with, mostly local but with a handful of Irish, were tough and funny, and remarkably indulgent of their temporary workmate. There was no resentment of the world of privilege I obviously inhabited in contrast to their own, nor of the future they imagined lay in front of me, whereas all they could look forward to was ongoing, bonewearying drudgery. In their place, I might have shown more than an academic interest in the Communist Manifesto and the revolutionary Left in general. But they were largely unpolitical, and strangely forgiving of a world in which their lot was far from what they would have liked it to be. The only complaint I heard, mostly from the Irish men, was that "the Queen" took half their pay packet every week even before it got into their pocket.

Conversation centred exclusively on two subjects, sex and football. Having no interest in football I had a gap to fill, and tried out various alternatives, sometimes with surprising success. One lunch hour, based on my conviction that everyone, regardless of origins or education, is interested in the "Big Questions" of life, I had got a lively discussion started about differing views on religion and life after death.

Don, our foreman or "ganger" as he was known, had been listening without comment on the fringes, and now leaned in to refill his mug of tea, observing: "Bloody 'ell, you're a dismal fuckin' lot today. Can't you talk about summat normal, like cunt?"

Well, he was the boss, so we complied. Conversation returned to the all-consuming topic of the day, the scandal starring Her Majesty's Secretary of State for War, John Profumo, and the sexy double act of Christine Keller and Mandy Rice-Davies. There was a somewhat academic discussion about the difference between adultery and straightforward shagging. Eventually it was agreed that for it to be adultery, at least one of you had to be married. Whereupon Don remarked, with a wolfish grin, that the good thing about being married was "you never miss a slice off a cut loaf".

I liked him.

Back in Oxford, my third and final year began. As the months of evasion, distraction, affairs and general amusement dwindled to a few remaining weeks before I hit the rock face of finals, I found myself confronting an unimaginable amount of catching up in a subject which bored me to death. Despite repeated reassurances from successful barristers that academic qualifications in law were not what counted in the making of successful advocates, and despite having won that mock trial which promised me excellent chambers and financial support in the early years of my career, I still had to scrape a degree of some kind. As the summer progressed, all attempts to cram my head with legal texts were increasingly hampered by the debilitating effects of the hay fever I suffered every season. Almost worse were the side effects of the antihistamine drugs that I took to control it, which in those days produced severe drowsiness. An overwhelming desire to sleep was something I could do without just then, so I paid a visit to my college doctor to see if there was anything he could do about it.

What he did was write me a prescription for some little pills with a name I didn't catch but which he promised would help. And they did. I barely slept for six weeks, enjoying a level of concentration that I found extraordinary, and an ability to retain what I was learning, at least in the short term, that seemed miraculous.

I stayed on the doctor's little pills all the way through finals, which were taken according to tradition in white tie, gown and mortarboard, and when the last exam was over I broke out the champagne like everyone else, and gave my remaining pills to a girl at Lady Margaret Hall who was also having trouble staying awake for round-the-clock revision.

This largesse turned out to be a mistake. Coming off "speed" as abruptly as I did brings one down to earth with a brutal thud.

Dextroamphetamine is a drug producing, according to the textbooks, "increased wakefulness and focus in association with decreased fatigue and decreased appetite". Withdrawal symptoms, I discovered – the hard way and not just from the textbooks – include "mental and physical fatigue, depression, anxiety, suicidal thoughts, and psychosis".

It would be impossible today, I am told, for a college doctor to prescribe such a drug at all, let alone without any warning about its side effects. As it was, I spent the next several weeks in a state of confusion. In London I was sleeping on the floor of friends' pads, drinking too much and starting to smoke marijuana – a late developer by modern standards. At home for a week or two in Brindle I was basically just sleeping, which only confirmed my parents' opinion that higher education was a corrupting and decadent experience which wiser members of the lower classes would do well to avoid.

One grey mid-morning, with the overnight drizzle still clinging to the ground, I wandered out into the garden, where I found Dad pruning his roses. Neither of us spoke, and I remember thinking he seemed rather incongruously dressed for such a task in a trilby hat and his second-best overcoat. After a few moments, without any preamble or overt acknowledgment of my presence, he came out with one of his pronouncements.

"It's no good thinking," he said, "that you can just come and live up here whenever you're broke."

With that, silence returned, broken only by the snip-snip of his secateurs.

Faintly taken aback though I was, I could see he was right. It was time to make my choices.

CHAPTER 8

I was shown into a high-ceilinged room with panelled walls and leaded windows overlooking a leafy courtyard. Facing me was a polished refectory table, on the far side of which sat about twenty stern-looking men in black gowns. These were the Master and Benchers of the Inner Temple, one of the four Inns of Court to which all barristers and judges have to belong. Presiding was the bulky, totally bald and immediately recognisable figure of Lord Goddard, a former Lord Chief Justice, generally known as "the hanging judge".

On my side, facing them, was a single straight-backed chair to which I was directed. I had been summoned before this august assembly to explain why I no longer wished to remain one of their number. The problem was the scholarship I had been awarded on the strength of that mock trial in Christ Church Garden more than a year earlier. Indeed, amongst the eyes now burning into me I recognised the high court judge who had decided I was worthy of the honour. Normally one law student more or less entering the profession would be neither here nor there, but I and not somebody else had been given this thing, so I was expected to account for my decision to throw away such an opportunity.

Inwardly convinced on some irrational level that I would be lucky to get out of the room alive, I began my stumbling explanation. I had, I explained, written a few one-act plays that had met with some success within the university and elsewhere. As a result, I had been approached by a couple of agents, and generally encouraged to persevere in what was, I acknowledged, a precarious trade. However, I felt in a way, a way I could not entirely ignore, an urge to try my luck in this direction, knowing that I was probably being very foolish. Nevertheless...

I didn't get much further because, to a man, the distinguished gentlemen rose from their seats and began to approach me around both ends of the table. This, I told myself, is where I make a dash for the door, find it locked, then take a header through the window before they string me up.

But then I began to hear what they were saying.

"My boy, this is a very brave decision."

"Entirely to your credit."

"D'you know, Gerald's never forgiven himself for not taking a shot at the professional stage."

This last speaker was Lord Goddard himself, and the "Gerald" referred to, I realized at once, was none other than the current Lord Chancellor, Lord Gardiner, who had been a famously gifted actor during his student days at Oxford.

"I always wanted to be a concert pianist," another voice piped up. "I was never quite sure I had it in me, but I still think about it."

The speaker this time was the very judge who'd awarded me the scholarship.

"D'you happen to know my friend Fabia Drake?" inquired a beaming QC with a comfortable girth and a magnificent head of bushy white hair. I did not know personally the distinguished actress, by then in her sixties, he was referring to, but I was certainly familiar with her work on stage and film. I listened in growing disbelief as he and others talked of how much they enjoyed "going round" to see their friends on opening nights in the West End, and of who in the room had played what role in some recent production of the Bar Drama Society. "You should come and see us some time!"

It was left to Lord Goddard to sum up the mood of the meeting. "Look here, my boy," he boomed with a geniality I had not been prepared for, "the best thing you can possibly do is go out and take a shot at something you really want to do. There'll never be a better time than when you're young. Most people go to the bar far too early anyway, and don't do themselves any favours by it. See how it goes, and if it doesn't work out you can always come back in a couple of years and have your scholarship back. You'll make a far better lawyer with a bit of experience behind you."

I shook hands all round, had my back and shoulders pummelled with expressions of good will, and left in a flabbergasted daze. However, relieved though I was by the way things had gone, I still faced an immediate problem: money.

What was I going to live on?

•

I went to see my bank manager in the hope of arranging a loan. I'd used Lloyds Bank in Oxford, so it had seemed natural to stay with them in London, and I'd chosen the South Kensington branch because I was dossing at that time on somebody's floor just five minutes away.

The manager, John Donnelly, was a large and rather frightening man, at least on first acquaintance. A cross between a Buddha and a giant bullfrog, he sat behind his desk in a windowless room to which visitors were led as though to the Holy of Holies in some ancient temple. He weighed me up through narrow, hard-to-read eyes that were folded into a broad, fleshy face. Before I could even start on my entreaties, he waved a handful of cheques which, he said grimly, he had paid, but which had taken me considerably beyond the meagre overdraft limit I was permitted. He demanded to know when further funds were due to be deposited into my account.

Doing my best to exude confidence and a positive attitude, I explained that I hoped to be in gainful employment very soon, and in the meantime trusted he would see his way to extending the aforementioned overdraft sufficiently to see me through. The cross-examination that followed was swift and deadly. Did I actually have a salaried position that I was about to start? No. Did I have any prospect of a salaried position? Not exactly, no. How "not exactly"? Well, I was working on a couple of plays and a TV script that I hoped might lead somewhere. Ah. Did I have access to any private money – savings, a trust fund, the likelihood of an inheritance? No, nothing at all. Would my family be prepared to help me? No, I explained, that was out of the question.

He sat back with arms folded and considered the situation for some moments. "You do realize," he said finally, "that you are destitute."

It wasn't so much a question as a statement of the obvious, implying at the same time a suspicion that he was quite possibly addressing someone too stupid to recognise the truth when it was in front of him.

The word seared itself into my soul as no other has before or since. I was branded. "Destitute." It felt like a prison sentence.

"Do you have any money at all," he asked, "I mean now, in your pocket?"

"N-No," I stammered, "except for some loose change."

I was afraid he was going to demand I hand it over to begin plugging the hole in my account. Instead, he heaved a long-suffering sigh and his attitude visibly softened. There was, I realized, a kindly man behind the gruff exterior. He reached down into a drawer of his desk and took out a five-pound note, which he handed over to me.

"Here," he said, "this should keep you going. Come back in a few days and we'll see if we can work something out."

I thanked him profusely and emerged from his tomb-like office into the bright sunshine of an early spring afternoon. For ever the optimist, I felt quite sure that my luck would turn and by the time I saw him again I would be able to wave a TV or film contract at him in the way he had waved my cancelled cheques at me.

And indeed, as though fate had decided to prove my point, I came across a group of men huddled over an improvised card table outside the entrance to Gloucester Road Tube station. I pushed forward far enough to see that they were engaged in a game of such utter banality that I at once realized I had stumbled on a fail-safe way of doubling or tripling my money in a matter of minutes. I hesitated just long enough to get the hang of the game. It seemed that any one of the onlookers gathered around the table was being invited to hand over a pound note, or even more, to a dealer seated on an upturned beer crate, who then slipped the note under one of three cups. He did this with careful deliberation so that no one could be in any doubt as to where the money was. He then pushed the three cups around in a way which he obviously thought was very clever, but which to my sharp eye was incredibly easy to follow. The person who had bet the money was then challenged to identify the cup under which his money lay hidden. I watched in amazement as two men placed their bets, then tapped what, at least to me, was clearly the wrong cup. I could barely believe their wide-eyed amazement when they discovered their error.

This was a breeze, I told myself. A complete steal. The man running this game was clearly an idiot and was going to lose his shirt. There should be a law against it. As I watched, a third man put down his money and, having followed the manipulations of the cups as closely as I did myself, tapped the right one, and walked off happily having doubled his money.

Despite my laudable feeling that the poor man on the beer crate needed a social worker to come and take him into care, I decided this was too good an opportunity to pass up, and put down my fiver.

As before, I watched the same inexpert bit of juggling, after which I reached out confidently to tap the cup under which my fiver had been placed. You may imagine my surprise when it turned out that I was wrong.

I was still scratching my head and trying to work out how I could have been mistaken when someone muttered "Scarper!", and the whole group around me, table, beer crate and all, vanished into thin air. I turned to see a police patrol car cruising slowly by, with the copper in the passenger seat gazing balefully out at me, fully aware of what had just gone on. It didn't even occur to me to make any protest or complaint, because I was already only too aware of my own stupidity.

Nevertheless, I had a problem on my hands. Having had a fiver for ten minutes, quite convinced it was about to become a tenner, I was now once again skint. What to do? There seemed only one course of action.

Eyebrows were raised in mild surprise when I reappeared at the bank fifteen minutes later, requesting a second audience with the manager. However, a phone call was made, and I was once again shown through to the inner sanctum. Mr Donnelly sat behind his desk as before, motioning me to sit down while he finished signing the papers in front of him. Then he lifted his gaze and spoke.

"So what can we do for you now?"

I had already decided to be completely honest about the situation, mostly because I could think of no alternative. I cleared my throat. "You won't believe what just happened," I began, and told him my story.

It was the first time I had actually seen anyone's eyes glaze over and cross slightly at the same time. Too stunned by the unfathomable depths of his youthful client's naivety, unable to muster even the mildest words of remonstration, he merely heaved another loud sigh and reached once more into his desk, took out a second five-pound note, and pushed it across to me. "Try to hang on to this one a bit longer," he said weakly, and dismissed me with a limp wave of his hand.

CHAPTER 9

A few years later, by which time I had started to make a decent living out of writing for films and TV, I took John Donnelly out for a lavish lunch to mark his retirement from the bank and to thank him for his kindness to me over the years. He was one of the last of his kind – a bank manager who knew his customers individually and not just as names on a computer screen, and took an interest in their lives.

But on that spring afternoon as I re-emerged from his office with my second fiver tucked safely in my wallet, wondering how long I could make it last, that word "destitute" still rang in my ears as nothing had before, or has since. My situation, I knew, was serious.

It would be absurd to pretend I was anywhere near sleeping rough in the park, though in darker moments I could imagine it happening if ever the kindness of friends ran dry. One of them, an Oxford contemporary called Leslie Megahey, who'd got himself on a BBC directors' course and would eventually become head of BBC Music and Arts, found me gazing hungrily in the window of a Ladbroke Grove bakery one morning, and rightly deduced that I didn't have enough in my pocket to buy even a sandwich. Incredibly generously, he not only bought me lunch but insisted on lending me money, and gave me the use of a room in his flat for as long as I needed it – which was a major improvement on the floors I'd been dossing on.

Further help came from another Oxford acquaintance, making me realize that the term "Oxbridge octopus" had not been coined for nothing. Although some nigglingly puritanical part of me tried hard to disapprove of this kind of privilege, another more pragmatic part snapped back, "Oh shut up and get on with it, and count yourself lucky."

Michael Beloff had been president of the Oxford Union in my first term at Merton College. I had always been rather in awe of him. By the time I met him, he already had a first-class degree in history and was by then studying law. He was a brilliant debater and public speaker, quick-witted and capable of being very funny. His background, too, was fairly daunting. His father, Max (later Lord) Beloff, was a world-renowned historian, a Fellow of All Souls, and Gladstone Professor of Government at Oxford. Michael had enjoyed a brilliant career at Eton, which had no doubt helped develop the easy-going social poise beneath which lay a razor-sharp and highly competitive intellect. It was not hard to see why a northern grammar-school boy like me might feel a little wary around the likes of young Mr Beloff.

We were never close friends, but, as a result of my taking part in so many Union debates, we knew each other reasonably well. He was generous with his praise when he thought someone had performed capably, and I remember feeling puffed up with pride on a couple of occasions when I received his congratulations. Having taken it for granted that, like him, I would be going to the bar after graduating, Michael was surprised to hear from some mutual friend that I had abandoned my scholarship at the Inner Temple and was going off to try my fortunes in show business. When I ran into him not long after, he inquired with genuine concern and down-to-earth practicality what I was going to do for money. I mumbled something about trying to get a bit of freelance journalism to tide me over, whereupon he said at once, "You must meet my aunt."

Nora Beloff was one of the most formidable figures in journalism, and that is without taking into account the fact of being a woman in a heavily male-dominated profession. She was by then senior political correspondent on *The Observer*, having earlier been posted as a foreign correspondent in various hot spots around the world. I anticipated a rather fearsome grilling from this charming but frighteningly clever woman, who had been described as "incapable of allowing a sloppy thought to slip past without a challenge". In the event, however, she seemed content to accept Michael's word for it that I was worthy of a helping hand, and I was waved straight through to the office of the paper's legendary editor, David Astor.

The Observer was at that time at the height of its influence as the home of cultivated liberal thought, its contents permeated by an attitude of tolerance, but a take-no-prisoners response to nonsense, whether from the Left or the Right. In fact, it was read and respected equally by people of all political beliefs, a persistent voice of sanity and reason in the clash of conflicting passions.

The editor and I talked for a while. He was slightly donnish, with a handsome, acquiline face and a faintly diffident manner. I already knew, however, that he was considered in Fleet Street to be the original definition of a steel fist in a velvet glove. Eventually he said that they could probably use me, on a freelance basis, not on staff. He made a call and sent me along to see a man called George Seddon, who edited a section of the paper called Briefing. This covered three or four pages of interviews with people in the arts, a handful of short book reviews, and a preview of whatever of interest was coming up during the week. Contributers were not given by-lines, but their names were listed at the end of the section. It was a good place to appear.

George Seddon, it turned out to my astonishment, had been at my old grammar school in Blackburn. And he'd hated it.

Pretentious, phoney would-be public school, encouraging the worst kind of ambition and snobbery, a launching pad for young men with no principles but an overriding ambition to "get on" in the world, but by the basest of standards and the most despicable of values.

Okay, right.

And furthermore, he went on, the headmaster in his day, Arthur Holden, who in *my* time was looked back on as a figure of near sainthood for his long stewardship of the school, had in reality been a fascist bastard who persecuted homosexuals.

Ah.

There was nothing camp about George. In our more enlightened day it would be unnecessary, indeed offensive, to make such an observation about a homosexual. Back then, however, notions like "effeminate" and "fairy" hovered over them, even among the most liberal-minded of heterosexuals, a category to which I liked to think I belonged. But I couldn't help being faintly surprised by the way George was at home with a pint of lager in front of him and a cigarette in his hand, a solidly built man with long-ish grey hair and horn-rimmed spectacles. His face was lined and lived-in, always displaying the hint of an ironic smile that couldn't quite decide whether to break out fully or not. He was married, but all references to "my wife" conveyed a suggestion that all was not well on that front. I think there were recently grown-up children, which may have had some bearing on the timing of the divorce which happened not long after.

George invited me that first evening to accompany him to a reception at the Westbury Hotel in Mayfair for the launch of some high-profile new novel by a member of the uberliterati. The room seemed full of famous faces from the media, politics, and the world of top to middling celebrity in general. The champagne flowed freely, interrupted only by the occasional bite into a drying canape. After about an hour, George asked if I fancied a spot of dinner at some place he knew nearby, so we could talk about my future.

Great.

The restaurant was low lit, its clientele fashionable, and its prices sky high. Soft flames, like lighted sambuca glasses, flickered along the walls. George, obviously well known there, was greeted effusively and we were seated at once, given more drinks, and enormous menus. I ordered some kind of complicated omelette that was wheeled up on a trolley and flambéed as I watched. It seemed like a pretty good end to an excellent day.

I couldn't help noticing, as dinner progressed, that George was talking an awful lot about men. From actors and dancers he thought were wonderful at one end of the scale, to Arthur "fucking" Holden and his like at the other. Why couldn't society mind its own business? What went on between two men in private was... etcetera and so on.

Awash though I was with considerable amounts of alcohol, I quickly worked out what was going on, and I was struck by an extraordinary thought. There I was, on the receiving end of what I had been handing out to girls for years. I was being courted by a man, gently probed to show signs of interest and encouragement, agreement and even willingness. It was a curious reversal of perspective, slightly disconcerting, and, frankly, very interesting. I'd always assumed homosexuals recognised each other by instinct or some kind of secret code, so how could George be so mistaken?

Unless, of course – a profoundly unsettling thought – I was the one who'd made the mistake. Could it be, although I didn't know it, that I was in fact, at least in part, gay?

But no. It took only a moment's reflection, even through the blur of alcohol, to realize that this was going too far. I had long suspected that most gay men I knew harboured somewhere a secret conviction that all men were essentially gay, or at least bisexual. And I, along with all my straight friends, held an equally strong conviction that this was simply not true. Completely at ease though I was with the fact of others being homosexual, I found it utterly impossible to imagine myself enjoying homosexual acts of any kind. Conclusion: gay men did *not* automatically recognise their own kind, and here was George proving it.

That left a faintly awkward situation, which I had to deal with. I vaguely remembered once hearing of an old music hall song (quoted in a speech by Harold Macmillan) about the girl who failed to spot the fatal switch between the moments when it was "too soon to say yes, and too late to say no". I began to feel a sense of urgency, gearing myself up for a speech along the lines of, "George, I think there's something you should know..."

As it happened, I was spared this awkwardness by events. Some time earlier an extremely attractive young woman had passed by our table on the way to the women's room. Now she came back. Long blonde hair, a tight-fitting dress on an impressive figure, bare shoulders. I'd clocked her the first time without thinking, and now I did it again just as automatically. George caught the look. Perhaps, this second time, I'd meant him to. If so, it had the desired effect.

"I see you're looking at that girl," he said.

"Yes," I said, "amazing, isn't she?"

George gave a kind of grunt in the back of his throat which didn't convey anything very much. I forget quite how the conversation went on from there, though I do recall George asking me earnestly if I was absolutely sure I wasn't just the least bit homosexual, and my saying no, I wasn't.

"And you never have been?"

"No. Never."

"Hm." George sat back in his chair, visibly disappointed, and said, "You've no idea how depressed I am to hear that."

"Sorry."

He reached for his glass and emptied it. "Tell you what," he said, "let's have another grappa, and call it a night."

Outside on the pavement, he pressed a couple of quid into my hand as taxi fair. "I insist," he said when I protested. "Call it expenses. Come and see me tomorrow, about eleven."

I was there on the dot, only slightly hungover. Any concerns I had about my job disappearing as a result of our conversation the night before were immediately banished as he introduced me around to the people I would be working with. His deputy was a man called Laurence Dobie, whose name I knew as the co-author of a couple of short-lived West End plays, and who had, probably wisely, decided to hang on to his day job at the paper. Another was a slim young woman with a bright smile and wiry blonde hair. This was Helen Dawson, who would go on to become the paper's arts editor a few years later, then, in the mid-seventies, the fifth wife of John Osborne.

Contrary to any fears about there being a lingering embarrassment between George and myself, I found we developed a relaxed, open and easy-going relationship from which I benefitted enormously. Under his tutelage I learnt the basics of journalism, with no shortage of bad jokes along the way.

George: "Oh, you didn't know he (some cabinet minister or leading public figure) was one of us? Good Lord, yes."

Me: "Oh, come on, George, you're making it up. Christ, you'll be telling me Danny La Rue's queer next, and I shall refuse to believe you!"

CHAPTER 10

Over the next eighteen months I met and interviewed people I would not otherwise have got close to if I hadn't been sent by *The Observer*. Among those who come most readily to mind is Dame Peggy Ashcroft, with whom I had a long and wonderfully poised, though relaxed, conversation in her dressing room at the Aldwych Theatre, where she was playing in *Days in the Trees* by Marguerite Duras.

In a dark-panelled flat overlooking Chelsea Embankment I chatted with Robert Bolt as he worked on the screenplay of *A Man for All Seasons*. The actual subject of the interview was his new play for children at the Royal Shakespeare Company, *The Thwarting of Baron Bolligrew*. I remember him saying how he'd thought it would provide some light relief after *Lawrence of Arabia* and *Doctor Zhivago*, but it had turned into the same "salt mine", as he put, that every piece of work did, whether comedy or drama. Like me, he was a northerner, and we exchanged views on the stifling puritanism up there which had made us both determined to escape at the earliest possible moment.

I also went to see the amiable Leo McKern, who was playing the title role in *Bolligrew*, and who chain-smoked small cigars, poured whisky, and gave out bursts of loud laughter during a very agreeable hour together backstage.

One highly enjoyable day was spent showing a young (thirty-nine) Neil Simon around London. He was over for the West End opening of his play *The Odd Couple*, which was already a smash-hit on Broadway. He was terrific company, and over a long lunch on expenses at Rules in Covent Garden he told me the most important thing he'd ever learnt about playwriting: the rule, which he attributed to Bernard Shaw, that the only way to write a convincing argument between two characters was for you, the author, to be genuinely convinced that both sides were right.

Another time I was sent to see Edward Bond, whose play *Saved* at the Royal Court, with its notorious scene of disaffected youths stoning a baby to death in its pram, had just scandalised half the theatre-going world and reduced the other half to gibbering superlatives. Instead of finding someone in a permanent rage against society, as I expected, knowing he was a Marxist, I was met at the door of his comfortable Hampstead flat by a charming, soft-spoken man in his early thirties who was clearly enjoying his fame, and the well-paid film-script offers that were coming with it, as well as the smart new sports car that was parked outside.

One morning I interviewed Paul Dehn, the distinguished poet, librettist and screenwriter (*Goldfinger, The Spy Who Came in from the Cold*, among many others). I was a little startled by the violent fragments of piano music which came thundering up from the basement of his Chelsea house during our conversation. Later I was introduced to the man he lived with, James Bernard, who composed the scores for all the great Hammer horror movies I'd been enjoying all my life.

I interviewed Hugh Paddick and Betty Marsden from radio's top comedy show *Round the Horne*, and spent a hilarous afternoon backstage at the Comedy Theatre, where they were appearing in a French farce. They actually gave me a private performance of one of their famous "Dame Celia Molestrangler and ageing juvenile Binkie Huckaback" sketches.

Famous faces became commonplace. On one junket at the Savoy for a picture called *The Quiller Memorandum* I chatted with its screenwriter, a rather shy Harold Pinter, a charming Alec Guinness, and a young George Segal, a little nervous about his first major leading role. Also there was Max von Sydow, who talked about the culture shock of going from Ingmar Bergman to Hollywood blockbusters. I tried to persuade the gorgeous Senta Berger to come and have dinner with me and do an exclusive interview for *The Observer*, but inexplicably she declined.

One of my fondest memories is of going down to Brighton to interview a thirty-two-year-old Richard Briers. He had already played in a couple of popular sitcoms on television and was becoming recognised as a young comic actor of brilliance. He was finishing a tour, with Sybil Thorndike and Athene Seyler, of *Arsenic and Old Lace*, which was due in the West End the following week. We sat on the sea wall across from the theatre and talked about acting. There was no difference, he said, between comic acting and any other kind of acting. Comedy was a technique that could be learnt like anything else. Whether your career went more in the direction of comic or straight acting depended on several factors, not the least of which was physical appearance. For example, he had recently played "the Dirk Bogarde part" in a stage version of Joseph Losey's 1964 film *King and Country*. The role is that of a young army captain in the trenches of World War One who is assigned to defend a shell-shocked young soldier unjustly court martialled on a charge of cowardice and desertion. It is a harrowing piece with no light relief whatsoever, and Briers had received glowing reviews for his performance. But he sensed a hint of reservation in his wife.

"Well," he said, "what did I do wrong?"

"Nothing, darling. You were absolutely fine."

"But..?"

"No, you were really very good."

"Come on, out with it."

"Well... you just looked so funny in the hat."

•

This was the stuff that kept me fed and watered for the best part of eighteen months. I also wrote occasionally for a couple of other magazines, but it was journalism as a means of survival, not an end in itself.

What I was really trying to do was write plays: stage plays, TV plays, screenplays. I'd got an agent, a sweet-natured lady called Elspeth Cochrane, who specialised in nurturing new talent; one of her young actors making a name for himself just then was Ian McKellen. She sent my work around to producers, directors and executives, and if they were at all interested I got a meeting. One of these days, I kept telling myself, I would actually sell something.

Despite my mounting impatience with the elusive holy grail of "success", I was still only twenty-three, and this was the sixties. It has become a cliché that anyone who remembers the sixties can't have been there. It isn't true, though I can see why it's said. Marijuana and cocaine were readily available and fashionable, as increasingly was acid.

I never greatly took to coke. For one thing it made my nose run for days, and for another, although it was an invigorating high, it lasted only for about half an hour before you had to top up with another dose. This made it both addictive and expensive. Marijuana, on the other hand, gave a high that lasted several hours. I discovered the incredible pleasure of listening to music while stoned, whether classical, modern or whatever. Also – and this I hadn't anticipated – a toke or two on a joint mid-morning or early afternoon would guarantee several hours of unbroken concentration and creativity. It was an instantaneous cure for writer's block, somehow opening up channels in the brain that had been previously sclerotic, and genuinely good work was invariably the result.

My first experience of acid (LSD) took place one weekend in the countryside outside Oxford. I was by then living in London, but a good friend had stayed on doing a PhD at Christ Church. He was a mathematician of near genius, and, perhaps because he was also an Indian, possessed of a deep interest in the mysteries of consciousness. Harsh (his first name) had rented an old stone cottage surrounded by fields and cows, and I quite often used to drive up from London on Friday evening and stay till Monday morning. He was a gifted cook and would prepare authentic and elaborate Indian food which was like none I had tasted before. We would smoke a little dope and talk for hours. Friends would come over, usually but not always from Oxford, and sometimes, like me, stay the weekend.

Mark and Karen were Americans doing postgraduate work in the sciences. They were very west coast, very Berkeley, very "beautiful people", without actually being all that beautiful themselves. (Except inwardly, of course.) She was dark, overweight (though not dreadfully so by American standards), with a wild shock of wiry hair and unshaven legs. She had a permanent wide smile on her face, as though she alone had discovered the secret of happiness and wanted everyone to know it. I don't think I ever once saw her not smiling. I remember her saying that most people didn't take happiness nearly seriously enough.

He, by contrast, was a slim, more contained individual, usually wearing a long embroidered coat, John Lennon glasses, and a Victorian smoking cap. He smoked his dope in a long-stemmed clay pipe, which he offered around to the assembled company, lending the occasion a certain elegance beyond the usual sharing of a bedraggled joint.

All three of them, my good friend Harsh and the two Americans, were experienced LSD users, and I felt secure in their company for my first trip. I'd read Aldous Huxley, Carlos Castaneda, Timothy Leary and others on the exotic benefits and hidden dangers of the drug's use, but nothing can fully prepare you for the experience itself. We each dropped a tab around ten-thirty on the Saturday morning of a grey, damp winter's weekend. I knew the whole thing would last up to thirty-six hours, and for the first forty minutes or so I sat around with the others in the living room of the little cottage, wondering when the thing was going to kick in.

By the time forty-five minutes had passed, I was beginning to suspect that the whole thing was a hoax and nothing was going to happen. Either that, or I was for some reason immune to the active ingredient in LSD and therefore wasting my time. I was on the point of making an announcement to my friends that nothing was happening, when it struck me what a strange statement that was. "Nothing was happening." How could *nothing* actually happen?

Then I noticed something odd. It took me some moments to figure out what I was seeing, but when I did I no longer had any doubt that things were really getting under way. Without noticing the transformation take place, I suddenly found myself inhabiting a strange kind of cubist universe, in which I was observing my companions from several angles at the same time. It made no sense, but it was unquestionably the case. The more I looked at them, the more clear it became. There was no distortion in my vision. It was nothing like being drunk and seeing double. My eyes were simply telling me that was how the world was.

I was, at that point, sitting with my feet up on a comfortable old sofa, and my companions seemed equally settled. Probably all of us had moved around somewhat in the past hour or so. Even if we hadn't got up and gone for a glass of water or something, we'd shifted in our places, turned this way or that, addressed a glance and a word or two to one of the others. All right, I managed to figure out, that's what's happening: I'm seeing all those angles and attitudes simultaneously, not sequentially as I normally would. Time was, in some way, out of joint.

But I'd been warned about that. I looked at my watch. I cannot say how long I stared at that curious mechanical device on my wrist, with its funny little pointers moving round and round, to no purpose, signifying nothing. Any notion of time's arrow, or the river of time, was not only wrong, but meaningless. Time didn't flow; people walked around in it.

Because of my interest in physics, developed soon after my abandonment of science studies in school, I already understood the essentials of relativity – that time and space were indivisible, not two separate things. At least I knew it intellectually, but to experience it directly was something else.

"Time exists to stop everything happening at once. Space exists to stop everything happening to me."

That was a quote from a brilliant physicist called John Wheeler who I'd been reading recently. It was Wheeler who invented the term "black hole". He also demonstrated that not only is observation essential to the resolution of quantum events, but that future observations can decide past events. As a result of which, he decided, it made perfect sense to say that the Big Bang did not take place until consciousness had evolved many billions of years later to become aware of it. All of which meant that we lived in what he called a "participatory universe".

"There is no 'out there' out there," he said, arguing that subjective consciousness and the unimaginable vastness of the cosmos were wrapped up together in a single process.

Heady stuff when you're on acid. But I patted myself on the back for being clever enough to understand what I was experiencing, therefore not overly alarmed by it.

Without warning, and with no sense of how I got there, I found myself in an open field.

This I didn't understand. It was impossible, I was going mad. I'd heard about people having meltdowns on acid...

On the verge of panic, I looked around. My companions were nearby, wandering around apparently disconnected from one another. But all at once they looked over at me.

Communication between us had a sixth-sense quality about it. I might be about to say something, and the other person would look at me in a way that confirmed they had heard the unspoken words. If anyone spoke, the others would often be sharing the same thought.

I don't remember the night, probably because it was no different from the day. I vaguely recall noticing that the sky had changed colour, but that was about all. I do remember a great mound of fried eggs we cooked up at some point and ate hungrily.

At another moment, I remember finding myself without shoes or socks. It seemed we had been talking about my anti-fetish about feet. I hate feet. Well, ugly ones, and most are.

There was a lot of laughter, broken now and then by wild Freudian theories. I joined in the jolliness.

The sky had changed back to its other colour (I would later remember it was called "daylight") when I found myself outdoors again and marvelling at the tiny flowers that were starting to bud at that time of year. One of them had fallen into an old wooden water barrel by the kitchen door. I watched, entranced, as it floated there, vibrating with a life and colour that burned into the eyes like a laser. I was suddenly afraid I would go blind, but my friends reassured me I wouldn't, and I should just go on enjoying the flower.

By late Sunday afternoon, I could feel myself descending gently back to planet Earth. It was reassuring to find it still there, but I felt the need to get my grappling hooks into it more firmly. The others declined to join me and warned me not to be too long, because they were going to prepare supper. I promised I wouldn't be late, then walked down the road to the village pub and ordered a double whisky and a cigar.

CHAPTER 11

Home at this time was a basement flat in Hammersmith, shared with an amiable young solicitor called James, who I also knew from Oxford. Girlfriends came and went for both of us, and although several of my friends were settling down into steady relationships (James would soon join their ranks), I felt no inclination to copy them. It was 1966–7, and as Albert Finney famously said about sex in the sixties, "It was *everywhere!*"

It's probably true that every generation thinks it has invented sex, but back then we must have had at least a fair claim to the title. With the pill freely available and women's liberation under way, it wasn't the same world that our parents had inhabited; not surprisingly, most of them, though they would never admit it, were bitterly jealous. I saw touching evidence of that one day.

Biba, in Kensington Church Street, was the trendiest fashion shop of its day. I was in there one afternoon with Nicky, a gorgeous seventeen-year-old Australian, and the place was packed as usual. I think there were changing rooms, but either they were always full or nobody bothered to use them, because lots of undressing and trying-on was done right there on the shop floor with no embarrassment and little discretion. The occasional boyfriend in attendance, like me, feigned lofty indifference to this exposure of flesh, a pose made easier by the knowledge that some of it was yours to touch and take home with you.

But that wasn't the case for the stocky middle-aged man in

a boiler suit who was trying to deliver canisters of gas to some place in the back of the shop. With each passage, pushing his way through this youthful crowd with a heavy steel container on his shoulder, he grew increasingly frustrated. Not only was he determined to preserve his dignity by not leering at the girls, he was also bitterly aware that no one in the shop had so much as noticed his existence. On the third trip through, with no one making the slightest effort to clear a way for him, he began muttering darkly about not having spent two years in the fucking desert fighting a war so a bunch of idle fucking kids like us could fuck him around. By an effort of self-control he managed not to smash anybody in the mouth or do anything else that might cost him his job, but it was a near thing. I felt for him.

It was, frankly, a time of extraordinary narcissism – or, to use the preferred term, "cool". The King's Road on a Saturday afternoon was a peacock walk of outrageous clothes and multicoloured hair, with everyone desperately competing for attention while affecting indifference. If you passed Michael Caine or Mick Jagger as you strolled along, you would die rather than be caught staring, or (heaven forbid) asking for an autograph.

Alvaro's, perhaps the most fashionable restaurant of the sixties, was also on the King's Road. The place was so chic it didn't even have a name outside, or anything to announce it as a restaurant. Its phone number was unlisted, and to get a table you had to know the owner personally, which meant being very famous or wealthy, or preferably both. Once admitted to the golden circle you were given a secret number to call for future reservations, along with a solemn injunction never to divulge it to anyone on pain of banishment. You were also handed a book of matches which carried no information whatsoever, just a photograph of Alvaro himself with his finger to his lips going "Shhhhh...!" I became a regular there for a short time, though not, thank God, at my own expense.

Peter Zoref billed himself as a film producer, though he had never up to that point actually produced a film. One of the speculative scripts I had written, and which my agent had been dutifully circulating as a "calling card", had come into his hands and he had liked it. He set up a meeting through my agent, and that was the first time I lunched at Alvaro's. I was very impressed. The place was a sea of famous faces. Among them was George Sanders, lunching alone, impeccable as ever but looking out of place and somewhat dated in that environment. Which of course he was. His career was by then in the doldrums and he was picking up whatever rubbish he was offered to pay off enormous debts following the collapse of a business venture he'd unwisely got involved in. A few years later he would commit suicide, sadly never living to see himself become the cult figure that he has.

My host that day was himself one of the best dressed and most perfectly groomed men I have ever met. Trim, poised and self-possessed, with a face that resembled a curiously handsome frog, Peter spoke perfect English, though with a slight accent that I never placed. I assumed from his name that he was Jewish, but he never talked about his background. Appearances were everything with Peter. He looked and behaved like a wealthy man, often with some well-known fashion model on his arm (he was particularly partial to models), though he later admitted to me that he and his business partner, the dashing French actor and director Christian Marquand, were leading a precariously hand-to-mouth existence at the time.

Peter explained, at our first meeting, that he was developing a comedy-thriller set in Swinging London. Well, lots of other people were doing the same thing, so why not? It was basically a "heist" movie, meaning an ingenious robbery, featuring a romance for somebody like, ideally, Warren Beatty and Susannah York, and a handful of juicy roles for famous supporting players.

Right.

I took home a script that he'd already had written but didn't think worked. I set about restructuring it and wrote a whole new opening. The cheque that was supposed to accompany this endeavor was, when I inquired of my agent, supposedly in the post.

My second lunch at Alvaro's took place ten days later, when I delivered my pages. I didn't say anything about the money because I felt it would be "uncool", and besides that was my agent's job. Why else was I paying her ten percent of nothing?

The next day Peter called me and said he liked what I'd written and I should continue. So I did. The cheque still didn't arrive, but I started getting invited to the parties that seemed to be a permanent feature of life at the huge apartment that Peter and Christian were sharing in Kensington. Frequently the evening would start with dinner at Alvaro's or some other fashionable hangout, often in the company of a movie star and other "faces". Marlon Brando joined us more than once. He was charming, reserved, much smaller than I'd imagined and nattily dressed in a lightweight suit and tie. Marlon and Christian had been close friends for almost twenty years. Marlon had named his first-born son after Christian.

The parties themselves were exotic affairs with people coming and going till dawn. There was an hallucinatory quality about them, due no doubt to a mix of alcohol and various substances and many other things, not least of which was the decor of the apartment: the entrance hall and enormous living room were lined with sheets of polished aluminium, upon which ceiling-fixed projectors flashed a stream of psychedelic images. Aside from that, I don't recall too many details. Although, as I already said, I don't subscribe to the cliché that if you remember the sixties you can't have been there, I have to admit that there are chunks of this period in my life which remain total blanks.

I did eventually get paid something: Peter was a decent man, and I liked him. But he never made the movie. Instead, a major deal that he and Christian had been working on for a couple of years or more finally came together, and they decamped to Rome to make a film called *Candy*. With Christian directing and Peter executive producing, and calling in every favour and pulling every string they could, they assembled a glittering cast that included Marlon Brando, Richard Burton, Walter Matthau, James Coburn, John Huston, Ringo Starr, and many others, including a breath-takingly pretty young non-actress called Ewa Aulin.

The film, released in 1968, was one of the most high-profile dis-asters of all time: witless, unfunny and boring. I heard from people who'd been there that most of the unit were stoned throughout the whole shoot, having a ball and convinced they were making a great movie. But, as the critic Pauline Kael put it: "One has visions of the [film] editor holding his head, his brains slipping through his fingers..."

I never heard from either of them again. Peter simply disap-peared off the face of the earth. The only reference to him I've ever found anywhere is as executive producer of *Candy*. Christian never directed again. During the seventies he lived for some years with the actress Dominique Sanda, twenty years his junior, and they had a son. He continued acting in increasingly small roles until the mid-eighties. After suffering for some years from Alzheimer's, he died in Paris in 2000, aged seventy-three, no doubt by then, poor soul, remembering not only nothing of the sixties, but of very little else.

CHAPTER 12

Michael York and I had continued to meet regularly for lunch or dinner. A few times we went out night-clubbing together, but Michael wasn't much of a drinker, or, indeed, inclined to the more louche side of life at all. He didn't smoke or do drugs. Unlike me, he never seemed to feel the urge to go off the high board once in a while just to see what happened. In fact he was more fastidious than me in more ways than one. "You'd better dip it in Dettol if you're going to shag that," was his parting remark at the end of an evening in some West End disco, where I'd made the acquaintance of a very charming girl who was letting me take her home. Unhelpful, I thought, at the time; and, as it happened, wrong. He would meet and marry the photographer Pat McCallum shortly afterwards, and from then on we confined our socialising to more respectable establishments.

He remembered the plays of mine he'd seen at Oxford, and he knew that ultimately writing was still what I wanted to do. Michael was always a generous friend, and what he did next was proof of that. Having got to know Dirk Bogarde and his partner, Tony Forwood, while shooting *Accident*, he had become part of a select group regularly invited to their home, Adam's Farm in East Sussex. One day Michael announced that he had spoken to Dirk about me and shown him one of my as yet unsold film scripts, and Dirk had suggested he take me down to lunch to talk about various projects he was thinking of developing.

So, on a dank and wintry Sunday morning early in 1967, Michael and I drew up in his gleaming new Mercedes outside an elegantly sprawling Tudor house surrounded by (I would learn later) nine acres of land, with an oast house and various outbuildings converted into guest wings and staff quarters. The door was opened by a middle-aged housekeeper in a starched white overall, who took our coats and disappeared, to be replaced by Dirk emerging from the living room to greet us.

There is a particular kind of anticipation involved in meeting movie stars. Memories of the roles you've seen them play run through your mind, moments of extraordinary intimacy you've shared with them while gazing up at some hugely magnified image of that face you know every inch of. You feel you already know the person, and yet you know you don't, any more than they know you. And suddenly there they are in front of you, instantly recognisable but in the unlikely shape of a perfectly ordinary human being: in this case a slim-built man of medium height, wearing jeans, a light blue shirt and a loose white cardigan. He welcomed us with warm handshakes and took us through to the main room, which was a long, high converted barn. A gallery ran along one side, with a refectory table beneath it. Opposite were huge windows looking onto a manicured lawn and immaculate garden. There was a fire, comfortable chairs, sofas and cushions everywhere, and a couple of somnolent dogs – a large mastiff and something smaller and collie-like .

Tony Forwood poured us all Bloody Marys, which was his preferred aperitif and which he mixed to perfection. He was a tall, effortlessly elegant man, with slightly old-fashioned matinee-idol good looks. In fact, he had started out as an actor, but his wife at the time, Glynis Johns, had convinced him he was rubbish. To be fair, it had been a view generally shared, and finally accepted by Tony himself. Since 1947, when he and Glynis divorced, he had lived with Dirk and functioned, very capably, as his manager.

We were joined shortly by other guests who had driven down for the day. First were the actors John Standing and his wife Jill Melford; she, for some reason, had been rather camply re-christened "Maude" by Dirk, which was the only name she now answered to. Then came the legendary costume designer Beatrice "Bumble" Dawson, a formidable figure with hair drawn tightly back, intimidating horn-rimmed spectacles, and a cigarette holder wielded, I felt, like a riding crop in the hands of some jack-booted film director of the Cecil B. DeMille generation.

Lunch was served by the woman who'd met us at the door and a similarly attired colleague. It was very English, very good, with both conversation and wine flowing freely. "D'you know," Dirk said as we got started, "I've actually been thinking for quite a while about trying to write myself."

"Oh," I said, "you mean a movie script maybe?"

"No, I'm bored with them. Well, sorry, I mean I enjoyed reading yours, but I don't think I'd be any good at it. I don't know, I'm just trying bits and pieces at the moment – essays, memories, mostly of childhood, a few portraits of people I've known."

This was just over ten years before he published the first volume of his autobiography, *A Postillion Struck by Lightning*, which would be followed by eight more, all critically praised as well as becoming bestsellers. He would also write six novels and many book reviews and articles before his death in 1999.

"I've always liked the idea of writing," he went on. "In fact I've always enjoyed talking to writers. I find them more interesting than actors."

This drew a sharp look from "Maude" across the table. She had already, I suspected, taken a dislike to me on principle as an interloper on privileged territory, and in particular for not knowing

who she was. When I had asked earlier if the distinguished character actor Jack Melford was any relation of hers, she snapped, "Only
my father," and swept off to talk to Bumble Dawson – who turned
out to be a sweet-natured old dear in contrast to the dragon lady I
had feared on first impression.

Dirk went on to develop his thoughts about writing. "I'm not
very well educated. I don't know very much, not like you and
Michael. But I do think with age (he was forty-six) I've developed
a kind of wisdom – I suppose that's the word I'd have to use for it.
Anyway, I'm giving it a try and we'll see what happens."

Then he got onto writers of his acquaintance, starting with Noel
Coward, whom he obviously revered as a man and as a talent.

"Noël would love to meet you. He just absolutely lives for bright,
clever young people. I don't mean sexually. Well, he might fancy
you, of course, but that's not what Noël's about. Unlike Terry,
who's just *so-o-o-o* vulgar – always fucking the milkman or
anyone else within reach. You'd hardly get in the door before he
had his hands down your pants."

This acidulous dismissal of the distinguished playwright
Terence Rattigan took me slightly by surprise, although his sexual
orientation was hardly a big secret in the theatrical world. What
was interesting to discover, however, was that despite the obsessive
secrecy with which Dirk conducted his own private life, homosexuality was by no means an off-limits subject in this house. Nor, on
the other hand, was it an obsessive or even central one.

He went on to talk about Harold Pinter, who had scripted both
The Servant and *Accident*, with a curious mixture of condescension and admiration.

"The first thing Harold did when he started making money was
get his house fitted out like some sort of Arab sheikh – gold-plated
fish-taps in the bathrooms, that sort of thing. And he was always
writing characters who ordered lobster thermidor in restaurants.

I said, 'Why are they always eating lobster thermidor, Harold?' He looked at me in a wide-eyed sort of way and said, 'Isn't that what rich people always eat?'"

In terms of playing the famously pause-laden Pinteresque dialogue, Dirk firmly believed he'd found the right, indeed the only, way to do it. "You have to throw it away," he said, "which doesn't mean mumble it, or get it wrong, or change it. Speak exactly what he wrote, but like a normal person speaking normally. None of this stilted, heightened way of playing it the way his wife does."

Pinter's wife at that time, Vivien Merchant, had been associated with his work since his beginnings in the late fifties, and had indeed developed a particularly arch way of playing him. As it happened, I myself was no great fan of Pinter, considering him a pale shadow of, and barely knee-high to, Samuel Beckett – who, to be fair, Pinter himself idolised. Months later, Dirk and I would have a bitter argument about the worth of Pinter in general and the film *Accident* in particular, but on that first day I was not about to get above myself by taking issue with my host. Besides, I was intrigued by Dirk's "throwaway" theory.

"You know," I said, "that reminds me of something I read a while ago that I found fascinating. Rex Harrison, when asked one time how he developed his famous 'throwaway' technique, replied with, 'First of all you need to work up a full head of steam.'"

"And that's exactly what it takes," Dirk said with enthusiasm. "How clever of Rex. I've never heard him say that. But you know, any time I don't know how to play a scene – any scene, comedy, drama, whatever – I always ask myself: 'How would Rex do this?'"

I found it interesting that a "serious" actor like Dirk should have such unbounded respect for someone known above all as a light comedian. In general, Dirk tended to be more waspishly critical than generous about his fellow actors. Stanley Baker, who had co-starred in *Accident* and had until then been more associated with two-fisted tough-guy roles rather than cerebral ones, was dismissed with an "Oh, please!" rolling of the eyes, despite having received excellent reviews for his performance. George Peppard was "*So-o-o-o* grand these days you can barely talk to him", which was why Dirk had turned down an offer to make a picture with him. Laurence Harvey, with whom Dirk had co-starred in *Darling* a couple of years earlier, "had taste only between his toes" – a peculiarly repellent remark that Dirk was fond of repeating. But Rex Harrison, widely acknowledged though he was as "a total shit" to work with, remained beyond criticism.

(Dirk wasn't alone in that opinion. A few years later, when Harrison played in a rather indifferent film I'd scripted, his fellow actors, all considerable names themselves but still intimidated by Rex, would gather discreetly on the edge of the set to watch him work.)

One of the other things I learnt about Dirk that day was that being a star was, for him, the whole point of being an actor at all. Forget any self-effacing talk about being a team player: that was something you could learn after you'd failed. As we sat around, listening to Broadway cast recordings of various recent and not-so-recent musicals (Dirk and Tony both loved show tunes and listened to little else), he developed the point with a story about Barbra Streisand. Dirk and Tony had seen the Boston opening of *Funny Girl*, and had been seriously underwhelmed by the event. Although possessed of a unique voice, she had poor stagecraft, in their opinion, and simply failed to make the impact she would need to if the show was going to work.

"So they took it on the road for a few weeks, and she worked like hell on that performance. Of course she was helped by the director and everybody else, but they can't do it for you. You're the one up there, you're the one who has to dazzle. And she knew it. She had guts, and she wasn't going to accept failure. By the time that show opened in New York she was a *STAR!*"

As the afternoon wore on and more drinks were consumed, we talked of other stars, including Judy Garland, with whom, a few years earlier, Dirk had made a film, her last, called *I Could Go On Singing*. He talked of the dramas on set, the midnight phone calls, the fights and the tears, and also of the weekends she'd spent at home with Dirk and Tony, relaxing, being herself, a sweet-natured, very funny woman. It was the first time I'd heard about how her drug problems had been created by "that monster Louis B. Mayer" when she was a teenage star at MGM. "He worked the ass off kids like her and Mickey Rooney, had them fed Benzedrine in the morning to get them up and working at dawn, then sleeping pills at night to knock them out in the studio dormitory, then more benzedrine in the morning to get them back to work. How she survived at all is a miracle."

Tony, who had been chatting with Bumble and the others while Dirk and I talked, now glanced at his watch and looked over. "You did talk to Viv this morning, didn't you?" he said to Dirk.

"Yes, she's definitely coming for tea." Dirk too checked his watch. "I don't suppose she'll be long."

I vaguely wondered who "Viv" might be. Not Mrs Pinter, I imagined, after the way Dirk had spoken of her earlier, but I didn't ask questions. A few minutes later the door opened and the house-keeper who had greeted Michael and me earlier in the day looked in to announce that Dirk and Tony's guest had arrived.

Vivien Leigh walked in.

The anticipation of meeting a movie star is one thing; coming face to face with a legend, without warning, is quite another. She was tiny, and exquisite, like a fine porcelain doll that had been somehow magically endowed with the power to move, smile and speak. I was mesmerised as Dirk introduced us, and looked on in awe as she floated with gossamer lightness between the other guests, giving a hug to Bumble Dawson who, I gathered later, was her oldest friend and closest confidante.

I didn't know then that she had suffered from tuberculosis for most of her life, but I noticed, as she sat down near the fire and lit a cigarette, that she suppressed a cough that came from deep in her lungs and sounded alarmingly fluid. But nothing broke her poise, part of which was a strange tightly coiled quality, like a fine watch-spring that had been wound to its limit and was now fighting to hold back and not run down too quickly and risk breaking apart. I did not know then that, in addition to tuberculosis, she had also suffered all her life from manic depression – bipolar disorder, as it would now be called – for which there was at that time no treatment, and which also perhaps contributed to the contained and slightly other-worldly quality she had about her.

She was accompanied by a tall man in the mould, rather like Tony Forwood, of a somewhat old-fashioned matinee idol. Jack Merivale was indeed an actor: not a star by a long shot, but accomplished and well liked, and an old friend of the Oliviers from way back. He had been Vivien's companion and, in effect, her nurse since the divorce from Larry in 1960. He had a quality of calm and great modesty about him, a consort who was content to remain in the background, ready to offer help when required, but never taking the lead. His devotion to Vivien must have been huge, because, as I learned later from people who'd known her for years, she had never got over the break with Olivier, even though it had been largely her fault due to her illness-based erratic and often impossible behaviour. Even that afternoon, within minutes of sitting down, her conversation turned to Larry and the "scandal" of his repeated failure to raise the money to film the *Macbeth* that he had always wanted to do, and which he and Vivien had played memorably on the stage at Stratford in 1955.

But the conversation drifted to other things, and soon she and Dirk went into a huddle and started to talk about gardening – when to prune and what to plant and how to plan for the spring. Before long they were swapping seed catalogues – a packet of something she'd brought over for him, something he'd been saving for her. It was a subject about which I knew nothing, so I contented myself with handing around the ginger cake and trying to keep my jaw from sagging every time my gaze returned to this extraordinary woman. She caught my look once, and gave me the most dazzling smile I've ever received.

It was a smile I would remember with a stab of real sadness when I heard, on a hot July afternoon less than six months later, that she had died suddenly at her London home. She was just fifty-three.

CHAPTER 13

What with one thing and another, Dirk and I never got around to talking about film development that Sunday, as had been intended. So, when Michael and I departed for London in the early evening, Dirk asked if I wouldn't mind coming to see him in a couple of days at Twickenham Studios, where he was shooting a film.

Mind? It would be my first time inside an actual film studio, and I was thrilled at the prospect. I took the train from Waterloo, emerging thirty minutes later from a suburban station into a landscape of terraced houses and small shops that seemed a million miles from the glamour of a film studio. Nor was there much glamour about the studio itself, which was a brief walk from the station. It looked more like a sprawl of drab warehouses than anything else. I entered by an unimposing gate and spoke to the guard in his little box next to it. Dirk had left my name, and I was given directions.

I found him in a dingy corridor talking with the luminously pretty Susannah York, who, though nearly twenty years his junior, was playing his love interest in the film they were shooting, *Sebastian*. It was one of several feeble and largely forgotten cold-war thrillers that Dirk had a curious proclivity for, and which he strolled through looking soulful and faintly cynical to subsidise his more "arty" work with Losey, Fassbinder, Visconti and the like. This one concerned a master codebreaker (Dirk) and his team of pulchritudinous female assistants. The strapline on the poster would read, provocatively: "We can't tell you what he does (it's an international secret) but he does it with 100 girls... and he does it the best!" Subtle stuff.

After Dirk had finished his conversation with Miss York (no relation to Michael), he led me down the corridor and across the corner of a sound stage where the set of the main codebreaking room (where Dirk and the girls "did it") was being struck, eventually arriving at his cramped and very modest dressing room. Tony was there, waiting to drive Dirk home as he did every day. He poured me a drink while Dirk went off to get out of his costume and take a shower.

Tony was an easy man to talk to. I could sense he had developed a talent for taking up the slack when Dirk, the inevitable centre of attention, was "off stage" and people were awaiting his return. When he did, Tony would discreetly step back, yielding the limelight with extraordinary grace to his famous partner. In private, however, theirs was a relationship of equals. In fact in many ways Tony was in the driving seat, guiding Dirk's career with impeccable taste and cool judgment. He handled the money, dealt with lawyers and producers, coped with household staff ("best to bring any problems you may have to me"), steered him clear of undesirables, and generally left him free to be what he was best at – being a star. This was a view based not just on my own observation but endorsed by those who had known them far better and for much longer, including someone who was in effect the third member of their tight little family.

"You must meet my son Gareth some time," Tony said. "He's an actor, about your age, just getting started. He often comes down to the house at the weekend."

"I'd like to," I said. "I look forward to it."

In fact I would get to know Gareth Forwood very well, not just through his father and Dirk but because he would be cast, quite by coincidence, in my first two television plays which would be shot the following year. He was a promising young actor whose career, and life, would end sadly. That was a tale yet to unfold, and yet somehow, looking back, inevitable.

Dirk returned and we had another round of drinks. Dirk's was Guinness. "All right," he said, "let's talk about what we might do. I'm thinking of directing – vaguely. I don't know if I will, or if I do what it'll be. It all depends on finding the right story. I haven't got any ideas, just some feelings, impressions, maybe a starting point. I've got this opening I keep thinking about, and perhaps you can make something of it."

He took a sip of his drink, and set the scene.

"It's dusk. A young girl, maybe fourteen, fifteen, is riding a horse round a paddock. She jumps a couple of practice fences, then a voice comes from a house beyond the trees nearby. It's a woman's voice, probably her mother, calling her name: 'Pamela? Pamela?' The girl reins in her horse, and turns to look in the direction of the voice. And that's all I have. I don't know where it goes from there or who the people are, or anything. It's just a feeling. A mood."

I nodded, I hoped wisely. It was indeed a feeling, a mood, and very little else. It was also, I thought, very Dirk: elegant, middle class, but with a sense of something perhaps a little troubling lurking in the shadows.

"I'll just leave it with you," Dirk said, holding up a hand to show he didn't require any immediate response. "Then there's this," he added, handing me a book from his dressing table. "I meant to give it to you before you left on Sunday."

It was a novel, I discovered as I began reading on the train back to London, about intense and doomed homosexual love in an English public school. I was astonished that Dirk was even contemplating involvement in such a story, especially after the extraordinary boldness he had shown six years earlier by playing a homosexual (though married) lawyer in *Victim*. That film had

99

not only shattered his romantic image as the "idol of the Odeons", but had very nearly ended his career. Only the insistence of the star, Alec Guinness, backed up by the director, Lewis Gilbert, had got him hired subsequently as second lead (and villain) in *HMS Defiant*, about a mutiny on a Royal Navy ship during the Napoleonic Wars. After that he had re-established himself somewhat with a war movie (*The Password Is Courage*) and another *Doctor* sequel (*Doctor in Distress*) before going on to make *The Servant*, which had won glowing critical praise, but which he had conservatively followed up with another comedy spy thriller (*Hot Enough for June*) and a pot-boiling war movie, *The High Bright Sun*. So, in view of his persistent denials, both publicly and privately, that he was homosexual, why on earth would he want to return to the subject in such an unambiguous way?

On my next visit to Adam's Farm a couple of weeks later I told him I hadn't much liked the novel, but asked him what it was he had seen in it of particular interest. He was curiously evasive, as he would be years later when insisting publicly that *Death in Venice* had absolutely nothing to do with an ageing homosexual's lust for a beautiful young boy, but was all about the love of spiritual purity and abstract beauty that comes with the nearness of death. In this case, he said, it was the formal setting of a public school with its rituals and rules that interested him, and the pressures and conflicts that could develop within such frameworks. He told me that in many ways the most satisfying period of his life had been his four years in the army during the war, in which he saw service in Europe and the Far East, finishing up as a major in the Intelligence Corps.

"You always knew where you were and what was expected of you. I liked that. It was reassuring and in a strange way liberating. It wasn't restricting, but you knew what the limits were, and within them you had the freedom to accomplish what you were supposed to accomplish."

It was a Saturday afternoon, and I was the only guest at the house that day. Tony had left us alone to talk, and now that the subject of homosexuality had been broached, albeit obliquely, I found Dirk touchingly open on the subject. He wasn't about to make any confessions, of course; at the same time, he wasn't putting up any strenuous pretence of being other than he was.

"But look," I found myself saying at one point, "homosexuality isn't going to remain a crime for much longer. The Arran bill to legalise it is going through parliament now. It'll be law in a matter of months, if not weeks."

Dirk moved over to pull a curtain across one corner of the window to block a dazzling shaft of sunlight that had just broken through the clouds. "It won't make any difference," he said. "The prejudice will last for at least another twenty years, probably longer."

He was right, of course, and I sensed a genuine sadness in him as he spoke. It reflected something he'd been saying earlier about how much he would have liked to have a child.

There was no suggestion that this might have been achieved by any method other than adoption, and he described to me how very nearly he had managed to adopt the child actor Jon Whiteley, who had appeared with him at the age of six in 1952 in the film *Hunted*, and again in 1956 in *The Spanish Gardener*. The child, Dirk claimed, had elderly parents who had never wanted him. Only at the very last minute, when the adoption papers were drawn up and about to be signed, had something gone wrong and Dirk's ambition to be a parent had been thwarted.

It was a touching story, one I learned later he had repeated on many occasions. But it was wholly untrue. The Whiteley family, when they eventually heard about it, were furious. Not only were the boy's parents far from elderly, but they were a close-knit and happy family, as would be later confirmed by the boy's younger sister. Why Dirk made up such a story, evidently convincing himself it was true by repeating it so often, remains a mystery.

Another mystery surrounds the exact nature of the relationship between Dirk and the beautiful actress/model Capucine. They had met on the set of Dirk's disastrous Hollywood flop, *Song Without End*, a crass biopic of Franz Liszt. They had become firm friends, sparking much press speculation that perhaps Dirk had finally met "the one" and that marriage was in the air. Neither he nor she had done anything to quash the rumours, but to anyone close to them the idea was unthinkable.

"That was a peculiar courtship," Dirk's sister would later say in a BBC interview commenting on some of Dirk and Tony's home movies, "all captured on film by Tony."

I never asked Dirk about Capucine, nor did he mention her himself. But, when he was showing me around the house one day on an early visit, I noticed a framed photograph of her on a window sill – placed exactly midway between Dirk's bedroom and Tony's bedroom. This, I suspect, summed up the truth: that she was a friend of them both, in the way that a single person often befriends and is befriended by a couple. It probably suited both Dirk and Tony to let the press and public speculate about a romance, just as it often suited them over the years to take Elizabeth, Dirk's younger sister, with them on holiday. A woman on Dirk's arm helped dispel any suspicions that might otherwise attach to two men travelling together, staying in the same hotels, and being photographed strolling through St Tropez or wherever they happened to be. She was the "beard", and knew it perfectly well. But the Bogardes were a sophisticated family, and Dirk had no need either to explain or excuse himself. It was only the press and general public he needed to be wary of.

In private he felt less need to mask the effeminacy that was part of his nature. A look, a gesture, a turn of phrase, all contributed to an air of slightly flouncing "camp" that he sometimes allowed to show. But nothing was ever said, nothing made explicit. "Fuck me!" I exclaimed angrily one day, after slicing my thumb on the steel cap of a champagne cork I was trying to remove.

"Not just now, thank you," came a response in clipped tones that managed to be slightly flirtatious and faintly reproachful at the same time. It was Dirk, one eyebrow coolly raised, entering from the kitchen with a tray of glasses.

CHAPTER 14

"Tote" was the affectionate nickname by which Dirk had addressed Tony for as long as anyone remembered. The origin of the name was unknown, unless, as some people have suggested, it was short for "totally gorgeous".

However, in his eight volumes of autobiography, not only does Dirk never use the nickname, he never refers to Tony as anything but "Forwood", as though they were a couple of crusty old bachelors sharing lodgings for convenience, like Holmes and Watson, or Higgins and Pickering – and just about as fictitious. Even as late as 1986, in a television interview with Russell Harty, only two years before Tony's death from cancer at the age of seventy-two, Dirk refused to concede that "Forwood" was anything more than a friend and business manager. Yes, they shared a house together, and had done so for over forty years, but there was nothing more to the relationship than that.

However, as Dirk conceded on numerous occasions when challenged about his reticence over this aspect of his life, "It's all there, between the lines, if you know how to read."

Which makes it all the more remarkable that the only person I ever met in Dirk and Tony's intimate world who did not accept that theirs was a sexual relationship was Tony's son.

Gareth Forwood was born in 1945 when his mother, Glynis Johns, was only twenty-two and already a movie star. His grandfather, Mervyn Johns, was a famous character actor and sometimes leading man of stage and film. By the time Gareth was two, his parents had divorced and his father, Tony, was living with Dirk in Chester Row, Belgravia.

There was no coyness about the arrangements. Dirk's younger brother, then a teenager and also by coincidence called Gareth, used to stay at the house sometimes and would take breakfast up to the two men who shared the same room and bed. Even before that, Glynis Johns, though still married to Tony, reassured a would-be lover, the director Ken Annakin, that "Tony's gone gay" and wouldn't give a damn if she had an affair.

Gareth Forwood had been largely brought up by his father and Dirk from early childhood, though he visited his mother whenever possible at various locations around the world where she happened to be working. After her divorce from Tony, Glynis would re-marry and divorce three more times by the end of the sixties. It was Dirk and Tony, with their settled domestic arrangements, who provided stability and continuity in the boy's life. It was Tony who would get his school reports and chastise him if they weren't good enough, and Dirk who would cheer him up as often as not with a bottle of Guinness.

As a child he played games with the likes of Judy Garland, Ava Gardner, Ingrid Bergman, Barbra Streisand, the Oliviers, Gregory Peck, Noël Coward and "Johnny" Gielgud. He would spend Christmas on Long Island with Rex Harrison and Kay Kendall, and be present when Alan J. Lerner sat down at the piano in Dirk's drawing room and played, for the first time ever with an audience, the whole score of *My Fair Lady*. It was, as Gareth would later describe it, "a charmed life".

I first met Gareth on a visit to Adam's Farm around Easter, 1967. As I hadn't made much of Dirk's "Pamela" idea or the novel he'd given me, he'd suggested finally that I write an original screenplay, for which he would pay me £200 (about £3000 in today's money).

I became, for the time being, a regular weekend guest. Gareth would pop down whenever he pleased; where Dirk and Tony lived had been home for him all his life.

Unlike his father, he wasn't tall and elegant. He was, by contrast, built along the lines of his grandfather, Mervyn Johns: short and physically rather stiff in his movements, with a pleasant though somewhat unformed face, and light-ish hair that was already starting to thin. He was no athlete; indeed he didn't have much of a physical presence at all. What he did have was a disarmingly self-deprecating manner that I found unusual in a young man of just twenty-two. Almost everything he said was accompanied by a smile that hovered on the edge of being somehow apologetic. And he had a way of speaking with his chin tucked in and a soft chuckle in his voice that seemed to invite his listener not to take anything he said too seriously. For someone brought up in such an incredibly sophisticated world (or so it seemed to me) he was strangely unsure of himself.

The other thing I noticed that first weekend I met him was that he drank a great deal. Not being a person of notable abstemiousness myself, I had no problems with that. Nor did Dirk or Tony, both of whom enjoyed a drink or three, though I never saw either of them actually drunk. Looking back, it was clear that Gareth was already on the way to becoming an alcoholic. For the time being, however, he was a convivial new friend of whom I immediately became very fond. We would meet up in London, go to a show, have dinner somewhere affordable in Soho. He had inherited his dad's and Dirk's love of musicals. More than once I got a call at the end of the afternoon to hear Gareth, fizzing with enthusiasm for some new show he'd just seen at a matinee. "I hope you're not doing anything tonight," he'd say, "because I came straight out and bought two more tickets. You're going to love it."

Throughout this period I was working not only on my

commission from Dirk, but on other plays and scripts that I was trying to sell, one of which finally hit the jackpot. Associated Television, one of the biggest of the independent television companies, bought a play called *Public Face*. To my pleasant surprise when I went to meet the producer and director of the play at ATV headquarters at Marble Arch, they proposed a young actor called Gareth Forwood for the juvenile lead. I was of course delighted, told them he was a friend of mine, and explained the connection. They were impressed: Dirk Bogarde was very chic in those days. The whole thing also stood me in good stead with Dirk. Now I was a professional, not just a "wannabe". I continued to go to Adam's Farm at weekends, but sometimes also at Gareth's invitation now.

It was on one of these weekends that Dirk and I had a somewhat vigorous difference of opinion. After the usual lengthy and bibulous lunch, Dirk was going on about how his role in *Accident* the previous year had been the most difficult he had ever played.

More difficult than Barrett in *The Servant*, somebody inquired?

"Oh, that was easy by comparison. I just walked through it. One of the easiest things I ever did."

"That doesn't make it any less good," I ventured.

"No, all right. But there was so much more going on in *Accident*. Layers, nuances..."

I had liked *The Servant*. It was small scale, edgy, somehow very much of its time. The characters were locked together in a shifting pattern of conflicts, power games and surprises. As drama, it was fairly basic, but with many memorable scenes, all held together by Johnny Dankworth's brilliant and haunting score. It was Losey, Pinter and Bogarde at their best.

Accident, however, was the same trio at their pretentious worst. Having sat through it once in dismayed boredom, I went again a few days later to be sure I hadn't been in some accidentally disadvantaged state of mind (like stoned) the first time round. But no, it really was that bad. Set in an Oxford where the crack of cricket ball on bat hung forever in the sultry afternoon air, where the characters talked in empty aphorisms, and were filmed endlessly walking through cloistered quadrangles, lolling in punts on the river, or puffing ruminatively on pipes in the library (Dirk never looked at ease with that pipe), it was a cornucopia of clichés linked together with lingering shots of empty spaces and deserted landscapes after the characters had walked out of frame. What was it all about? What did it amount to? Aside from the fact that it had helped make my friend Michael York a star, I could see no virtue in it.

The trouble was it had been hailed as a masterpiece by almost everyone from the critics to the art-house public. And here was Dirk being exceedingly self-congratulatory about it all, and everyone agreeing with him. What does one say in such circumstances?

A sensible person shuts up and goes with the flow. I, however, was in that dangerously articulate mid-point between loosening your buttons a little, and tripping over your trousers.

"*The Servant*," I persisted, "was at least about people you could understand, if not like. And you liked all of them a bit at different times. At any rate, you felt you knew them enough to care, or at least have some interest in what happened to them. Unlike in *Accident*."

Dirk continued to insist that *Accident* was a far more intelligent, profound and in every way superior piece.

"Well," I said, "I didn't believe in a single moment of it. Not a word. Not one character in the whole thing."

"All right," he replied, a slightly sarcastic edge creeping into his voice now, "you've been to university, you're the expert. Tell us why not."

"Well, for one thing," I said, "it had nothing to do with any university I've ever known. That story could have been set anywhere and it wouldn't have mattered."

The eyebrows went up. "Meaning?"

"None of you gave any sign of actually belonging to the world around you. It could have been Oxford University, Newcastle, or Ford Motors in Detroit. Nor did the characters have any relationships to each other, for that matter. You just all walked round in a daze, spouting this flat Pinteresque dialogue like speak-your-weight machines."

Whoops! Well, that's cleared the air, I thought, perhaps a bit optimistically. But there was no going back now, so why try? Besides, I had read somewhere – I think it was Cocteau – that the only thing to do when you've gone too far is to go further. This seemed like as good a time as any to test the theory.

"I think you're completely wrong," Dirk was saying crisply, "and I can tell you, as an actor, that role took more out of me than almost anything I've ever done."

Even at this point, I suppose, I could still have backed off with some floundering anodyne comment, and let the subject drop. But the next thing I heard myself saying was, "Well, that's probably because it wasn't working. You know? It felt uphill all the way because it wasn't real."

"Oh?" The eyebrows way up now. "And what would you know about 'real' in acting?"

I thought I knew at least something. "You're playing an academic philosopher, right?"

"Mmm."

"That means you've spent all your life thinking about stuff."

"Stuff?"

"Philosophical stuff. Logical problems, moral questions, definitions, ambiguities, the meaning of language, and the meaning of 'meaning'. You've read a stack of books and given a thousand lectures. At the very least you've published a few academic papers of your own."

"So..?"

"So one way and another, you've thought about pretty much every kind of question it's possible to think about. You've been doing it all your life, it's your job. You'll have come up with a few tentative conclusions about this and that, but nothing final – you're too smart for that. But the point is you'll always have a starting point to reflect on what's happening now, and that point will be the result of everything you've thought about so far. And that's what I didn't see in your performance."

His reply was a crisp, "I'm still not sure I know what you mean."

I tried to clarify. "You were reacting to everything that came along, large or small, as though it was totally new and nothing like it had ever crossed your mind before. You had no starting point. You weren't coming from anywhere."

Dirk, I recall, tossed his head scornfully a couple of times, puffed on his cigarette, and stared out at the garden. But he said nothing. Nobody said anything.

Feeling, perhaps wrongly, an obligation to fill the silence I had created, I decided to switch to a more conciliatory tack, even a flattering one.

"The thing is," I said, "you did what you always do on screen, and which you do brilliantly. You have this extraordinary ability to show the audience what you're thinking, to actually draw them into your thought process. It was just that in this case, it was your thought process itself that was the problem. There was nothing there."

Gareth, who had listened to the whole exchange while gazing into the fire and nursing a large cognac, came over and poured the same for me. Dirk was clattering about with drinks and coffee cups for other guests by now, signifying that the entertainment was over and the afternoon would now be moving on. I really hadn't meant in any way to alienate him or even to appear rude, but I had, in a way that surprised me, come to a point where I was not prepared to stay silent merely out of politeness or, even worse, deference.

In the evening I was driven back to London by the agent Terence Baker and his wife "Boatie" Boatwright, also an agent of some importance. A few years later Terence and I talked about that afternoon, which he remembered well. He thought that, quite apart from whether I was right about "fucking *Accident*" or not, I was obviously mad.

I trusted his judgment. I had to: he was my agent by then.

CHAPTER 15

The same television company, ATV, that had bought my first play *Public Face* commissioned a second one even before the first had gone into production. It was a vote of confidence in me as a writer and gave me a great deal of encouragement. To my surprise, I was invited down to Adam's Farm again a few weeks after my outburst about *Accident*, though more as Gareth's guest than Dirk and Tony's. Gareth assured me, however, that they were firmly behind the invitation and would be happy to see me. Nonetheless, feeling the atmosphere might be a little strained, I declined.

During that summer of '67, frustrated by the time-lag between the purchase of my first two television plays and their going into production, I finished the original screenplay that Dirk had commissioned and posted it off to him in September. It was the story of a young couple becoming dull and middle-aged before their time, who split up and go through many "liberating" adventures before meeting up again, by accident, as dramatically different people. Their response is to start a new relationship as though they have never known each other previously. I called it *Fairy Tale*.

Dirk's response was prompt and considered. He wrote me a letter typically full of spelling mistakes, but also containing the kind of lively metaphors and vivid similes that would become characteristic of his professional writing some years later. He was generally complimentary, very specific about certain things he liked and one or two he didn't. There was sometimes a sharpness in my dialogue, he said, which could border on the vicious, and he suggested I might add a little sugar to the lemon juice on my strawberries, or something to that effect. Foolishly, I didn't keep the letter, but I do remember that rather complex thought about lemon juice and strawberries, which I was never quite sure I fully understood.

I only saw Dirk and Tony twice again. The following year, late '68, I ran into them in a restaurant in Rome, where Dirk was filming *The Damned* with Visconti, and I was working on a screenplay for an Italian producer. Then, in the summer of '72 when I was staying in the south of France not far from where they were by then living, I got a surprise invitation to go over for a drink one evening. Apparently Gareth, who was in London, had told them I was down there, and I was genuinely touched by their initiative. I took my girlfriend Laurence with me (in France "Laurence" is a girl's name, pronounced with the emphasis on the second syllable, Lau-*rence*. Its masculine equivalent is "Laurent"). After a hot day at the beach the traffic was dreadful, and my rather dodgy Renault chose that moment to develop some clutch problems. As a result, we arrived over half an hour late. Dirk, a stickler for promptness, was not best pleased.

"Well, I suppose you're not *that* late," he said, making a big point of consulting his watch. Leaving me to chat with Tony, he swept Laurence, whom he hadn't met before, up to the far end of the terrace, where they got through a bottle of champagne together. Laurence said afterwards that he'd been an utter delight and she'd had a lovely time.

Gareth, by this time, had set up house (in fact a poky little flat in Fulham) with a charming and pretty French girl called Veronique. Despite the fact that work was thin on the ground, just a few minor TV and film roles and a couple of out-of-town plays, he seemed happy and was drinking less. A son was born, and to make ends meet Veronique found herself having to take up waitressing. She would put the baby to bed, leaving Gareth in charge, then go off to work, returning about midnight.

Before long Gareth had started to hit the bottle again. Every night she would find him spreadeagled on the floor with an empty flagon of cheap wine nearby. One night she returned to find the street cordonned off and police cars everywhere. An IRA terrorist bomb had gone off. When she explained she lived there, they let her through. She found baby Thomas standing up in his cot, miraculously unharmed even though the window had been blown in and there was broken glass everywhere. Gareth was, as usual, dead drunk in the next room, unaware that anything had happened. By the time he woke up in the morning Veronique had left him, taking the baby.

Feeling himself a failure now on a personal as well as a professional level, Gareth's life spiralled further out of control. I was not the only one of his friends to get phone calls at one or two in the morning from some restaurant or bar across town where Gareth was legless and unable pay the bill. Having driven out one night to settle things and get him home, I found him so drunk he couldn't even explain where he was living, which was invariably in a shabby room somewhere, a borrowed flat, or a mattress on somebody's floor. So I took him back to the flat where Laurence and I were living in Primrose Hill. He stayed a week, recovering. But that was nothing. His loyal friend the actor Jeremy Child told me much later how Gareth once came for dinner with him and his wife, passed out drunk, and stayed a year.

I lost touch with him in the late seventies, by which time I was living mostly in Hollywood. He died almost thirty years later, two days after his sixty-second birthday. His funeral, I learned, had been organised by his son Thomas, by then in his thirties. About a hundred people had attended the service in St Paul's, the actors' church in Covent Garden, though Gareth's mother, Glynis Johns, felt too old at eighty-four to make the journey from Los Angeles. She did, however, suggest that they set up a video link and play her recording of "Send in the Clowns" before she said a few words about her son. Thomas did not take her up on the offer.

Only a few weeks earlier he had called her to say that Gareth was dying in a squalid room in Earl's Court that someone was letting him have free of charge. "Gareth hadn't seen his mother in twenty years," Thomas told me, "but I managed to get in touch with her to say we needed money to get him into somewhere decent, or rehab, or anything. She told me to contact her business manager."

He hadn't taken her up on that offer either.

•

Why did Gareth Forwood's life implode in the way it did? His childhood was unusual, but no worse, and in some ways a great deal better, than many. Although his mother was a distant figure, there is no doubt that his father and Dirk did their level best to give him all the attention and affection that a child needs.

Was he destroyed by the shadow of the greater talents he grew up surrounded by? Perhaps. To be honest, I was never sure how good an actor he really was. He never lit up either stage or screen, though he was perfectly competent and might well have matured into an interesting character actor like his grandfather, whom he came increasingly to resemble with age.

But something held him back. Something very deep-rooted had fatally undermined him. But what?

The answer lies, I suspect, in his curious refusal to accept that the relationship between his father and Dirk was anything more than a business arrangement between good friends. I never challenged him on that assumption, nor did anyone I knew; it would have been presumptuous and plain bad manners to do so. Besides, everybody understood that, in the early fifties when Dirk became a star, if there had been the slightest hint that the "idol of the Odeons", mobbed by adoring women wherever he went, was homosexual, he would have been hounded to ruin (if not worse) by the press. Certainly, the "charmed life" that Dirk and Tony had created for themselves, and that the young Gareth had shared, would have been, overnight, a thing of the past.

So it was crucial back then that Gareth, close as he was to the two of them, should do nothing, however unintentionally, to "spill the beans". That meant, in effect, that he had to know nothing. Consequently, it was drilled into him from earliest childhood that the relationship between his father and "uncle Dirk" was absolutely nothing more than the facade they presented to the outside world. Not for him, an unreliable child, the tacit understanding that was shared with their adult friends and family. Gareth, not yet ten years old, could not be trusted with the truth.

But why, at the age of fifty-five, twelve years after his father's death and a year after Dirk's, was Gareth still repeating the story that had protected them during the danger years when there had been everything to lose? Filmed in 2000 for the BBC'S *The Private Life of Dirk Bogarde*, he persists in his conviction that their relationship was platonic: "As I saw it, this was a profound friendship based both in a professional way, and a personal way, and I think that was the only important factor of it, and I would suggest that was the only factor of it anyway."

As he speaks, he swallows as though suffering from a suddenly dry mouth, and his eyes are constantly flickering nervously. It isn't hard to see a man who is unsure of what he is saying, yet remains determined to believe it.

Why?

The reason, I believe, wasn't that he couldn't bear the truth about their relationship with each other. It was that he couldn't bear the truth about their relationship with him. It was too painful for him to admit that the most important part of his childhood had been founded on a lie, or at best a half-truth. Others might have been kept at arm's length for various reasons, but Gareth had always felt that he was closer to his father and Dirk than anyone else in the world could be. Surely they would have kept no secrets from him. They had been his parents. How could they have lied to him?

And if they had, what did that say about him? That he had been unworthy of the intimacy he had always, with hindsight perhaps mistakenly, taken for granted?

In the that same BBC documentary, Gareth is asked:

"Did you remain in contact with him [Dirk] after your father died?"

"No."

"Why?"

"I don't know. It was something on his side, something on mine." His eyes flicker uncertainly here and there as he speaks. "Maybe he was trying to sweep the decks, maybe I felt I needed to get from under various shadows. There was no malice in it. It just kind of went that way. I did try and make contact with him, but there was no response... I feel sad about that."

According to Gareth's son Thomas, that attempt to make contact had been a drunken midnight phone call from Gareth which had convinced Dirk, ageing and ailing as he was by then, that he could no longer cope with the relationship. But, greatly to his credit, Dirk showed remarkable generosity to Thomas, then just fourteen years old and living in France with his mother.

"They had more or less disowned Gareth," Thomas told me. "When they found out that Veronique had left Gareth and was flat broke, living in a women's shelter with me, they helped out with

118

money and in every way they could. Tony was incredibly kind to me, and when he died I got a letter out of the blue from Dirk asking if I would accept him as 'a proxy grandfather' – which of course I did. From then on, I saw him regularly until he died. I could talk about anything with him. I quite often watched him being difficult and prickly with other people, but never with me. When he was given his honorary fellowship of the BFI (British Film Institute), he even took me along as his date for the evening."

By contrast, Thomas had known his father barely at all. "I did manage to track Gareth down in his last years and create the outlines of a relationship, but he didn't make it easy. He was really in bad shape and had discharged himself from the hospital against his doctors' advice. I tried to go round to see him. I rang him up, and he said he wouldn't let me in the door unless I brought him a crate of Guinness. So I had to."

Thomas is now a successful screenwriter living in Paris. He agrees with my view of why Gareth's life fell apart, and provides an interesting bit of evidence to support it. Although by the end of his life Gareth had lost just about every material possession he had ever had, he clung on to two books. One was a collection of poems by Jacques Prévert, which he had always loved; the other was a short story by Graham Greene called "The Basement Room".

This is the story of a small boy whose parents go on holiday, leaving him alone in their large London house in the care of a sympathetic butler and his harridan wife. Gradually the child gets caught up in a history of betrayal and jealousy involving this couple and the husband's younger mistress. Unable though he is to understand what is going on or the intensity of the emotions involved, the boy finds himself being forced to keep secrets for, and from, all sides in this triangle. When the wife accidentally falls to her death after a quarrel, the boy, though doing his best to avoid causing trouble, blurts out something to the police that gets the butler accused of murder. The story is told from the perspective of the boy as an elderly man sixty years later, having failed throughout his life to create any successful relationships as a result of the psychological scars left on him by this complex situation in childhood.

Gareth was fascinated by the story and wanted desperately to make a film of it, playing the butler himself. In fact the story had already been filmed by Carol Reed in 1948, with Ralph Richardson as the butler. Nevertheless, Gareth felt he had something forceful and new to bring to the story, though he never managed to explain to his son or anyone else what that was.

And, of course, he never succeeded in getting the film set up.

CHAPTER 16

I lay on the hard-tufted grass gazing up at the sky and the willowy outline of Primrose in jodhpurs and tweeds. On her face was that faintly amused, slightly mocking expression that I had come to know well. It was borne out of no unkindness or malice; Primrose just found much of life faintly amusing, and most of it the better for a little mockery.

"I can't understand what you're doing wrong," she said. "You start off looking perfectly all right, then suddenly you're on the ground."

Disdaining her outstretched hand I struggled stiffly to my feet and glared at the horse from which I had just fallen for the sixth time that morning, and which was now grazing placidly nearby.

"Conceivably the problem might be you're a bloody useless teacher," I snarled uncharitably.

"Don't be silly, I've been riding all my life."

"All you do is stick me up there, whack the horse on its bum, and tell me to hang on."

We decided to call it a day, and retired to the house where Primrose's mum made Bloody Marys to rival those of Tony Forwood. She had been widowed for ten years, and lived alone on the family estate in Wales, surrounded by a pack of Jack Russells, several horses, and a handful of staff. To their credit, neither she nor Primrose had raised an eyebrow when I informed them that the only four-legged creature I had ever sat on was a donkey on Blackpool sands. Once.

"Never mind, there's nothing to it. You'll pick it up in no time," Prim had assured me breezily, but accepted defeat with her usual grace and good humour.

I was twenty-four; she was a couple of years younger. We had met at a party in London and found that we lived near each other, she on the King's Road in Chelsea, me in a less salubrious part of Fulham. Most evenings I would walk over for dinner, picking up a bottle on the way, and usually stayed the night. It was a lovely time.

My days were spent writing and going to meetings with TV and film people to discuss possible new projects, though nothing much was happening – until one morning in March '68, about three weeks after my twenty-fifth birthday, my agent, Elspeth, called with an odd question. How I would feel about going to Romania for three months?

"They've just started principal photography on a Roman epic," she explained, "with a big international cast and a terrible script. They're all having fits and they need somebody out there to re-write as they shoot."

I would learn as time went by that such an idiotic-sounding situation was by no means unique. Many films are financed by an extraordinary patchwork of deals which involve preselling the as-yet-unproduced movie in various territories around the world. This pre-selling is generally facilitated not by questions like "How good is the script?" or even "What's the story?", but "Who's in it?" Some stars are a draw in Europe, some in the Far East, some in South America, some in the USA and Canada, and so on, allowing local distributors to raise money up front on the star names alone.

In this case a very successful German producer had put together a deal to make a sprawling Roman epic of the kind that were popular at the time. He had signed up, amongst others, Laurence Harvey, who was still an international star though his career was perceptibly on the slide. Only three years earlier he had been billed above Dirk Bogarde in *Darling*, the film that had made Julie Christie famous. Before that, throughout the fifties he had played leads in a respectable list of British pictures, finally breaking out worldwide with *Room at the Top* in 1959. "From now on," he had crowed triumphantly to reporters, "you're going to have to say which one you mean when you say 'Larry'. Me? Or Olivier?"

Nominated for an Oscar, he went on to play in a string of big pictures alongside such names as John Wayne, Elizabeth Taylor and Frank Sinatra, reaching a level of international stardom that Dirk had never got close to. But by the late sixties, just as Dirk was becoming a universally respected and something of a "cult" actor, Larry's career was running out of steam. After several high-profile flops he had been reduced most recently to playing in an unreleasable Italian thriller alongside Ann-Margret. To him, a breathtakingly extravagant high-liver, *The Last Roman* (or *The Battle for Rome* as it was alternatively called) represented a much-needed and very big pay day. But also perhaps, just perhaps, a chance to escape the doldrums towards which his career seemed unavoidably headed.

Also signed up were the Italian star Sylva Koscina, Britain's Honor Blackman, famous for *The Avengers* and more recently *Goldfinger* with Sean Connery, the Swedish Harriet Andersson, who had until then played mostly in Ingmar Bergman art-house movies, and various others. All had received assurances that once their deals were made the script would be pulled into shape. But it took Larry's arrival on location to ensure that the promise was delivered on. I was told he would be flying from Bucharest to London in a few days' time to interview writers.

Elspeth had explained to me that other agents were putting up other writers for the same job, most of them more experienced and better known than I was. The money was seriously good, and a screen credit on a big picture was a tempting prospect for anyone. So I tried not to get my hopes up too high as I turned up at Harvey's flat in Park Lane on a drizzly and grey March morning.

I was met by Larry's London agent, Maggie Parker, an elegant woman in her mid-fifties who had previously been a well known actress under the name of Margaret Johnston. She asked me to wait in a small-ish pastel-coloured and antique-filled sitting room, and disappeared for a few minutes. I filled in the time by poking around, as I have always had a habit of doing, in things that were none of my business, my excuse always being that as a writer nothing was off-limits, and as a very discreet person there was no chance of my blabbing to the world at large any gossip or scandal I might accidentally unearth.

Surprisingly, despite the time of year, there were several Christmas cards still displayed on one side of the room. Peering inside, I saw a number of famous signatures that would have quickened the heart of any autograph hunter, including Burton and Taylor's and the Kirk Douglases. But the one that struck me most bore on the front a pen and ink sketch of an ornate garden fountain, the centre of which came together in the unmistakable features of David Niven, lips pursed in comical disdain to squirt a stream of water into a pool beneath. Inside was written, "Dearest Larry, this is pretty much how I feel about the business at the moment. Never mind, onwards and upwards. Love David and Hjordis."

Hearing a sound at the door, I stepped back and turned to meet my host. Larry entered, followed by Maggie. I saw right away that he was the kind of actor who liked to make an entrance, even for an audience of one. Tall and impeccably dressed in a dark green velvet jacket, black trousers and collar and tie, he held a long cigarette holder in one hand, and in the other a few ice cubes wrapped in a handkerchief and clasped to his forehead. The star had a hangover.

We sat opposite each other as a secretary appeared with a tray and poured three cups of coffee. Larry took a sip, then set his ice cubes aside and focussed on me.

"Have you read the script?" he asked.

Indeed I had. From the names on the cover I concluded that it had its murky origins in Hungarian and German versions, after which a couple of English writers had given it a quick going over to make it at least readable. The plot, however, remained largely impenetrable, and the dialogue veered between the stilted and the unspeakable.

"Yes," I said, "twice."

A drag on his cigarette. "What d'you think?"

I was obviously prepared for this and had settled on what I thought was the only reply in the circumstances. "I think it's fixable."

He took another drag on his cigarette, his rather Slavic eyes narrowing to peer at me through the smoke and his hangover, and waited for me to expand.

"The story's there, and all the characters, but they need bringing out. I think there are quite a few scenes we could cut, which would help. And the dialogue of course, well, it needs a complete re-write of every scene."

We talked a while longer, maybe fifteen minutes, with Maggie filling him in on the exceedingly modest details of my career so far. I departed with a polite handshake from both of them, and zoomed home to phone Elspeth.

"Have you heard anything?"

"Not yet, dear," she said with her usual kindly patience. "They're seeing people all day and some more tomorrow. Try and forget about it for now. I'll call you as soon as I know something."

Forgetting about it was more easily said than done, but I did my best, only calling Elspeth four times over the next two days to say, "You *must* have heard *something.*"

Elspeth's composure never slipped as she gracefully fielded my impatience. On the third day, having white-knuckled it until eleven-thirty in the morning, I was about to cave in and call her yet again, when she rang me.

"Start packing. You're flying out to Bucharest with Larry tomorrow."

CHAPTER 17

My instructions were to make my own way to Gatwick Airport and meet Larry at the desk of Tarom Airlines, the Romanian national carrier, which operated out of the furthest and most obscure corner of the airport there was.

There weren't many people around and Larry was not hard to find in a bright orange jumpsuit, cigarette holder stylishly poised as always, and accompanied by the young secretary, Sandy, who had served coffee three mornings earlier, and Brian, a cheerful Londoner about my age who was Larry's chauffeur, valet and general amanuensis.

The plane we were to travel in was at first glance disappointing, and at a second glance rather alarming. A twin-engined turbo-prop of a certain age, its fuselage was dirty and worryingly dented, and a large oil stain was spreading on the tarmac beneath one of the wings where two engineers were working furiously to plug a leak.

"Too much oil in the engine," we were assured by an English-speaking (but only just) member of Tarom's ground staff who had shown up to greet the airline's celebrity passenger.

"Bloody miracle there's any oil in the engine at all looking at that mess," was Larry's only comment. Nonetheless, he gamely mounted the steps to the plane's interior, bolstering my confidence (it was only the second time I'd flown) by observing that he'd always had a premonition he would die young, and probably in a plane crash.

Whether there was any real difference between first class and economy was hard to discern, except that maybe half a dozen passengers, including Sandy and Brian, were scattered around in economy, with only Larry and myself in first. We buckled ourselves into seats facing each other across a table, more like in a passenger train than an aircraft. The thing shook and snarled its way into the air more or less on time, and Larry lit a cigarette without waiting for the no-smoking sign to go off.

We enquired about alcohol, only to be told by the sweet and well-meaning hostess that there was no champagne or Scotch, but several Romanian wines that we might like to try. These turned out to be poisonous, so we settled on a native plum brandy, not something wisely consumed in any great quantity, but it served to break the ice.

One of the first things I couldn't resist asking Larry, after a glass or two of this fire water, was what had prompted him and Maggie Parker to choose me for this assignment as opposed to any of the other candidates up for it. He looked faintly amused and glanced out at the clouds we were beginning to climb above.

"It was something you said in the interview."

"Really? What?"

"Well, we asked everybody more or less the same bunch of questions, including 'Tell us something about the way you write'."

I couldn't recall being asked the question, but I must have been since he remembered my answer.

"Most people came up with some balls-ache like, 'I'm rather of the school of Rattigan', or 'I write somewhat after the fashion of Pinter'. When we asked you, you just said, 'As simply and clearly as possible'. As soon as you were out of the room I turned to Maggie and said, 'He'll do'."

So why hadn't they told me right away instead of waiting three days?

"Maggie said we should see everybody on the list or the producer wouldn't think we were serious. And he was paying."

In all honesty, I'd never much rated Laurence Harvey as an actor in the past, finding his performances often wooden, shallow and one-note. To his credit, I would find out later that he didn't have much of an opinion of himself either, but that self-knowledge was something he was always at pains to hide beneath the carefully manufactured bravura that he showed the world in general.

I had also picked up on the show-business grapevine that he was considered by many colleagues, acquaintances, ex-lovers and his former wife to be a shameless, copper-bottomed, grade-A, total shit.

But that day, rattling through the skies in that dreadful and patently unsafe plane, I began to discover that I was going to like him in person quite a lot.

•

We made it to Bucharest by the end of the afternoon, though only after an unscheduled stop in Brussels to re-plug that oil leak from one of the engines. Larry had drunk enough plum brandy by then to start recounting some of his favourite and blackly funny flying stories, and I had drunk enough to enjoy them.

There was one about Harry Cohn, the thuggish head of Columbia Pictures who most Fridays would take a private plane from Burbank to Las Vegas to screw a few show girls. Before take-off he would have his doctor administer an enormous shot of vitamin B-12, supposedly the Viagra of its day, to get him ready for an evening of orgiastic pleasure. One time, when Larry had gone along for company, a fog had descended over Vegas forcing the plane to circle endlessly, waiting for it to disperse. Larry's impersonation of Cohn's mounting panic that his B-12 shot might wear off before he even laid hands on a girl was a classic piece of comedy. Finally Cohn had ordered the pilot to land almost blind: a case, as Larry put it, of a man "not just ready to die for a fuck, but willing to kill for it too".

Then there was the time on a commercial airliner when Larry was travelling with Otto Preminger and a few other big names in Hollywood. As they were coming in to land the captain announced there was a problem with the landing gear which was refusing to lock in place. They circled for more than an hour while the crew tried to resolve the problem from the flight deck, and on the ground preparations were made for a crash landing.

Conversation among the movie titans, however, was confined entirely to who would get top billing in the obituaries if the whole thing ended in disaster. Preminger took violent exception to the prospect of being upstaged by a "fucking no-account actor" who'd only had a couple of hits compared with Preminger's long career and many major pictures. According to Larry, a couple of agents and a senior executive who were also in the party tried to draw up a legally enforceable document in which Larry graciously conceded first place in the death notices to Mr Preminger, he himself taking second position, though in equal size print. Then they asked a pale and jittery hostess if she had anything fire resistant, some metal container from the galley perhaps, in which the contract might have a chance of surviving the conflagration to come.

Obviously, in spite of everything, the flight was concluded safely, as was ours to Bucharest. But by the time we got there I had seen a side to the actor Laurence Harvey I had never suspected before, certainly not from any of his performances. He was capable of being very funny. Some weeks later, when I knew him better, I asked, "Why don't you do more comedy?"

His face fell as though the question had touched a sore point.

"I'd like to," he said, "I've a pile of scripts I'm trying to get off the ground, but nobody thinks I can do it. And you know what, maybe they're right. Every time I get in front of that fucking camera, I freeze up. I can feel it happening. The face tightens up, the voice, whole bloody body goes rigid."

It was a remarkable confession, one of a surprising number I heard him make that summer, "the summer of my fortieth year" as he would intone in a doom-laden voice from time to time – not entirely seriously, because he was never entirely serious about anything.

All the same, during the three months I was in his company almost every day, there was an oblique admission behind much of what he said that he knew the game was up, professionally, personally and financially. And in truth it was.

But, while it lasted, what a game it had been.

•

Larushka Mischa Skikne was born into a Jewish family in a small town in northern Lithuania on 1 October 1928. He was the youngest of three brothers. His father was a casual house painter and builder who emigrated to South Africa shortly after Larry's birth, leaving the boys to be brought up by a strict and domineering mother. Five years later, when Larry was six, the rest of the family went out to join their father in Johannesburg.

Larry never cared much for schooling, and by all accounts was a street-wise hooligan by his early teens. At fourteen he ran away to Cape Town and joined the navy, lying about his age. His mother came down and dragged him back to Johannesburg. A year later he ran away again and joined the army. This time his family let him be, realising they had little alternative.

According to Larry he saw active service in Italy, though he was a little vague about the details and there may have been a degree of exaggeration in his story. What is certain is that by the end of the war in 1945, at the age of only sixteen, he was a sergeant in something called the Union Defence Forces Entertainment Unit and stationed at a base camp outside Cairo. From there he negotiated a grant from the army of around £700 (in today's money about £25,000) to send himself to England, where he had somehow got himself accepted into the Royal Academy of Dramatic Art.

He was still only seventeen when he started at RADA, completely alone in London and living in a rented room in Chelsea – at that time still seriously bohemian and tacky. Tall and gangling, and with an accent you could cut with a knife, he nevertheless had a notable stage presence and before long had been signed up by a leading agent. By the time he was nineteen he had played a season of classic and new plays at the Library Theatre, Manchester, and had been given a contract by Warner Brothers in London, which led to his first supporting roles in modest British B-pictures.

So far he had been working under the name of Larry M. Skikne, but the film world decided this would no longer do for a budding star. According to Larry, he himself chose the name "Laurence Harvey" by checking into an expensive suite (which, naturally, he couldn't afford) at the Hyde Park Hotel in Knightsbridge, and ordering up a bottle of champagne which he consumed while sitting on his balcony and contemplating the city spread out before him under the night sky. Gradually his focus narrowed onto the big department store on the opposite side of the road, Harvey Nichols.

"Laurence Nichols?" he wondered aloud to himself. "Nah!"

But "Laurence Harvey..?"

Well now... yes, not bad.

A few weeks later on the set of one of his first films he would meet Hermione Baddeley, a rather blowsy but famous and well-connected actress who was twenty-two years his senior. He moved into her house in Belgravia, spent her money and shamelessly exploited her connections in the business.

Largely through her he got his first season at Stratford playing second leads, during which time he began an affair with Margaret Leighton, only six years his senior and one of British theatre's aristocracy. As a consequence, she was divorced by her publisher husband and married Larry in 1957.

According to Ms Baddeley, Ms Leighton had been reduced to "a gibbering bag of nerves" by the time she divorced Larry in 1961 on the grounds of "irreconcilable differences". At the forefront of these "differences" was the affair he was openly having with Joan Cohn, this time seventeen years older than himself, and the widow of the aforementioned Hollywood mogul Harry Cohn.

Not only was she one of the wealthiest women in America, but an alliance with her offered Larry the tantalising possibility of taking over Columbia Pictures and becoming a mogul himself. However, by the time he married Joan in October '68, his English girlfriend Paulene Stone, who was only twenty-five and had been with us for a large part of our summer in Romania, would be already pregnant with their child. When Joan discovered that he had installed this new family in a large and extravagantly remodelled house in London, in large part at Joan's expense, she decided enough was enough and started divorce proceedings in early 1972. On the last day of that same year Larry finally married Paulene, but was dead from colon cancer eleven months later.

By any standards "a shameless, copper-bottomed, grade-A, total shit", just as I had heard him described, and which so much about his behaviour seemed to confirm.

So why did I like him so much? It certainly wasn't a matter of being star-struck. As I've said, I'd never rated him as an actor and hadn't even seen most of his films since *Room at the Top* nine years earlier. To his credit he didn't bat an eyelid when this became evident. "Don't worry," he said, "you and a few million others. Sandy here thinks I'm box-office poison."

A spluttered denial from his secretary across the terrace on which we were enjoying the Romanian sun met only a dismissive wave. "Relax, you're not fired."

It was that surprising element of self-deprecation in him, quite unexpected in such an obvious narcissist, that made me recognise something in myself. We were both totally self-created personalities, with all the uncertainties and insecurities that go with the territory. Admittedly, his journey had been rather more extreme than mine, though as Noël Coward once said, "Larry claims his parents were Lithuanian Jewish peasants, though we all know the truth is his mother was Gladys Cooper and his father a Ruritanian prince."

CHAPTER 18

1968 was a dramatic year worldwide. The war in Vietnam was causing political upheaval across America and Western Europe. In France rioting students and striking workers had united to take the country to the brink of revolution. Meanwhile in Eastern Europe communism was showing a new and more human face in the Prague Spring, an experiment which would be brutally snuffed out by the Soviet invasion in August.

Romania, under the communist dictatorship of Nicolae Ceauşescu since 1965, was at that time looked on favourably by the West because of its refusal to toe the Moscow line and condemn the independent-minded Czechs. I was soon to learn, however, that there was no comparable liberalisation taking place inside Romania, which was why the Soviet leadership left the country alone. So long as Ceauşescu maintained a ruthless police state at home, thereby risking no destabilisation of the Eastern bloc, he was free to say what he liked to the outside world and posture as a world statesman to his heart's content. Which was one of the reasons why President de Gaulle happened to be on a state visit to Romania when Larry and I arrived in Bucharest. The French flag and the General's photograph were everywhere.

We were initially installed in the Plaza Athenee Hotel in the centre of Bucharest. It was considered to be the country's finest, a reasonable facsimile of Western comfort, although I found the combination of beige, browns and oatmeal fabric throughout faintly depressing.

As it happened, we weren't the only movie people staying there. Omar Sharif and the director Terence Young were also resident. Young was riding high from having created the James Bond franchise by directing *Dr No*, then *From Russia with Love* and *Thunderball* in quick succession. Currently he was making *Mayerling* with Sharif, Catherine Deneuve, James Mason and Ava Gardner. The main shoot was over and had not taken place in Romania, but they were spending a few days at Buftea Studios, where our picture was based, picking up a few shots with Omar and some extras that Young had decided he needed.

Terence Young had directed Larry in a British film, *Storm Over the Nile* in 1955, so naturally enough they arranged to meet in the bar, along with Omar who knew Larry from Hollywood. I was invited to join them.

Young was a tall, suave Englishman of the kind that was already even then going out of style – a style on which, I suspect, Larry had built much of his own persona. As, up to a point, had I for that matter.

Omar Sharif, by comparison, had been born into a wealthy Egyptian family, inheriting naturally the kind of suavity and elegance that Larry could only aspire to and largely only carica-ture. Also unlike Larry, Omar was at the top of his career, with *Lawrence of Arabia*, *Doctor Zhivago* and *Funny Girl* only recently behind him. Actually, I'd never thought much of him as an actor. He shared some of Larry's woodenness and limited range; but at least you got the impression there was something going on behind the eyes, a hinterland, something more than mere surface. It was not for nothing that he was a world-class bridge player, something he took far more seriously than acting.

I'd assumed my invitation was just for a drink, then the "grown-ups" would go off for dinner, but Larry insisted I join them, which I found generous of him. We were driven to somewhere recommended by one of our film company's local fixers, whose job was to ensure that we got the best of everything while in the country. This included an officially non-existent black-market restaurant that catered exclusively to members of the central committee, their families and associates. It served simple but extremely good food, and the wines were the best in Bucharest.

Conversation between Larry and Terence was mostly about "the business". Terence boasted about his work ethic, how he never sat down on the set, and how he had just directed Audrey Hepburn in *Wait Until Dark* and now she wanted to make a deal for three more films with him (it never happened). Larry talked about all the projects he had in development, including a comedy with Robert Mitchum (which also never happened), offers he had turned down, some of which I suspected were more imaginary than real. There was a touching transparency to him at times. Nobody was going to believe his claim that they had really wanted him for the Christopher Plummer role in *Fall of the Roman Empire*. And when he talked about certain actors' performances in other recent films, it was obvious how much he had coveted the role himself.

"Rod Steiger? He was okay, but what that part needed was somebody tall, elegant, sophisticated..."

The film under discussion was called *No Way To Treat a Lady*, a considerable success at the time. And the "somebody" the film had really needed, one was left to assume, was Laurence Harvey. Later he would actually tell me that he had been approached to play Omar's role in *Mayerling*, and I did my very best to look like I believed him, though I don't think he really expected me to.

Omar had little interest in Hollywood gossip. I would later hear him described as a great ladies' man, "the number one swordsman in town" as one show-business lawyer I met put it admiringly. But he couldn't have cared less about which studio head was about to be fired, or how many zillions the Burtons got for their last movie – a constant preoccupation of Larry's. Omar asked me about my life and told me something about his. We talked about Oxford, and about Cairo University, from where he had graduated with degrees in mathematics and physics, making him, to say the least, a somewhat out-of-the-ordinary movie star. I also discovered that he spoke at least half a dozen languages fluently, and was well read and articulate.

Later in the evening we all repaired to the town's number-one disco, which was housed in the basement of our hotel. This also catered chiefly to the privileged offspring of the party elite, plus any sufficiently well-heeled visitors in town. The appearance of movie people, especially Omar, caused quite a stir among the women there, not all of whom, I noted, were escorted by boy-friends; and not all of whom, I also noted, were professional hookers, though there was a generous supply of those discreetly available at the bar. We stayed a while and had another drink. Omar and I danced with some of the girls; Larry and Terence Young, above such cavortings, remained seated. Everyone had an early start in the morning, so we went to bed not much after one.

•

I was up, breakfasted and ready by nine-fifteen, and waiting for the car that was supposed to drive me the twenty kilometres out of town to the studios, where I was to meet the director of our film for the first time, a respected Hollywood veteran called Robert Siodmak. After half an hour I was still waiting for the car when one of the German production staff came puffing in, red-faced, to tell me that the traffic was in chaos and my visit to the studio would have to wait until the afternoon. The reason was that the French president, having cut short his state visit to deal with "*les evenements*" at home, was being given a hurriedly arranged send-off, with a long motorcade and thousands of citizens ordered from their homes and places of work to line the streets and cheer. I went out to take a look.

It was one of those occasions which showed how efficient totalitarianism can be. Buses and coaches were discreetly parked around corners and behind buildings, having disgorged their cargoes of obedient citizenry from the outlying parts of the city and the suburbs. No one complained about the inconvenience or made cynical remarks, largely because of the overwhelming numbers of soldiers, armed police and the hated plain-clothes *"securitate"* patrolling the streets.

As sirens and the roar of motorbikes approached, I climbed some steps behind the six-deep cheering and flag-waving crowd and got a good view of the passing spectacle. And quite a spectacle it was, with President de Gaulle, all six feet five of him, sitting in the back of an open car alongside the diminutive Ceauşescu, five feet five, who looked like a pet mouse despite the elevator cushion he was habitually perched on. Both waved regally to the crowds, and then they were gone.

It was after two in the afternoon when I finally got to Buftea Studios, a sprawl of buildings on the edge of a large natural lake. I was taken to see our director, who was finishing a simple lunch of sandwiches and salad in his room. Robert Siodmak was German by birth, but like many of his Jewish contemporaries had fled the country in the late thirties and wound up in Hollywood, where he had made some of the most stylish "films noir" of the forties and fifties. He had discovered Burt Lancaster and made him a star with *The Killers* in 1946, working with him on a couple more highly successful films including *The Crimson Pirate* in 1952. I was excited to meet him, but not sure what to expect.

What I found was an anxious, elfin-like little man, still sprightly for his age – sixty-eight – but looking harassed and tired. The previous year he had directed a Cinerama epic called *Custer of the West*, with Robert Shaw and Robert Ryan. It had not been a success, and I suspect he knew he was at the end of his career. Ours would be the last film he made; he died five years later in retirement in Switzerland.

It quickly became apparent to me that anything I did with the script was fine by Robert as long as it kept the actors happy and didn't screw up the shooting schedule too badly. I pointed out a few scenes that I thought were repetitive and we could delete. He readily agreed, partly because this gave him more time, and perhaps money, to spend on other more complicated scenes.

From that day on, although I saw him frequently on the set or out on location, and quite often had dinner with him in a small group of Larry, the producer, and one or two others, we never had a conversation about anything I wrote. I merely handed him the pages, and they would be typed up and circulated. If any of the cast wanted to discuss any aspect of the re-writes, I was available; but by and large they didn't.

The bulk of the re-writes involved Larry, not surprisingly as he was in almost every scene of the picture. He was, he warned me, a slow reader, adding that for years it had been his habit to study his script for the day while sitting on the lavatory each morning, which he did for between one and two hours, being a lifelong sufferer from chronic constipation. This was more information than I felt absolutely essential for the fulfilment of my duties, but it didn't surprise me. Despite being a lover of fine food, and also an excellent cook, Larry had a terror of putting on weight. Today I have no doubt he would have been diagnosed with an eating disorder. He ate like a bird, often just picking tiny morsels from other people's plates and washing them down with generous glasses of dry white wine (usually Pouilly-Fuissé), of which he consumed two or three bottles a day, convinced as he was that white wine was less fattening than red.

I was pleased to find that Larry liked what I was doing on the script. Only occasionally did he appear with a few pencil marks editing some of the lengthier speeches I'd given him, usually where he was addressing the senate or urging on his troops. I was quite relaxed about this, since like most writers I have always preferred to overwrite in the first place and then edit; and Larry's edits were, in fact, very shrewd.

CHAPTER 19

Larry and I moved out of the beige but limited splendours of the Athenee Palace after about a week. The production had arranged for us to be housed in something called the Ştirbei Palace – a real palace this time, not a hotel. This was a nineteenth-century Gothic monstrosity set in extensive grounds overlooking the same lake as Buftea Studios, which at least made it convenient for work. Although cars were always available, one could walk between the two in a matter of minutes.

The interior was all dark panelling and great stone fireplaces. Tapestries depicting hunting scenes hung on the walls, and the high vaulted ceilings were painted with images from folklore. Tall windows relieved the threat of Stygian gloom, bathing the interior in surprising amounts of light. We were told the place had been refurbished some years ago, since when the likes of Khrushchev and other great socialist leaders had stayed there.

The furnishings were totalitarian plush: large, square, but surprisingly comfortable. Larry and I were each provided with vast suites of rooms on higher floors, accessed by a great double staircase sweeping up from a hall the size of a minor cathedral. Larry's secretary and driver were housed in further recesses of the building, as was the pretty twenty-one-year-old Ingrid Boulting, who had joined us to play Larry's daughter in the picture.

I found myself with an airy sitting room and a pleasing view of the lake, an adjoining bedroom the size of a tennis court, with a bed of commensurate proportions, and beyond that a mausoleum-sized bathroom in white tiles with modern fittings and plentiful hot water. No Iron Curtain discomforts or shortages here. The whole place came fully staffed with servants who would materialise anywhere in the building at the press of a button, but were otherwise invisible. Meals were prepared in a gleaming modern kitchen in the basement, where we were invited to inspect the wine cellar and cold-storage facilities.

Within days I had settled into a comfortable routine. I would have breakfast in my sitting room around eight each morning, then work on the script, sustained by a constant supply of coffee until lunchtime. Then I would either saunter over to the studio, or Larry and various members of the company would come over to the house to have lunch on the terrace that ran along one side of the building. Sometimes various friends of Larry, like the actor John Ireland, would fly in for a day or two just to see their old chum, and they would be housed in another of the seemingly endless suites of rooms we had available.

All was going swimmingly. The only problem I'd had so far was getting sick for two days from an overdose of caviar. Traditionally the great bulk of Romanian caviar, which was of excellent quality, was exported to Paris, but owing to the current riots there this had become impossible. As a result, the shelves of every food shop in the country, normally suffering from shortages of everything including the most basic provisions, were groaning under kilos of choice caviar at knock-down prices. Terence Young bought so much he had to charter a plane to get it out of the country. Relatively unaccustomed to caviar, I piled in with abandon. Larry prepared it with baked potato skins, sour cream and chives. It was one of the best things I'd ever tasted, until I began to feel unwell. I've never been able to touch caviar since.

Larry's girlfriend, the model Paulene Stone, arrived from

London a couple of weeks later. She was carrying the Sunday papers, which she kept hidden from Larry because they contained some of the worst reviews he'd ever received. Two years earlier he had led what he called a "scratch company" in a performance of *The Winter's Tale* at the Edinburgh Festival. The critical reception had been devastating, but Larry's name, along with Jane Asher's, had sold out the run. However, any hopes he may have nurtured that this effort might re-open for him the prestigious doors of the Royal Shakespeare Company or even the National Theatre, both of which had pointedly ignored him despite their love of showcasing big stars, lay in ruins.

Ploughing on regardless, Larry had been instrumental in raising the money for a low-budget and quickly shot film version of the production, which had just been released. The reviews were even worse than for the earlier stage version, with Larry's performance being compared by one critic to a parody of Peter Sellers doing his Indian voice while impersonating a ham actor trying to play Shakespeare.

In spite of Paulene's best efforts to protect him, Larry got the reviews by post a couple of days later. I sat with him on the terrace that evening watching the sun go down across the lake. We were drinking Larry's "sledghammer" Campari sodas, which involved adding a large slug of vodka to the usual mix.

"To hell with them," I said, indicating the crumpled newspapers on a table nearby. "You're a movie star, that's why they hate you."

"Movie star," he repeated in a tone that poured acidulous scorn on the term. "I'm not a big star." There was a pause before he went on with, I thought, a touch of wistfulness in his voice. "The thing is, though, if you've had any kind of career in Hollywood, even a pissy little one like mine, you'll always work somewhere – road shows, dinner theatre, whatever. Your name's always worth a buck or two. You won't starve."

I got the impression he needed to reassure himself by saying it out loud. Then, brightening slightly, he told me how he'd been offered a tour of *My Fair Lady* only the previous year.

"We started talking money, and I said, 'Wait a fucking minute, how much did you say you're offering me? That's no more than you paid Mickey Rooney last time out. You're not telling me I'm not worth more than Mickey fucking Rooney!'"

And he was off, doing the voices, playing all the parts.

"But Mr Harvey... Laurence... can I call you Larry..?"

He created a compelling little vignette of a sleazy, hand-wringing small-time producer.

"Larry, you don't understand. We're only talking here about what's *on* the table. Let me tell you about the concessions, the back-handers, the parts of the arrangement we don't put on paper. You know what I'm saying?"

He had cheered up considerably by dinner, which we ate in our palatial dining room at a vast round table that always made me think of *Camelot*, a show he'd done for six months at Drury Lane in London only four years earlier. It had been a happy time for him.

"We were up and down to that fuckin' palace non-stop. Buck House we called it. Princess Margaret loved a party. Queer for horses, you know, all those royals. Queen, Queen Mum, Margaret. You'd go in those royal stables, and there were all these rows of fucking horses with lipstick marks all over their bums."

Then he'd start into some hilarious impersonation of Dame Flora Robson covering her ears on a film set in response to Larry's foul language and begging, "Will you *please* stop using that word!"

After which there was a story about his friend Paul Newman, who had shown Larry a letter he was writing to a gifted but psychotically paranoid writer called Meade Roberts, who had co-scripted *Summer and Smoke* which Larry had made at the top of his career seven years earlier. "Thanks for dropping off the script, Meade," Newman had written, "and we really enjoyed having you for the weekend. However, we're very sorry to hear that you're still putting it around that Joanne and I are trying to poison you. I assure you that you are mistaken in this."

Each anecdote would be polished and told to perfection. The best nights were when there were only three, four, or at most half a dozen of us around the dinner table. Once a week or so we'd have guest night, with up to twenty people in attendance. But it was in the small "family" setting that Larry talked most freely and funnily and sometimes touchingly.

Like a lot of vain but insecure people, Larry harboured a conviction that everybody he met, especially homosexuals, was in love with him. Gilbert Harding, dangerously overweight and asthmatic, had made a guest appearance in the film *Expresso Bongo* that Larry had made with Cliff Richard in the mid-fifties. "He wouldn't leave me alone. I kept telling him, 'Gilbert, you're just going to lengthen your cock and shorten your life.'"

Tennessee Williams, according to Larry, had followed him around during the shooting of *Summer and Smoke*, jumping up like an adoring little dog. "I had to bat him off all the time and keep telling him to stop it."

Somerset Maugham, whom he went down to visit on Cape Ferrat as he was embarking on the disastrous remake of *Of Human Bondage* in the early sixties "was in love with me".

It has been widely assumed that Larry was bisexual, but, having known him, I'm far from convinced. Certainly he camped it up outrageously sometimes, but always in my experience for comic effect while telling some bad-taste joke that certainly didn't glamorise homosexuality.

I do think, on the other hand, that he would have had sex with a porcupine – or anything else for that matter – if it would have furthered his career. From his early twenties he had maintained a close relationship with the homosexual film producer James Wolf, who had been an invaluable mentor to him until his (Wolf's) death in 1964, at which point Larry's career had begun to falter. Whether there was a physical aspect to that relationship is anybody's guess, though, as the openly gay actor John Fraser puts it in his autobiography, "Larry's whoredom was so blatant it was disarming."

Bisexual or not, there was one night when we reached a potential precipice of confession that I quickly realised I did not care to go over. It was very late, and the only remaining drinkers were Larry, myself, Brian the chauffeur and Sandy the secretary, and somebody else who had fallen asleep. We had been telling some extremely politically incorrect (a notion which did not then exist) "queer" jokes and laughing uproariously. Suddenly Larry fixed me with a teasingly quizzical look and said, "What would you say if I told you I was queer?"

Brian, I noticed, had quickly fixed his gaze on the ceiling as though nothing else in the room was of the slightest interest to him. Sandy appeared to be studying her fingernails. The sleeping guest snored gently. It was down to me, I realised, to field and deal with this one.

"Well, I'll tell you what I'd say, Larry," I began after a moment's reflection, choosing my words carefully. "I think I'd say, pull the other one. And that isn't an invitation."

CHAPTER 20

The routine of palace to studio, studio to palace, was broken now and then by a day out on some location shoot surrounded by hundreds of extras on loan from the Romanian army and dressed as Roman soldiers. A couple of times sudden and vicious sand storms had blown up, and I'd found myself protected on four sides by members of the crew holding up deck chairs and tent flaps so that I could get on with banging out a quick re-write for the next scene. But I was comfortably on top of things and beginning to think what a relatively easy gig this was and how fortunate that I'd brought along a stack of books to read during the many hours I found myself not working.

But then a new challenge emerged on the scene – a large and intimidating one that cast a long shadow. In fact "The Shadow" was one of the radio characters he had made famous as a young actor in New York in the late thirties.

He was better known as Orson Welles.

•

I had been told initially that the part of the Emperor Justinian was going to be played by the German actor, Curt Jürgens. He was at that time an international star, often described as the handsomest man in the world, and had played opposite leading ladies as various as Ingrid Bergman and Debbie Reynolds. I looked forward to making his acquaintance, but wasn't all that excited. Then for some reason he dropped out, and the hunt was on for a replacement. I found myself included in the discussions between the director, the producer and Larry as to who we might go after. Names were listed as desirable but unlikely (Laurence Olivier); possible and quite likely (Christopher Lee); and acceptable but not very interesting, including Larry's friend John Ireland, who I'd taken a great liking to during his recent visit and certainly wasn't going to vote against.

But when the producer murmured the words "Orson Welles" in an uncertain, oddly tentative way, everyone fell silent.

Orson Welles? Well, obviously. Of course. How could there be anyone better for the role?

But would he do it?

And if he agreed, could we cope?

Robert had already turned pale at the prospect of having to handle the man who had made theatre and film history several times over, and who had the reputation of bawling out lesser directors and taking control of their set if he thought he could do a better job. Robert had in his long career handled difficult actors like Charles Laughton and the already mentioned Burt Lancaster, but Orson Welles was in a class of his own. In every way.

After a legendary stage career as both actor and director in New York in his early twenties, Orson had stormed Hollywood to make *Citizen Kane* at the age of only twenty-five, followed by *The Magnificent Ambersons* the year after. Despite battles with the studio system which left him struggling to raise finance on his own, often from highly paid acting jobs such as his unforgettable Harry Lime in *The Third Man*, he had directed and played in, amongst several always interesting films, remarkable versions of *Othello* and *Macbeth*.

Making a return to Hollywood in 1957, he had scripted, directed and, along with Charlton Heston and Janet Leigh, starred in *Touch of Evil*, a movie which the studio had tried to bury when it came out, but which had gone on to become a classic. Its famous opening sequence in one long unbroken crane shot is still talked about by cineastes everywhere. There followed Kafka's *The Trial*, and the film he was most proud of, *Chimes at Midnight*, in which he had given the world a magnificent and definitive Falstaff.

Larry had worked with Orson only recently on one of Orson's several unfinished films (owing as usual to financial problems) called *The Deep*. Shot in Yugoslavia, it had co-starred Jeanne Moreau and Michael Bryant, an English actor who I would work with myself and get to know well just a few years later. They were all prepared to work for little or no money just for the opportunity of being part of an Orson Welles picture. Larry, however, claimed that his involvement in the film had cost him a good deal of money. Aside from never seeing a fraction of his negotiated fee, he'd had to pay his own expenses each time he'd flown over to do a few more days' shooting. On top of that, he'd been asked to bring with him large quantities of the very expensive Havana cigars that Orson chain-smoked, which were also never paid for. Nevertheless, Larry held no grudges, and realised at once that if Orson's name were to appear alongside his above the title of our film, that could only be a good thing.

Phone calls were made to ascertain the whereabouts of the peripatetic Mr Welles, and it turned out he'd been last heard of in London, but had left for some unknown destination in Europe. He was, according to his secretary, "travelling incognito".

This brought a bark of laughter from Larry. If there was one person in the world who might have a problem travelling incognito it was Orson, with that unmistakable bulk and instantly recognisable voice.

By the end of the day he had been tracked down to – by happy coincidence – the producer's home town of Berlin, though his exact whereabouts remained unknown.

"If Orson's in Berlin," Larry said, "he'll be at the Kempinski and nowhere else."

It was the best hotel in town, and he was, of course, there. The producer flew off to meet him and talk money.

I could barely contain my excitement at the prospect of meeting a man I'd been in awe of ever since *Citizen Kane* had bowled me over when I'd first seen it only a few years earlier. Orson Welles. Oh, my God!

Star-struck? You bet.

Of course, I kept telling myself, it wasn't going to happen. As a safeguard against disappointment I thought about how much fun it was going to be having that nice John Ireland around again for a few weeks.

Then the news came. Orson had agreed – in principle – and would be with us in three days. I barely had time to absorb the fact that it was actually going to happen before I found myself the focus of anxieties from all sides: producer, director, production manager, line producer, unit manager, right down, it seemed, to script girl and make-up. They had all developed a bad case of nerves. If Orson turned up and wasn't happy with his part, which the producer had promised would be re-written and expanded for him, there were going to be ructions that nobody wanted to have to deal with.

In other words, I had three days to re-write every scene he was in, adding a couple of new ones to ensure his talents would be exploited to the full.

Right, onwards.

A few years later I would be told by the great comic actor Alastair Sim that the worst parts he had ever been offered were the ones that had been specifically written for him. All they did, he said, was exaggerate his worst tics and habits, giving him nothing interesting or original to work with. Cheerfully unaware at the time of this danger, I set about turning the Emperor Justinian into everything I thought Orson Welles at his most mightily unleashed might bring to the role. From rumbling introspection to roaring tongue-lashings, from smirking conspiracy to towering rage, from seductive charm to brutal dismissal, it was all there.

Curiously enough, nobody showed the slightest interest in reading what I'd written. Robert waved my pages airily aside, saying he'd wait to hear what Orson thought and then discuss it with both of us, and went on supervising the lighting set-up he was preparing for a scene with Honor Blackman and a young German actor.

The producer made a peculiar yodelling sound and waved his arms around as though trying to take flight, saying that the script wasn't his area of expertise, especially in English. The line producer and production manager both reacted like vampires being offered a bowl of garlic soup. Even Larry felt he shouldn't interfere with things that were entirely another actor's affair.

Gradually it dawned on me that I was being very deliberately left out on a limb. Towards the end of the afternoon I was informed by a production secretary that a car would be collecting me from the studio in an hour's time to take me to the same hotel in Bucharest that Larry and I had stayed in initially, where I would meet with Mr Welles and present him with my scenes.

Just me, I enquired?

Yes.

No producer, or director? Or anyone?

No. Just me.

So that, I realised, was the strategy. If Orson turned out to be unhappy with what he'd signed on for, let the kid get it in the neck. Why risk more valuable lives?

My first five years, round and round...

Mum and dad's wedding. Harry and Marion, not yet
married, on their right. Granny Fairclough on their left.

The remarkable Tom Crehan. Me, aged fifteen, third on his left.

Hamming it up in 'The Government Inspector'.

Aged 16, invited with the parents to some municipal knees-up.

Photographed for my play 'SIEGE' in 1972.

Summer hats.

Winter hats.

Aged 16, invited with the parents to some municipal knees-up.

Photographed for my play 'SIEGE' in 1972.

Orson Welles. © AF Archive/Alamy

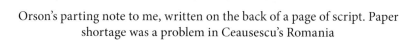

Dear David

As you see, I'm still suffering from a paper
shortage...

Thanks for all your great help and congratulations
on the heroic salvaging job . .

My permanent address:
care

Mrs Ann Rogers
36 Warwick Ave.,
London W. 9.

Orson's parting note to me, written on the back of a page of script. Paper
shortage was a problem in Ceausescu's Romania

Kirk Douglas, in 'The Final Countdown' in 1980. © Movie Store collection/Alamy

Laurence Harvey. © Keystone Press/Alamy

Cyril Cusack. © Everett Collection /Alamy

Dirk Bogarde. © Moviestore collection/Alamy

Alastair Sim. © AF Archive/Alamy

With Laurence at our house in France in the mid-nineties.

Summer hats.

Winter hats.

CHAPTER 21

My finger hesitated, anticipation vying with trepidation, before I pressed the buzzer alongside the door of his suite. Perhaps I only imagined the sound of approaching footsteps on the carpeted floor, but they seemed to coordinate perfectly with the handle turning and the door opening. And there he was. Tall, a surprisingly trim figure despite his bulk, with a neat grey beard and wearing a kind of tailored Mao suit, and drawing on a ten-inch cigar that had obviously just been lit. He invited me in with a grunt and I followed him down the narrow hall to his sitting room.

In the centre of the room, with its familiar colour scheme of beige, brown and oatmeal fabric, was a table scattered with papers and books, and a typewriter. There was also a bottle of whisky and a bottle of Perrier water.

"D'you want a drink?"

It was well after six, so I thought why not?

"Yes, thank you," I said.

He poured me a large tumbler of whisky and said I could add some water if I wanted. Then he poured himself a tumbler of straight water.

"Doctor's orders," he said. "On the wagon."

It didn't seem to improve his temper, and he was scowling darkly as he held out a hand for my pages.

"Let me see."

I handed them over, and he started to read. There was no sound in the room except for the rustle of paper as he turned a page, giving the occasional grunt, which for all I knew could have signified disgust or grudging approval. He picked up his cigar from the ash tray in which he had briefly set it down and puffed out a great cloud of rich-smelling smoke. I reached cautiously for my glass of whisky, half-hoping he would forget I was there.

Suddenly Orson gave a louder grunt than previously, and I realised something was wrong.

"I can't play this scene," he said, tapping the page with a hint of irritation. "It's the whole wrong way around. You've got me reacting to everybody else. It won't work. I'm what the French call a 'King actor'. I've got to be the focus of the scene. I don't mean I can't play it, or won't, it's just not what I do best."

He took up a pen and started scoring out some of my dialogue, putting brackets and circles around other parts of it, then adding arrows this way and that.

"I should have this line here," he said, adding as an afterthought, "Who's playing the Empress anyway?"

"Sylva Koscina," I said.

"You explain to her will you – why you're giving me her line, I mean?"

"Er... yes, of course."

"And who's playing this character, Cethegus?"

"That's Laurence Harvey."

"I'd better have these couple of lines you've got him saying. Larry won't mind. You'll tell him too, okay?"

"Um... sure."

He passed the scene back to me, and I saw at once that it wasn't simply a question of Orson wanting the most lines, or even the best ones. It was, as he had implied, a question of balance. With just a few skillful changes his character had gone from watching something happen to making it happen. I made a mental note to remember the trick.

Silence resumed as he read on. After a further twenty minutes or so we were both finished, me with my whisky and he with my scenes.

"That's fine," he said, leaning back and visibly relaxing. "There's a few things we can talk about later, but it's fine."

Desperately hoping that the ballooning sense of pride I was feeling at this hoped-for but barely expected imprimatur was not too obvious, I started to gather myself together, intending to thank him for his time, and leave.

But before I could, he said, "So where are we going for dinner?"

Once again I prayed that my face didn't betray what I felt, which was complete and utter shock. No one had mentioned that I might be expected to entertain the great man for the evening. I doubt if it had crossed anyone's mind. Certainly, no one had thought of setting up a welcoming party for him, in case, perhaps, things didn't work out as well as might have been hoped. But now the matter was in my hands.

And I was thrilled. But I had to get it right. I thought fast. "We could eat in the hotel," I said, "but it's kind of dull. On the other hand..."

I fumbled through my wallet for the slip of paper on which, thank God, I'd written the phone number of the "secret" restaurant where I'd eaten with Larry, Terence Young and Omar Sharif just recently.

"May I use your phone?"

"Go ahead."

I dialled the number and asked for the manager. We spoke in French, which I had discovered was the universal second language in Romania; there were cultural ties, apparently, that went back a couple of centuries or so. In fact Bucharest at one time had been

157

called "the Paris of the east", though I could see little resemblance aside from the spacious avenues and boulevards that both cities shared.

Fortunately the restaurant manager remembered me, and more especially the company I'd been in. I asked him if he could fix me up with a table for two for dinner that evening, which was by no means an easy thing to get even for the cognoscenti, both political and artistic, of that city. I very deliberately didn't mention Orson's name, being acutely aware that he was listening to me while sorting out the various books and papers on his desk. When the manager said he would do his best to fit me and my guest in if we came along in half an hour, I thanked him and hung up.

"I think you're going to like this place," I said, sensing that I'd scored another point or two by not dangling Orson's name as a calling card to get in.

The studio car that had brought me into town was waiting downstairs to take me back to the palace at Buftea, but I told the driver we were going somewhere else and we had an extra passenger. His jaw dropped when Orson got in.

Orson sat back, looking, I thought, increasingly content with the world. He lit up another cigar, and as we drove through the night he gazed out at the drab, dimly lit streets of Bucharest. Then he turned to look over at me.

"So tell me," he said, pausing for another puff on his cigar, "what does a young man like you do for fucks in this town?"

•

As an ice-breaker, I thought the question took some beating. I answered by pointing out that there were several attractive girls working on the production, aside from which Romanian girls,

158

being denied the right to travel abroad, found foreigners attractively exotic. We moved on to other topics. He asked how I found Larry, what I thought of Robert Siodmak, and other things, so that by the time we reached our destination I was feeling already quite at ease in his company.

I led the way into the restaurant, which was in a windowless semi-cellar with a vaulted stone ceiling. As usual it was full and the decibel level was fairly high, but the whole place fell silent as people realised who was following in my wake. The manager, his eyes out on stalks as I introduced him to my guest, led us past the modest table he had prepared for us and, despite my protests that it wasn't necessary (Orson standing innocently by, not saying a word), ordered a larger table in an alcove to be vacated and its diners rehoused elsewhere. Nobody raised the slightest objection, and Orson and I took our places graciously.

"So what's good here?" he asked when I explained there were no menus.

"They've got a choice of two main dishes," I said, "both of them fantastic. There's a great big filet of pork, and you've never tasted pork like it. They also have a fish, kind of like a huge goldfish, it's called 'Crap', but don't let that put you off."

"Let's have both."

"But... they're quite big..."

"That's okay."

Normally either dish would have served three or four people, depending on appetites. But having heard about Orson's eating habits, and looking at the evidence of it seated opposite me, I didn't argue.

The manager, anxiously standing over us to take our order, made a note without batting an eyelid.

"And what about some kind of starter while we're waiting?" Orson asked next.

"Best thing they do," I said, "is a tomato and mozarella salad, and the tomatoes are..."

"Let's have that right away."

I nodded to the manager and he started towards the kitchen, only to be called back by Orson.

"Bring a bottle of vodka, will you? And let's get some wine." He looked at me. "Why don't we get whatever it was you had last time?"

Orson, I could see, had decided that a few hours on the wagon were more than enough, and was preparing to fall off it with a resounding thud. He continued to brighten by the minute as the vodka arrived, most of it disappearing down his throat with dazzling speed. The wine arrived along with a more-than-generous tomato mozarella salad on a big oval plate. I managed to salvage a few pieces before that too was gone.

By the time our main orders arrived we were well into a second bottle of wine, and launched on what promised to be, at least for me, a very special evening. I still couldn't believe that I was sitting with Orson Welles, hosting him to dinner, and talking with such ease. Before long I was pounding him with every question I could think of about his films. Was it true that he had learnt everything it was possible to know about a movie camera in one afternoon? Perfectly true, he said, anyone could do it, adding only that it took "a certain amount of application". And, of course, he'd had an exceptional teacher in Gregg Toland, one of Hollywood's greatest cinematographers who went on to shoot *Citizen Kane* for Orson.

And was it true that he had watched John Ford's *Stagecoach* thirty-seven times before starting work on *Kane*? Yes, it would have been about that much, he said. "Ford was a master at handling movement on the screen."

Had he really been surprised when he scared America witless with his mock-documentary *War of the Worlds* on radio in 1938, or had he planned it all along?

160

A secretive smile, followed by, "Well, I thought there was a pretty good chance it might stir something up."

Then I was asking about those fantastic shots in the ballroom scene of *The Magnificent Ambersons*, where the camera gets in among the dancers, waltzing with couple after couple in long unbroken takes of a breathtaking elegance. How had he figured all that out?

With a rumble of laughter he told me what a nightmare those shots had been to achieve. "The floor we were shooting on was terrible, creaking and groaning like it was going to cave in any minute. I had to dub the music and dialogue in later because we couldn't use direct sound."

We talked about the battle scenes in *Chimes at Midnight*, where he'd never had more than a hundred or so extras to play with, but by dazzling editing had created two whole armies out of them with some of the most powerful fight scenes ever filmed.

Some of what he told me that night has since been repeated in books about Orson; indeed I would hear some of it repeated by Orson himself in various interviews and on talk shows he appeared on later in his life. Many people who met him said he never wanted to talk about his films in private, but that wasn't the case that night.

It's probably worth remembering, however, that this was 1968. Orson was still a relatively young man at fifty-three, and the great vogue of media studies and film schools that we are familiar with now had barely begun. If he gave an interview back then it would more likely have been to a gossip columnist than someone with a real interest in film-making. Perhaps that was why he was so indulgent of my endless pestering questions: he seemed to like my enthusiasm, and he had already discovered for himself that I knew at least something about how to put a scene together.

At the end of a long and unforgettable evening, as I paid the bill and asked for someone to get us a taxi, having let my studio driver go home hours ago, I heard myself delivering perhaps the most banal and naff line I'd managed all evening, something to the effect of, "Christ, Orson, I can't believe you'd done everything you had – all that incredible theatre, *War of the Worlds*, *Citizen Kane*, *Ambersons* – all by the time you were my age."

He gave a chuckle and came out with a remark I would later get to know as his routine self-deprecating response to anyone who made such a comment.

"I know," he said. "I started at the top, and I've been working my way down ever since."

But he also gave me one piece of advice in the course of that evening that I have never since heard repeated either by Orson himself or anyone else. When I told him I hadn't yet been to Hollywood but certainly hoped to work there soon, he said, with a great wheezing laugh, "Just remember when you do, David, everything you've ever heard about Hollywood is true – including the lies".

Thirty years later I would adapt that remark, with proud acknowledgment of its source, as the title for a collection of short stories I would write called *Hollywood Lies*.

CHAPTER 22

Our pink-faced, pop-eyed production manager's eyes were even wider with anxiety than usual when he sought me out the following morning to find out how my meeting with Orson had gone. His relief was palpable when I told him, with studied nonchalance through a pretty formidable hangover, that we'd got along fine, and I'd even taken him to dinner. On hearing this his mouth fell open to form, along with his eyes, three perfect circles, like an only slightly less disquieting version of Munch's *The Scream*. He scurried off to spread the news around the studio that all was well.

I was never reimbursed for that dinner with Orson, though no doubt I would have been if I'd asked. In fact, even if I'd been offered the money I suspect I would have turned it down. I liked the feeling that I'd had the privilege of entertaining this extraordinary man as my personal guest and not just on behalf of the production. Also, to be frank, the cost, though high in terms of the Romanian currency (lei), was negligible. The official dollar-lei exchange rate at that time was eight lei to the dollar; however, because our movie was bringing millions of dollars into the country everyone associated with it was given a special rate of forty lei to the dollar, which made one's daily living allowance go an awful long way. Another triumph of totalitarian pragmatism.

Orson turned up around eleven for a costume fitting in a genial mood. He exchanged a big hug with his friend Larry, and greeted

Robert Siodmak with all the respect and courtesy that one might hope to find between one distinguished film-maker and another.

For my own part, despite having puffed out my chest somewhat in the course of the morning, I found myself harbouring a slight anxiety that I might possibly have overstepped the bounds of permissible familiarity once or twice the previous evening. As a result I kept my distance when he arrived. A couple times I caught him shooting me a sideways glance which could have meant either, "Oh, Christ, not him again!"; or, more optimistically, "He doesn't look too bad after the amount he drank last night."

All the same, not wishing to put myself in the way of a humiliating come-uppance, a reverse version of Falstaff's rejection by Prince Hal in *Chimes at Midnight*, I approached him with caution and made a point of addressing him as "Mr Welles", until he said, "Oh, stop it! Who's this 'Mr Welles' you're prattling on at? It's still 'Orson' for God's sake!"

I was much reassured.

In fact he was in a pretty good mood for most of the time he was on the picture. I saw him throw a rip-roaring tantrum only twice. The first came a few days into shooting when he found he'd been given the wrong pages of script to learn for that morning and was now expected to master a wholly different scene in a matter of minutes. Standing in his flowing robes on a built-up stage alongside the emperor's throne, with his hawk-like plasticine nose and fearsome eyebrows (Orson always did his own make-up), he delivered a tirade against everything that was wrong with the world, which somehow came down to focus on the unfortunate script girl who was responsible for the mistake.

The script girl was in fact a very nice middle-aged woman who was married to a good-looking younger man who was employed as one of the extras on the set that morning, and who had to be restrained by a couple of assistant directors from stepping up and taking a swing at Orson.

Robert, the director, was full of spluttered apologies, which Orson ignored as he stormed off the set and beckoned me to follow him.

Back in his dressing room we shuffled through pages of script to find the correct scene.

"Where the hell are we? You got the scene?"

I found it and handed it to him. He read it through.

"Now where am I supposed to have been before this? Where are we in the goddamn picture?"

I found the relevant previous scenes, which hadn't been shot yet, and he quickly got his bearings.

"Go tell them I'll be ready in fifteen minutes."

I hurried back to the set to find a white-faced director, sprawled in his chair and trying to calm his palpitations, and a gibbering production manager looking at his watch and waving his arms, afraid that the whole morning's shoot was going to be lost.

"It's all right," I assured them, "he'll be back in fifteen minutes."

And he was, word perfect and ready to go. He offered no apology to the humiliated script girl, but a couple of days later he made a point of insisting that she and her husband have lunch with him in the studio canteen and they all had their picture taken together. Peace and harmony were restored. It was typical of Orson. He was not by nature a bully, and didn't like himself when frustration drove him to behave like one.

I saw this generously long-suffering side of him again some time later. It was a blisteringly hot day and we were shooting on location in desert-like terrain, a real dust bowl. We were surrounded once again by hundreds of Romanian soldiers playing Romans in a huge battle scene; I couldn't help thinking how Orson would have loved such facilities for his own movies. Once his scenes for the day were in the can, he asked someone to get his car to take him back to Bucharest. It was nowhere to be found. Owing to some misunderstanding his driver had gone off with the car on some errand, leaving Orson stranded. Everybody feared a nuclear meltdown if Orson got his hands on whoever was responsible; but when this turned out to be a humble Romanian assistant who had simply made a genuine mistake, Orson remained perfectly calm and sat patiently on an upturned camera box for half an hour, perspiring in his heavy costume and smoking a cigar, until another car could be found to get him out of there.

The only other great tantrum took place one morning in the studio, and was, I regret to say, at least partly my fault.

Orson arrived one morning on a large and ornately decorated set only to stop short and gape in horror at what he saw. Everywhere he looked were images of peacocks: stuffed peacocks, peacock feathers, pictures of peacocks on the walls and tapestries, peacock motifs worked into the tiled floor. It was, the designer had decided, the Peacock Salon. (All of which had nothing to do with me. My blunder came later.)

"Are you insane?" he bellowed. "I can't work on this set!"

Silence.

I had accompanied him with the usual stack of pages under my arm, and he turned to me as though for support.

"Will you look at this?" he boomed. "Can you believe it?"

I looked back at him blankly.

"Um... what's wrong?" I ventured uncertainly.

"What's *wrong*?" he roared, and I could swear I heard the rafters rattle. "No actor in his right mind would appear on a set like this with peacocks everywhere! It's death! Terrible! A disaster!"

"You mean they're unlucky?"

"Of course they're unlucky. Don't you know?"

"Well, no."

Obviously our director didn't know either. He was standing on the set looking stricken.

166

"I'm sorry, Robert," Orson said to him, "but you're going to have to redress this whole set before I set foot on it."

In the background I could see the production manager, his pink face turning puce. I thought he was going to faint. Orson started for his dressing room, and I walked with him. I had heard or read somewhere that Orson was superstitious, but was nonetheless a little surprised at the power it obviously had over him.

"So this thing about peacocks being unlucky," I said as we walked, "where does it come from?"

"I don't know. They just always have been. It's something you've got to know about if you're an actor."

"You mean like never saying 'Macbeth' in a theatre."

Orson stopped in his tracks, both hands shooting up to clasp his head.

"Shiiiiiiiiiitttt!!! Now you've done it! Oh, Christ!"

"But... but we're not in a theatre; this is a film studio."

"It makes no difference! Oh, dear God! Somebody get me some salt – fast!"

Nobody moved.

"Did you hear me? Salt! Right now! *Move! Anybody!*"

Several people began a stampede in the direction of the canteen. I merely gazed at Orson, too taken aback by his reaction to feel as intimidated as I might otherwise have. He, meanwhile, remained rooted to the spot as though unable to shift from it, muttering imprecations under his breath. After a few moments someone ran up to him, nervously holding out a tiny salt cellar and jumping back in fear as Orson's great paw snatched it from him.

I continued to watch in amazement as he began to revolve slowly, reciting some kind of incantation in Latin while throwing salt over each shoulder alternately. After a couple of minutes he was done, and began to breathe normally again.

"Tell 'em I'll be in my room," he said, and disappeared down a corridor, displaying, I couldn't help thinking, the body language of a man who had just survived a brush with something worse than death.

Or was it a joke?

I didn't believe he would waste the production company's time and money simply to amuse himself. I could just about imagine it if they had treated him badly and he had some grudge against them; but that wasn't the case here, and arbitrary malice wasn't in his nature. Besides, I had seen for myself that he had been genuinely alarmed on seeing those peacocks.

But how about my Macbeth gaffe? Could he have been kidding about that? After all there was nothing to lose by then. He had already created a delay in shooting, and maybe now he was just amusing himself by filling in dead time.

And yet if he was superstitious enough to be scared by peacocks, he would certainly be in thrall to the best known of all theatrical superstitions – that you must always refer to *Macbeth* only as "the Scottish play".

A few days after all this excitement, following which his scene on the de-peackocked set had gone smoothly and without further incident, I wandered down to the kitchen of our Gothic palace around eleven one morning and found Orson raiding the fridge. He had already consumed the remains of last night's dinner and was starting on a piece of cheese.

"I get tired if I'm hungry," he said, as though feeling he should explain himself. "Can't concentrate, can't work. I have to eat."

There was something vulnerable about him that morning. He had been shooting early and was still wearing his emperor's costume, but he had removed his false nose and wiped off his make-up. Somehow this wasn't the Orson Welles the world normally saw. Instead of a man whose presence filled the room, whose roar of laughter swept away solemnity, and whose icy disdain made phoneys tremble, I was looking at someone strangely subdued and somehow lonely. Perhaps it was just that, as he had implied, his blood sugar was low.

I made some coffee and we sat at the table together. He finished eating and lit a cigar. I was still struggling to understand how a man as brilliant as he was, as well read in everything from Shakespeare to the sciences, as widely travelled and worldly wise, could be a prey to such superstitions as he apparently was. I felt that if one understood that, one might understand something important about him.

"About that peacock thing the other day," I said, "you know, I've really never heard about that before. I've always known about not mentioning – "

Orson's eyes flashed a warning.

" – the Scottish play, but nothing about peacocks. Where does that come from?"

He shrugged. "I don't know. But you ignore it at your peril."

"Have you ever known anyone who did that? Ignored it I mean?"

He gave a dry laugh. "Sure I have. Some people in Dublin decided to build a theatre once and call it the Peacock Theatre."

He looked at me as if that in itself was the clinching argument of his case.

"So what happened?"

"It burned down," he said, surprised I even had to ask.

Some time later I checked out the story. It was true that the Abbey Theatre in Dublin had, in the twenties, created a small experimental theatre called The Peacock. But it was almost thirty years later that a fire occurred. Even then it wasn't the Peacock Theatre that burned down but the Abbey itself. The Peacock Theatre continues to exist today as a small experimental theatre forming part of the rebuilt and still-flourishing Abbey. Hardly conclusive proof of the malign power of peacocks.

I wondered later if this side of Orson's character wasn't mirrored in his lifelong love of magic. He was an accomplished magician, specialising in elaborate illusions involving "loaded" guns, randomly selected playing cards made to vanish and reappear inside a block of ice, and the sawing in half of beautiful women – most frequently Marlene Dietrich.

Magic, like superstition, it has always seemed to me, represents another collision of reason and unreason; except that with magic we remain safe in the knowledge that reason is in control. Everyone accepts there is a rational explanation for the "impossible" things we are witnessing. In a way it is superstition in reverse: perhaps, even, an antidote to it.

I suspect Orson might have found such a discussion too theoretical for his liking. He had little time for abstractions, including philosophy. He never talked about magic while I knew him, and never volunteered any tricks to entertain his fellow guests at dinner. But I did once, one evening, catch him performing some very dextrous sleight-of-hand.

Larry had organised a dinner party in Orson's honour. The producer and director were there, some of the cast, one or two Romanian dignitaries and their wives, and a couple of big-deal American show-business lawyers who had come over to see Larry about something. All in all, we were about twenty at the big round table in our palace by the lake. Orson had an attractive, middle-aged and expensively dressed blonde woman on his left. She was obviously thrilled to be in his company, and he was keeping her enthralled with a non-stop string of anecdotes and gossip – so enthralled and glued to his magnetic eyes that she had no idea what was going on.

Having polished off his own dinner in record time, Orson, his hands nimbly and all but invisibly criss-crossing the space between the two of them, was eating hers right off her plate.

CHAPTER 23

"Ah, I see the problem," Orson boomed, "you don't understand ambiguity."

We were seated at a rickety folding table in a deserted corner of the studio, going over a scene I'd written that morning.

"Ambiguity is a scalpel, not a smokescreen. Not something you hide behind when you don't know what you want to say. It's something precise and exact, which looked at one way means one thing, and looked at another means something else."

I think that's more or less how he put it. Certainly it was illuminating at the time, and I have never since forgotten that key insight: "ambiguity is a scalpel", something to be used with clinical precision.

We would often have chats about scenes I'd written, not just scenes involving him but in general. He was generous with his time and showed me how to make an otherwise flat scene interesting, how to make exposition happen dramatically instead of just spouting out of somebody's mouth, how to cut away deadwood and get into a scene (and out of it) at the optimum point.

I was, in short, getting a one-on-one course on screenwriting from Orson Welles. Not a privilege enjoyed by many, I suspect. Of course, being young, I took it all for granted at the time; and, indeed, Orson made it seem like the most natural thing in the world.

We talked about some of the movies he'd been in, many of them just to raise finance for his own productions. He told me how he always tried to balance the money he was getting for acting jobs against any potential damage to his name.

"You have to be careful, no matter how much money they're offering just to have your name up on the marquee, which is often all they want. If you do too much of that, you're just going to lose all credibility."

It was an attitude that obviously governed his work on our film; I was well aware of how seriously he took his role, determined to give the best performance he possibly could. Plus he was reassured by the fact that the director, though little more than a competent journeyman by now, enjoyed a distinguished reputation and had done good work in the past. And, of course, Orson was in the company of an internationally known cast and therefore wasn't carrying the whole thing on his own shoulders.

I mentioned a film he'd made in England the previous year, *I'll Never Forget What's'isname,* produced and directed by Michael Winner. Orson gave a loud snort.

"A great producer. *Great* producer. But he should *never* direct."

I ventured to say that I'd seen the film only recently and rather enjoyed it. Orson merely grunted and changed the subject, as he did sometimes when he considered the topic under discussion exhausted.

We talked about many things other than movies during the time we "hung out" together, from the principles of nuclear fission to whether or not it was Marx who first defined capitalism. A couple of times I got my knuckles rapped for holding forth on subjects I was insufficiently qualified to have a worthwhile opinion on. After expatiating at some length one day about how the plays of Bertolt Brecht were little more than sloppily thrown together pieces of political propaganda, I was informed in no uncertain terms by Orson, who had known Brecht (of course) and worked with him on a couple of productions of his plays, that they were constructed with immense care and subtlety, and that Brecht was at least as concerned with aesthetic questions as with political ones.

On another occasion I expressed some firm views on Arthur Koestler's book *The Ghost in the Machine* based on two reviews and a quick glance at the first few chapters. Orson, who – again, naturally – knew Koestler and had read the book from cover to cover, shot down my bullshit in full flight and taught me a valuable lesson about not opening my mouth until I had sufficient confidence in what was about to come out of it.

There were also casual snippets and throwaway tips that I remember vividly. One day, as he and I were strolling across the backlot of the studio during a break in shooting some outdoor scenes, we came across our director of photography seated behind a giant Mitchell camera mounted on a large crane. He was a big man around sixty, bald on top and with long white hair streaming out from the sides of his head. His face wore a permanently sour expression, as though it was being sucked into his thin-lipped mouth and was in danger of being swallowed. Appropriately enough, for a man who went around looking at such odds with life, his name was Richard Angst.

As Orson sauntered up to him I saw Herr Angst's face tighten even more than usually, anticipating, I assumed, some unwelcome piece of advice from the great Orson Welles. And indeed Orson did have a suggestion, quite a modest one, and it was very modestly offered in a quiet voice that defied any possible charge that he was trying to take over other people's jobs. I didn't grasp the details at the time, but it was something about how the rather plodding fight scenes that were currently being filmed might be made more interesting by an ingenious bit of camera work. Herr Angst listened in disdainful silence, then shook his head and said, "No, it's impossible. It can't be done."

Rather than make an argument of it, Orson merely shrugged

and strolled off, puffing on his cigar and with me still trotting alongside like Sancho Panza. "That's another thing you should always remember, David," he said as soon as we were out of the grumpy Swiss's hearing, "anyone who says something can't be done is a second-rater by definition."

Good enough, Orson, and a piece of advice that has cost me as many headaches over the years as perhaps you intended it should.

•

The day on which I drove an elderly Mercedes into a ditch and tipped Orson Welles and Laurence Harvey out in a tangled heap began like any other. Shooting had started early in the studio, but stopped abruptly around ten-thirty when there was a power failure. On top of that the reserve generators broke down within minutes of being started up, so there was nothing to do except wait around until things were fixed.

Larry, Orson, and the American actor Michael Dunn were all in full costume and make-up and ready to do their next scene. Michael was playing General Narses, a brilliant and devious strategist in both politics and war. He and Orson had many scenes together, and considering that Michael was all of three feet ten, the physical contrast between them was, to say the least, striking.

A highly intelligent, educated man with a handsome and perfectly normal head on a shockingly small, misshapen body, Michael had his demons and sometimes created problems, though never on set. On this particular morning he was in good spirits as he waddled along at knee height between the tall, elegant Larry and the even taller and more massive Orson. They made quite a picture as I ran into them heading for Larry's dressing room.

"Come on in," Larry said, waving me to join them. "Nobody's going to be doing anything till they get this fuckin' power fixed."

We sat down on an assortment of folding chairs, a battered sofa, and an old leather armchair. The walls were a pale institutional green, broken here and there by little white eruptions of dampness. The steel window frames were rusting and hard to open. It was all a long way from Hollywood luxury, but these three were troupers who went where the work was and didn't complain – at least not excessively. And I was just very happy to be there with them.

Orson pealed off his false nose, which was beginning to itch, and placed it on what passed for Larry's make-up table, on which a mirror stood propped against the wall with a string of light bulbs around it – which of course were not working at this time.

Larry himself had curled up in the armchair, not at all on good form and nursing a pain in his gut that had already laid him low twice during the few weeks I'd known him. With hindsight, I realised five years later when he died that these regular attacks almost certainly had something to do with the colon cancer that killed him. But he didn't like doctors – a prejudice, I suspect, with its roots in the Lithuanian peasant stock he came from – and refused to have a proper examination until it was too late.

"It's nothing, I've had it all my life," he said to anyone who expressed concern about his condition. "It lasts a couple of days and goes away."

"It's the booze," Orson told him that day, with the cold resignation of mid-morning sobriety.

"It's not the booze," Larry protested. "It's just this gut of mine."

Orson gave a rumble of laughter. "It's the booze," he repeated. "Put the blame where it belongs. You're like all of us, walking around saying 'It's not the booze, it's not the booze, it's anything else but the booze', till one day your liver explodes in a million phosphorescent pieces, and you finally have to admit it was the booze!"

The rumble of laughter grew to a roar, which drew a weak smile from Larry. Somebody bustled in with a pot of coffee and a tray of custard-filled pastries that Orson had had the presence of mind to send for immediately the lights went out. An hour or so later word came that the power was likely to remain out for some time yet, and it was impossible to say when it might be restored.

"Fuck this," Larry groaned, uncoiling his long frame from the armchair and standing up carefully to avoid provoking yet further the pain that was gnawing at him. "Let's go back to the digs and get comfortable."

His driver, Brian, was despatched to get the car, then drove us the short distance to the palace, where we surprised the staff by saying we would be in for lunch after all. They set about preparing it without complaint; but then in communist Romania, if you were Romanian, you didn't complain about anything.

Drinks were brought out automatically. All three actors exhibited a laudable caution: no matter how much they enjoyed a drink, it was a bad idea to be drunk while working.

But they had been assured they wouldn't be working for at least two hours. So maybe a small one. Larry said red wine, in his condition, was softer on the stomach than his usual white, so he would stick with it.

Half an hour later, Larry and Orson, their arms around each others' shoulders, were doing a softshoe shuffle, vaudeville style, across the spacious floor of our main drawing room. What had started it all was Brian mentioning something he had been told by one of our Romanian production assistants, namely that the palace we were staying in was bugged and all our conversations were recorded and listened to. It had been meant not as a warning against bad-mouthing the Ceauşescu regime and getting ourselves arrested, which was highly unlikely, but to avoid mentioning any Romanians who might have voiced such criticisms to us. The risk to them from such loose talk could be very great.

Initially I had thought the idea was both paranoid and silly, but

I had poked around a little in search of evidence. To my amazement I had found two men wearing headphones in a basement room accessible only from the garden. I stared at them and they stared back at me, all three of us unsure what to do next. I gave them a brief smile and a wave, turned and left them to it. I thought I might hear something more about the incident, but I never did.

It was this reference to bugging that got Orson onto the story of how Harry Cohn (again) had bugged Orson's office at Columbia Studios when he was making *The Lady from Shanghai* with his ex-wife, Rita Hayworth.

"Once I'd found where the microphone was hidden, I had everyone play into it. When we came in every morning we'd kick off with, 'This is the Mercury Theatre welcoming all of you out there to our show for today'. Then at night we'd finish with, 'We're signing off now, but the Mercury Theatre will be back with you tomorrow, same time, same wavelength, and we hope you'll join us'. Then we'd harmonize a few bars of some tune to close the show, and go home."

This gave Larry, who was now feeling much better after several glasses of red wine, the idea of playing disc jockey and putting on some music for our own captive audience listening to us in the basement. Frank Sinatra had just made his first bossa nova record with Antônio Carlos Jobim, and Larry had brought it with him. Orson, like Larry, was a good friend of Sinatra, and the two of them listened to that familiar voice negotiating with consummate skill the (at that time) less familiar and subtle rhythms of bossa nova.

"He's pretty good, isn't he?" Orson said with genuine admiration, his body swaying gently to the music.

Larry agreed. And then they were off, the two of them, shuffling across the carpet in an improvised and surprisingly inventive dance routine.

Just as we were sitting down to lunch a call came to say they wouldn't be needed for at least another two hours or even more.

Three hours later, with Tony Bennett playing now, it was obvious that the likelihood of their being called at all that day was vanishingly small. So maybe just one more drink, then a nap before the evening.

The call came just before the nap. Orson and Larry were needed, not Michael, which was just as well since he was deeply asleep on a sofa beneath the window.

Brian was also by now asleep upstairs, so I said I'd drive. I'd driven that car several times already, and after all it was a private road between the palace and the studio, so there wasn't any risk from, or even to, other traffic.

I was doing fine, negotiating the gently winding road through the palace grounds with care and concentration – until I came to a bend where the view ahead was blocked by a big laurel bush. Rounding it at only moderate speed, I came abruptly upon a Romanian soldier in full uniform with a clumsy-looking rifle slung over his shoulder. He was one of a group who patrolled the palace grounds in a round-the-clock security guard. Normally they remained discreet and unseen, but this one was planted in the middle of the road, daydreaming as he gazed up at some birds fluttering in a tree.

Realising his danger at the last split-second, he leapt with a crash into the laurel bushes, while I swung the car away from him and, with a far greater crash, hit a tree, ripping off the front near-side wing of the vehicle and winding up nose down in a ditch. I didn't so much tip Larry and Orson out of the car as they tipped themselves out, opening the rear door at an angle from which they could only roll onto the grass.

I thought they would be furious, but when I stumbled out from behind the wheel I saw that they were both on their backs, helpless with laughter. The astonished soldier was on his feet and looking down at us from the road. He stayed just long enough to be sure no one was hurt – drunk, certainly, mad quite possibly, but not hurt – then hurried away.

Larry and I helped Orson to his feet, then I fell over and Larry helped me up. A brief glance was enough to see that the car would have to wait for a tow truck, so we set off on foot to cover the last few hundred yards to the studio, both my erstwhile passengers still cackling and wheezing with laughter. Orson gave himself a coughing fit by remarking what an epitaph it was to an actor's career – driven into the ditch by a fucking writer. And so on and so forth.

We were all a little calmer, and slightly more sober, by the time we reached the set. Orson was the only one with any real cause for concern that afternoon. All Larry had to do was stand in one place watching Orson in the distance. Orson himself, on the other hand, had to deliver the longest single speech in the whole movie. We had talked about it a couple of days earlier. "I know," I'd said, "it's not how I'd have done it ideally. It's a bit of a chunk, but the audience absolutely has to know what you're thinking at this point, otherwise the whole next part of the plot won't make sense."

He gave something between a growl and a laugh. "You and your goddamn Byzantine plot."

"It's not my plot. I'm stuck with it and trying to make it work."

"All right, all right, you're right. I'll learn it."

And he did. If they'd shot it before lunch he would have been word perfect. But now..?

Pressing his false nose once more firmly into place and getting a dab of powder from the make-up girl, Orson studied his script. After a few moments he lifted his gaze to take in the set, which was a large cloistered area with a few flaming torches on the walls. He started walking around to get the feel of it.

Robert, the director, took this as his cue to explain how he saw the character moving, pointing out the "marks" he'd had taped on the floor. "You start here, say the first part of the speech standing still, then you walk to here, pause, then come around this way, and you finish up over here. The camera stays on you all the way. Okay?"

Orson nodded, happy to move as the director wanted. Then he looked up to the lighting gantry and pointed.

"Put me a pin spot right here, will you?" he said, "and another over here, directly above me. A pin spot takes weight off the face – makes me look thinner on screen."

He carried on making lighting changes for a few minutes more. At first I assumed it was all about taking weight off his face as he'd said. Then I saw what he was also doing: planning to move from light to shadow, from shadow to light, and so on several times, to punctuate the speech and illustrate the mood swings and vacillations his character was going through. It was simple and brilliant. Robert Siodmak knew it, having made moody "film noir" lighting something of his trademark in his earlier career. He made sure everything was arranged, quickly and efficiently, just as Orson wanted it.

They went for a take. Orson dried after a few lines.

They went again.

He dried again.

It happened a third time. It was quite clear that Orson's memory, undermined as it was by his long lunch, was not going to be working on all cylinders before the next morning. But he was determined to persevere. He didn't get angry, either with himself or anybody else. I thought I might get some more flack about Byzantine plots and how we should have done this another way, but not a word. He just made a Herculean effort to concentrate and get it right. He took a few moments to study the script again, and they went for a fifth take.

He got a little further than before, but still dried.

I could see the production manager standing in the shadows with his teeth clenched and hands clasped tightly beneath his arm pits, as though trying to generate enough internal pressure to finally pop his eyes right out of his head.

Robert remained calm, springing out of his director's chair to reassure Orson that it didn't matter; they could shoot the scene in sections, which would allow Orson to deliver the whole speech a few lines at a time.

But Orson wanted to do it in one take as it had been envisioned, and for which he had now arranged the ideal lighting.

Robert, despairingly, said it just wasn't going to work.

Then Orson had an idea.

"David, will you get up on the camera? If you can throw me – silently – the first word of every line, I'll get through it."

The camera, manned as usual by the redoubtable Herr Angst, was once again on a large crane so that it could move with Orson and get the whole scene in one shot. I clambered up alongside him and his operator, one hand clutching the script and the other hanging on to the side of the crane as it rose, dipped and tracked across the floor.

With a certain amount of ducking and weaving, I managed to stay in Orson's view at all times, mouthing the first word of each line with the exaggeration of someone addressing a stone-deaf lip reader. He picked them all up seamlessly. Once or twice I could see he was about to dry in the middle of a phrase because his eye line had moved to where it took me in. I was ready, script in hand, with the next word for that split second when he looked at me for a prompt.

This time he got through the take in one, and it couldn't have been better. Vastly relieved, he came over to me as I stepped down from the camera crane. "Thank you, David," he said, with what sounded like real gratitude. "That was a great job, just what I needed. Not everybody could have done that."

I tried not to swell too obviously with pride, but I'm afraid I wore a grin from ear to ear for the rest of the day, and possibly told the story a couple of times – until Larry, a little cranky now because his gut was playing up again, said I was getting on his nerves.

But me and Orson Welles? Blood brothers, mate.

CHAPTER 24

It's probably a rather silly form of inverted snobbery, but I've always avoided getting my picture taken with celebrities. I cringe with embarrassment at the thought of asking for a photo opportunity with a famous face, and my first instinct when I see a camera within range of me and someone recognisable is to step out of the frame.

When I look at the walls of people's homes displaying pictures of themselves with presidents, prime ministers and movie stars, I have mixed feelings. In one way it's a shortcut to impressing people; in another way it strikes me as a curious kind of insecurity and somehow rather demeaning. Snapshots of a formal handshake with some world leader, or of a casual conversation with a star, usually mean your acquaintance with the personality in question lasted just about as long as it took to get the picture. The first thing you saw when you entered my parents' house was a photograph of themselves standing in a long line to meet the Queen at a Buckingham Palace Garden Party. I knew how much it had meant to them to be invited (because of my father's long service on the county council) and I was pleased for them. Nonetheless, I hated the "de haut en bas" feeling about it. It wasn't that I was a revolutionary republican or anything like that: more that as a fully fledged snob, albeit a self-made one, I firmly rejected the idea of playing Uriah Heep to anyone.

At any rate, for whatever mixture of reasons, my own walls

remain denuded of any evidence of my ever having been on hob-nobbing terms with anyone worth knowing. Interestingly, the only famous person who made a point of having the two of us photographed together was Kirk Douglas, with whom I made a picture (*The Final Countdown*) in 1980. My wife Laurence and I were invited for the weekend to celebrate his sixty-second birthday at his and Anne's weekend house in Palm Springs. After dinner one night he asked his son Peter, who had produced the movie, to get a photograph of the two of us together with Kirk's arm around my shoulder.

It happened again on another occasion when I was invited to the Dougalases' main home in Beverly Hills for Thanksgiving. In this one I was wearing a full-length butcher's apron, leant to me by Anne Douglas, and wielding a large knife as I carved the family turkey. In the picture Kirk is peering over my shoulder with rapt interest; Spartacus, it seemed, although a dab hand with a broad sword was all thumbs with a carving knife, and I had volunteered to stand in. Peter, much amused, had grabbed a camera.

Needless to say, I subsequently lost both photographs, which is a pity.

I never had my picture taken with Orson, despite the fact that it seemed almost everyone else did. Sometimes members of the unit would ask the production stills photographer to sneak a quick one while they were in Orson's presence; sometimes people just asked outright if they could have a picture taken with him, and he always agreed graciously. On one occasion he was photographed holding the two-year-old daughter of one of our Romanian production assistants. When the photograph was developed and presented to him for an autograph it, he inscribed it generously: "To Doina, from her daddy's friend Orson Welles".

Perhaps because he'd noticed this streak of self-denying

puritanism in me – and very little escaped him – he did something rather touching to make up for it. As I was passing the open door of his dressing room one morning towards the end of his time on the production, he called me in. It was as spartan as all the other dressing rooms in that place, and he was hunched over a small typewriter which he was picking at with two fingers.

"I've got something for you, David. Wait a minute, will you?"

He finished typing, pulled a single sheet out of the machine, signed it with a flourish, and handed it to me.

"I want you to have this."

On the back of a page of our script (part of a scene between himself and Michael Dunn) he had written:

"Dear David,

"As you see, I'm still suffering from a permanent paper shortage..."

(We had in fact had terrible trouble getting adequate supplies of writing paper throughout the shoot.)

He went on:

"Thanks for all your great help and congratulations on the heroic salvaging job..."

Underneath that he gave me what he called his permanent address, which was care of his full-time secretary in London. Anything sent there, he assured me, would reach him.

His signature "Orson" was a blue swirl from a felt-tip pen, with a squiggly line running down from the final "n" and turning into the smoke rising from the tip of a long cigar which was clenched in the jaws of a clever little cartoon of himself, in full costume and make-up, as the Emperor Justinian.

I still have that faded yellowish page of poor-quality paper, and treasure it now as much as I always have.

Sadly, however, I have lost the correspondence I kept up with Orson for the next year or two. The first time I wrote to him was very soon after we had gone our separate ways from Romania, sending him a play by the Hungarian writer Julius Hay, who I'd spoken to him about and who I considered superior to Brecht while dealing with similar subjects. Orson read the play and wrote back promptly. He agreed that Hay was a fine writer, regretting only that "his kind of excellence, sadly, is out of fashion at the moment", therefore the chances of Orson putting the play on somewhere and playing the leading role himself were slim.

I wrote to him about various other things and possible projects, always through the secretary in London, and always receiving a thoughtful reply from wherever he was in the world. Once I sent him Iris Murdoch's first novel, *Under the Net*, which had been published fifteen years earlier and had a great part for him in it. He agreed, but as neither of us could see any prospect of getting the picture set up, the point was academic. He sent me one or two other books that he had long wanted to film, though without success.

Gradually the correspondence came to an end, but I count myself an absolute fool that ten years later, by which time I was working in Hollywood, I didn't look him up. He was by then acting in fewer films and doing more voice-overs, commercials, and talk shows. He was a regular on the *Dean Martin Comedy Hour, Celebrity Roast*, and other things. I felt on the one hand it was better to leave the past where it belonged – in the past. A call or note from me would probably have been kindly received, but I didn't have any projects to propose to him or anything specific to talk about, and Hollywood is a company town where all relationships are bounded and defined by the limits of mutual usefulness involved.

Looking back, I can see I had been infected by the atmosphere of the place more than I had realised, especially as I've since been told that he might well have welcomed a visit that was not purely and simply about "the business".

Too late now. I remember the morning in October 1985 when I heard he was dead. I was staying at my parents-in-laws' house outside Lausanne in Switzerland and listening to the morning news in bed. He was seventy years old, though I was surprised he'd lasted even that long with all the weight he carried around. And I was saddened to think that any lingering chance of seeing him again had finally slipped away, owing entirely to my own negligence.

Orson's eldest daughter Christopher (Orson's whimsical choice of name) has written a charming memoir of him in which she relates how upset she became over all the betrayals and disappointments he'd had to endure, especially towards the end of his life. Orson, she said, would comfort her with the words, "Don't worry, darling girl, they're going to love me when I'm dead."

Hell, Orson, it didn't take that long.

CHAPTER 25

I stayed on in Bucharest for a couple of weeks after the principal actors had departed. One reason was a handful of minor scenes that remained to be shot and which needed attention. The other reason was Vicky.

We'd met in a bar in Bucharest – frankly, a pick-up joint for the better-off and well-connected offspring of the communist middle class. All of them seemed to despise the regime, and despite their relatively privileged lives did not find it easy to leave the country either for a holiday or permanently. As I'd told Orson in response to his very direct question about these matters, foreigners arriving in this closed society had the advantage of appearing faintly exotic.

She was just twenty-one, with a very pretty face, and a body that offered the abundant fulfilment of T.S. Eliot's "promise of pneumatic bliss". Her father was leader of the Bucharest Symphony Orchestra. She shared a flat with two other girls – also amazing lookers – in one of the better parts of the city. We communicated exclusively in French, which neither of us spoke particularly well, but that proved no impediment to the enjoyment of our time together.

It was with more than a touch of regret that I boarded the brand-new BAC-111 jetliner with which Tarom Airlines had replaced the dreadful old rustbucket on which Larry and I had flown into the country a little more than three months earlier. I seriously contemplated returning in a week or two to see Vicky again, and we spoke a couple of times on a crackly phone line between London and Bucharest. But I was due in Rome soon to start work on a new script. In Romania Larry had been visited by the director of his unreleased thriller with Ann-Margret and an Italian producer who had an idea for a picture they wanted to get Larry involved in. Seeing how well we got along together, and how happy he was with the work I was doing on our epic, they made a note of my name and my agent, and eventually I got a call from Elspeth in London to say that my next job was all lined up. As anyone in show business knows, having your next job lined up before the current one ends is just about as good as it gets. I was beginning to nurture illusions of being a dashing international screenwriter.

Before I left London for Rome, I broke up with Prim. I'm not sure exactly why, except it seemed to me that all romantic relationships had to break up after a few months. I think I had persuaded myself that they were actually programmed to do so. My fear of entrapment into domesticity remained as strong as ever. I was touched when Prim failed entirely to conceal a sniffle of disappointment at this development, but she knew as well as I that it was bound to happen. I was not the stuff of which stable relationships were made – not that she was specifically looking to get married and "settle down", but she was less inclined to the pursuit of sexual adventure for its own sake than I still was at that point. She knew we would have come to grief sooner or later, and this kind of clean, clear break somehow allowed us to remain friends without any lingering bitterness.

Somewhat to my surprise, a girlfriend of hers came up to me a day or two later and congratulated me on "doing the decent thing", adding that she'd never believed until then that I had it in me.

A compliment of sorts, I suppose. Anyway, that's how I chose to take it.

The Parco dei Principi was a hotel much favoured by the film community at that time. It struck me as wonderfully exotic, surrounded by umbrella pines, terraces, and with a huge swimming pool. It was on the edge of a beautiful park called the Villa Borghese, only a short walk from the Via Veneto and the fashionable heart of the city.

Rome at that time was at its height as one of the world's great centres of film production, routinely described in the press as "Hollywood on the Tiber". The studios at Cinecittà were full to capacity with stars and directors from all around the world, many of whom, I would discover, were staying at my hotel. I knew nobody in the city except for the director and our producer, from whom I found a message saying he would come to collect me the next morning for a meeting with the writer he wanted me to work with, a poet called Edith Bruck. I'd been told that she had completed a rough first draft, but what was needed now was someone with a stronger sense of dramatic structure to pull it into shape.

That evening I took a walk alone down the Via Veneto. I felt like I had stepped into a Fellini movie. Everywhere I turned I saw images that were straight out of *La Dolce Vita*. I passed James Mason in an immaculate lightweight suit strolling with a friend. Tony Curtis was at a pavement table drinking with a group of people. All around the girls combined sexiness and chic in a way Italian (and French) girls seem able to do better than anyone in the world. It was a perfect moment, with the setting sun casting a warm glow over the whole scene. In an hour it would be dark, and I felt a pang of regret that I would be dining alone, an outsider in this glittering city.

Then I thought I heard my name called. I glanced around, but could see no one I knew. I had imagined it. Wishful thinking, probably. I walked on. And it happened again.

This time I stopped and looked around more carefully. And there, pulled up on the far side of the road was a gleaming Rolls-Royce in pastel blue and white. A tall man with film-star good looks had stepped out from behind the wheel and was waving me over. It was Lang Jeffries.

Lang was a Canadian-born actor who'd played a key supporting role in our Roman epic. He was a likable guy in his late thirties who'd had some success in American TV, then gone to Rome in the early sixties to star in a succession of low-budget "sword-and-sandal" epics. In one of them he had co-starred with Rhonda Fleming, a few years older than himself but still the "flame-haired Hollywood goddess" she had been since the forties. They had married, but it had lasted only a couple of years. His current wife, Gail, was an attractive and down-to-earth brunette who I'd met when she came out to visit him on location in Romania. She was the ex-wife of John Paul Getty Jr, heir to one of the world's largest fortunes, by whom she had four young children. Between them, she and Lang were clearly well funded enough to be living the high life with some style. I got a touchingly warm welcome from them both, and was bundled into the back of their Rolls and taken to dinner.

CHAPTER 26

We were joined in an elegant restaurant – a sea of white table-cloths and sparkling silver on one of the city's great piazzas – by another American actor, Brett Halsey, and his German wife Heidi Brühl. Heidi, a strikingly pretty blonde of twenty-six, was, I knew, a big recording and movie star in her native Germany.

Brett, already on his third marriage at the age of thirty-five (first wife a former Miss Germany, the second an Italian former Bond girl), was tall and possessed of what are usually described as smouldering good looks, though his expression always reminded me more of a spoilt boy about to burst into tears. Like Lang, Brett was an actor who had parlayed a modest success in the States into minor stardom in Europe. What they and others like them dreamt of doing was repeating the astounding success of Clint Eastwood only four years earlier. Coming off a long-running TV show called *Rawhide*, Clint had been offered a "spaghetti western" which had been turned down not only by Charles Bronson, but by a list of small-time actors no one had ever heard of even back then, let alone now. The script was called *A Fistful of Dollars*, a low-budget Italian production to be shot in Spain, for which Eastwood was being offered peanuts. But he saw something in it. Directed with flare and imagination by Sergio Leone, it had catapulted him to international stardom. Clint's friends and contemporaries, a group which included Brett Halsey, had observed this phenomenon with green-eyed envy, and headed for Rome.

To be fair, I felt that Lang was rather more relaxed about it all than many. I got the impression that he regarded himself simply as a jobbing actor who turned up on time, knew his lines, and considered himself lucky to be getting paid for it.

Brett Halsey was more complicated. Hungry for major stardom, he knew that every passing year made the likelihood of its happening more remote. His conversation that night, and on subsequent occasions, revolved around his frustrated efforts to negotiate three-picture deals with slippery Italian producers, or to agree complex profit-sharing arrangements in order to make potentially breakout pictures for little or no money up front.

Lang knew how unlikely it was that any of these schemes would work out. Ever the pragmatist, his advice was to take the best flat fee you can get, do the movie, and don't worry about profits because even if it's a hit they'll rob you; but if it is a hit, you'll be able to negotiate a better price next time out. It was good advice. I don't know if Brett ever took it, but he certainly never got the breakout movie he was looking for. A few years later he was back in America, divorced from Heidi and working in daytime soaps and episodic television.

Lang and Gail's marriage had also broken down by then, which surprised me: they had seemed like a good couple enjoying life and each other to the full. Not long after the divorce Gail became front-page news around the world. In the summer of 1973 her oldest son, sixteen-year-old John Paul Getty III, who I'd known in Rome as a happy twelve-year-old, was kidnapped. Beside herself with fear, Gail begged the Getty family for help in raising the seventeen-million-dollar ransom demanded of her. Her pleas were refused by her autocratic ex-father-in-law on the grounds that by paying up he would simply be guaranteeing that all of his remaining fourteen grandchildren would also be kidnapped. In response, the kidnappers cut off the boy's ear and posted it to an

Italian newspaper. Getty senior relented, and a lower ransom of three million dollars was negotiated, of which the elderly billionaire contributed two point-two million, that being the maximum he could claim in tax relief. The rest of the money to make up the total he loaned to his son, Gail's ex-husband, at an interest rate of four percent.

The boy was released and found wandering in a daze south of Naples. He never fully recovered from the ordeal and became a drug addict, suffering a massive stroke after an overdose at the age of twenty-five which left him blind and paralysed until his death in 2011 at the age of fifty-four. He had, however, fathered a son in 1975 who is now the actor and musician Balthazar Getty.

But that night in Rome in the summer of '68 there was nothing in the air to foreshadow such future tragedy and pain, no way of knowing that both Lang and Heidi would die too young of cancer, she not yet fifty, he just a few years older. That night life was good and the future full of promise for everyone around that table.

After dinner we all piled into the Rolls and headed for what I would discover was the film colony's favourite late-night hang-out. "Dave's Dive" was located down a stone staircase beneath a building just off the lower end of the Via Veneto. Dave was Dave Crowley, a former lightweight British boxing champion, a Londoner but with an Italian mother. Always in immaculate black tie and dinner jacket, he presided with grace and good nature over his little kingdom. He was good friends with a number of heroic boozers when they were in town, Peter O'Toole and Richard Burton among them, but was not a drinker himself.

The place was busy, but Dave spent a good ten or fifteen minutes talking to me and making me feel welcome. He was clearly fond of Lang and Gail, and any friend of theirs was all right with him. Eventually he said there was someone I should meet, and he led me over to a corner booth, where I found Peter Sellers sitting

195

alone in a deep armchair, a beatific smile on his face, obviously very stoned.

Although drug-taking on the premises was not allowed, what people got up to on their way there (or sometimes in the lavatories) was nobody else's business, and I suspected that Sellers had taken full advantage of that freedom. He was charming and approachable, but talking to him was rather like taking part in one of those television conversations between someone in the studio and someone else halfway around the world: there was a measurable delay between what was said to him and his response to it. But, allowing for that, the conversation flowed easily – especially when I told him that a few days earlier in London I'd seen Mel Brooks's first film, *The Producers*, entirely on his (Sellers') recommendation. A small budget independent production with no big stars (though Gene Wilder would soon become one) the picture was in danger of sinking without trace when Sellers happened to see it in a private screening. At his own expense he had taken out adverts in several newspapers, including *Variety* and *The Times*, to write his own review and sing its praises. As a result, although it was showing only in one cinema just off Leicester Square, I had got into a packed midnight showing and had howled with laughter along with everyone there.

Sellers was delighted, and immediately went into a replay of his favourite moments from the picture. Brilliant mimic that he was, it was as good as the original: in fact in some ways better. There I was, I told myself in disbelief, being entertained by this comic genius who I'd listened to on *The Goon Show* at home in Brindle only a decade earlier, with the volume turned down because Dad couldn't stand them: "It's not funny, it's just daft, all them damn silly voices."

It was after three in the morning when I finally took a taxi back to my hotel. My producer was due to pick me up at nine-thirty to start work.

Thanks to the remarkable resilience of a youthful constitution, I was waiting in the hotel lobby after breakfast and an early morning swim by nine twenty-nine. As a producer, more specifically an Italian producer, he was straight out of central casting: an expensive silk suit, slicked-back hair, and a perma-tan. We drove in his chauffeur-driven car through the narrow streets of a residential district where imposing old buildings had been turned into elegant apartments. My co-writer, Edith Bruck, lived in one of them. The director was already there, and the four of us chatted for about twenty minutes before the two men departed, leaving their writers to get on with the script.

I sensed at once that there was something out of the ordinary about this woman I was to work with, though it would be some time before I understood what. In appearance she was, I would have to say, plain, but in the sense of unadorned rather than unattractive. Her hair was pulled back and fastened unfussily behind her head. She dressed simply in neutral colours and wore flat-heeled shoes. And yet she was wholly and appealingly feminine.

At thirty-six, only eleven years older than me, she had about her an air of gentle, quiet self-possession that I found almost disturbing. But unlike so many members of the sixties' "peace and love" generation, there was no hint of smugness attached to this quality of inner stillness, no sense of having attained some higher ground from which she could look down indulgently upon the rest of us.

On the contrary, there was an effortless humility about her combined with an unshakeable sense of who she was. Because she had no need to hide or pretend to be anything other than herself, she displayed an openness and generosity of spirit towards everything and everyone around her. It was as though she knew something about life that the rest of us didn't, certainly not me.

The truth about her, I would discover later, was that this was a woman whose soul had been forged in Hell. She was twelve when her family – the poorest of poor Jews in a Hungarian village – were rounded up by the Nazis and deported to Auschwitz. Her mother died in the gas chambers there, her father and brother shortly afterwards in Dachau. Edith and her sister somehow survived both camps and then a transfer to Belsen-Bergen, living through experiences beyond the comprehension of anyone who had not shared them. After the war she returned to Hungary to look for what remained of her family. Having been raped by a cousin, she had an abortion while not yet fifteen. At sixteen she married and emigrated to Israel. After divorcing at seventeen she married a man who abused her, leading to another divorce. She married a third time, but this marriage too had ended by the time she was twenty. Barely twenty-two, she emigrated to Italy, where she met Nelo Risi, twelve years older than herself and a respected poet and film-maker.

All of which makes it an even greater pity that the enterprise Edith and I embarked on that late summer morning was doomed to failure from the outset. For me it was a lesson in how not to go about making a movie. The whole thing was a product of opportunism and little else. From the producer's point of view the name of Laurence Harvey, though well past its sell-by date in Hollywood, was still useful in putting together a deal in the international marketplace. For Larry, it meant having something written at no cost to himself and which might conceivably offer him a decent role. To the director it meant a second shot at directing instead of going back to being an assistant director on run-of-the-mill Italian movies. To Edith, who for all her hard-earned wisdom was a naive outsider in the shark-infested world of commercial film-making, it was a pay cheque that a poet would be unwise to turn down. And to me, well, I was in Rome having a fine time and getting paid for it.

In my defence I have to say I did the best I could with the material to hand. Unfortunately it struck me as more suitable for a mid-afternoon radio play than a full-length feature film. I can't even remember the story. It was so meandering and inconsequential that no amount of "dramatic structure" was going to hide the fact that we were making bricks without straw: no conflict, no compelling characters, no suspense (which cannot be imposed from without if it is not innate to the story), and absolutely no humour other than the odd moment of gentle whimsy.

We worked every weekday from ten till twelve-thirty, and every afternoon from around three till six. Either I would take a cab to meet someone for lunch, or sometimes I would be invited to join Edith and Nelo. She would always have something simmering in the oven in readiness for his return from the editing room where he was putting together a rather solemn-sounding semi-documentary called *The Diary of a Schizophrenic Girl*. Nelo, being an intellectual, affected a down-to-earth manner, eating with his shirt sleeves rolled up, his elbows on the table, and tearing his bread into manly chunks. He didn't have a lot of conversation, and I always suspected he rather disapproved of me. I probably struck him as an insufficiently serious sort of person. He was probably right.

Indeed, I could find little to be serious about during my stay in Rome, so I settled for having a good time. I met a lot of people and made many friends around the pool of my hotel or in Dave's Dive. One afternoon I shook hands with Federico Fellini, and the same night had rather a lot of martinis with Eric Sykes. An attractive girl I was chatting up on the terrace one day took me over to meet her father, who turned out to be Ernest Borgnine. He was very charming, but dropped a couple of casual remarks to make sure I was aware that his daughter was rather younger than she looked, having just turned sixteen a couple of weeks earlier. Considering that this was the man who had beaten Frank Sinatra to death in *From Here to Eternity* and had played more tough-guy roles than I could remember (*The Dirty Dozen*, *The Wild Bunch*), a hint was all it took to keep me in line.

Later on Ernie introduced me to the Hollywood screenwriter Millard Kaufman, who had written *Bad Day at Black Rock*, the classic Spencer Tracy movie in which Ernie had played a thug the year before winning his Oscar for *Marty*. Millard had written a number of movies in the past that I had seen and greatly admired, and I was proud to get to know him. He was a tall, broad-shouldered ex-marine in his early fifties, almost certainly a good deal tougher than any of the tough-guy actors he'd written roles for. We would remain good friends for more than thirty years.

It was one Sunday afternoon by the pool with Millard, his wife Lory, who was a psychiatrist with a practice in Los Angeles, and their two teenage children, that I had the most unexpected encounter of my time in Rome. I spotted a very attractive blonde girl in a bikini lying in the sun by herself. At least everything I could see suggested she was very attractive, though she was lying face down at the time. Making my excuses to the Kaufman family, I edged my way over so that I would be close enough to start up a conversation should the opportunity arise. After a while she turned over lazily, as I had supposed she would, and I was ready to pounce.

Then I saw who she was.

It was Sue Lyon.

This was the girl who had played Kubrick's "Lolita" only a few years earlier. She'd been sixteen then, which made her twenty-two now. And just about the most gorgeous thing I had ever set eyes on.

All the cool chat-up lines I'd been preparing went out of my head as though somebody had flicked a switch – which she had. Possibly because she was accustomed to having this effect on young men, and presumably also middle-aged and older ones, she took the initiative and gave me a sweet smile, and said, "Hi!"

I pulled myself together enough to say "Hi!" back, feeling my face freeze into an idiotic grin that I feared I might never shake off.

In the easiest and most graceful way, she simply took over for the next few minutes, making casual conversation until I'd had time to regain my equilibrium and get some sort of thought process re-started in my head. And then the afternoon just flowed. We took a swim and goofed around, had a couple of drinks, and went back to lie in the sun. Never in my life before or since have I met a less "actressy" actress, or a less self-involved star. She had by then, in the six years since making *Lolita*, worked with the likes of Richard Burton and Ava Gardner, Anne Bancroft and Frank Sinatra, and been directed by heavyweights like John Huston and even John Ford. Yet there was nothing of the movie star about her, no barrier of narcissism between herself and the world around her. She was as down-to-earth and straightforward as anyone I'd ever met, including in the proudly down-to-earth and straightforward Lancashire that I came from.

It was that quality of normalness, I came to suspect later, that helped sink her career over the next few years. There was no doubt she was talented, and no doubt audiences responded to her; she just didn't have what it took to take herself seriously. Or, more precisely, to take being a movie star seriously. Her life, from all I've read subsequently, has been pretty complicated and far from ideal: five mostly short-lived marriages, a child by a stunt man, and a rapid professional descent through episodic television to an unbilled two-minute role (in which she was very good) in a low-budget exploitation movie called *Alligator* in 1980.

But that day in 1968 she was on top of the heap. Millard could barely wait when I ran into him next morning to ask: "That girl at the pool, was that..?"

"Yes, it was."

"I thought so. My God, wow."

"Wow indeed."

"You seemed to be having a great time."

"Oh, we were."

"And... did you..?"

"No. No, sadly. I mean, I'm not saying it would have definitely happened, but... well, she had to meet people and was leaving this morning. I had a dinner date too, which of course I would have broken..."

"Who wouldn't!"

"Yeah. You know what, I think I'm in love."

"Of course you are."

"If I don't see her again I may kill myself."

"I understand."

"I know you do."

We walked on through the Villa Borghese, until Millard broke the silence with a perfectly timed suggestion.

"On the other hand, we could just have lunch."

"You're right," I said. "Where shall we go?"

CHAPTER 27

I got back to London in late October '68, just as my first television play, *Public Face*, was about to go into rehearsal. Despite the eventfulness of the year so far, this promised for me to be a major highpoint.

The "television play" as we knew it back then no longer exists today. From the late seventies it began to be replaced by the "television movie", originally a kind of low-budget B-picture but which has become increasingly sophisticated over the years. Before that, however, the TV play was closer to a piece of theatre than film. Studio-bound and taking place usually on no more than half a dozen sets, the story and characters would unfold at a leisurely pace, with relationships being developed more through dialogue than action, and conflicts established through carefully constructed scenes. Film inserts, if any, were used sparingly and only if essential to create a sense of place, or to convey some piece of information or aspect of character that could not be achieved any other way.

Rehearsals took place as for a stage play over three weeks or a month, depending on whether it was an hour-long piece or longer. At the end of the rehearsal period everyone would move into the studios – which might be as far away as Manchester, Norwich or Leeds, regionalism being much in vogue at the time – for a day's technical rehearsal on the sets, followed by another day, two at most, on which the production would be taped for later transmission.

My play, being ninety minutes long, was accorded a month's rehearsal. I took the Tube from the tiny flat I had just started renting at the wrong end of Chelsea to a rehearsal room in Brixton. I still find it strange, no matter how many times I've done it, to walk into one of those dreary and unwelcoming places to find famous actors sitting around on folding chairs, gratefully accepting mugs of tea or coffee from production assistants and looking more like the inmates of a charity shelter than stars of stage and screen.

Gareth was there of course, along with John Castle, who at twenty-eight had just completed a co-starring role in *A Lion in Winter* with Peter O'Toole, Katharine Hepburn and Anthony Hopkins. Instantly recognisable was Cyril Luckham, a silkily benevolent actor in his sixties who had the main role in the play. Also there for one of her first leading roles in television was a very pretty young Scottish actress called Hannah Gordon, who would soon become a major and much-loved star, even to the extent of being a guest on the *Morecambe and Wise Christmas Show* a year or two later.

Public Face was set in an Oxford college. It didn't, however, reflect my experience as an undergraduate so much as what I had observed of the subtle, complex and sometimes vicious competitiveness that existed between professional academics. I had a good friend, Michael Gearin-Tosh, who was just three years older than me and who was already a lecturer in English at Magdalen College when I first came up to the university as a freshman. We met because he saw the first one-act play that I wrote at the end of my first year, and also because he had seen me as a regular participant in Union debates, and found the combination of these two activities odd and interesting. As result, although I was only once invited by my law tutor to dine on high table in my own college, Merton, I became a frequent guest on high table at Magdalen, where I got to know the college president and many of the fellows, especially the scientists and philosophers, who I found the most interesting. All of this did nothing for my law studies but proved infinitely more valuable in the long run.

The central conflict in *Public Face* was between a man in his late twenties, Donald Webster, who had just been given a fellowship in a college very clearly based on Magdalen (where we shot the exteriors), and the master of the college, Sir William ("Willy") Ince. With curious precision I had placed Ince's age at precisely sixty-eight. Worldly, charmingly feline and politically astute, he was based so closely on the president of Magdalen at that time, T.S.R. ("Tommy") Boase, that I became seriously worried about the prospect of a libel suit as the play's transmission date approached. I needn't have worried; he did actually watch the play and apparently enjoyed it. I have subsequently observed on a number of occasions that people almost never recognise themselves in plays or novels. The most they ever say is, "D'you know, I once knew somebody just like that."

•

In my next play, *The Innocent Ceremony*, I abandoned the narrow world of Oxford academia and returned to the even narrower world of my origins in the north. It was a pattern I would follow through the next half dozen years or so of my writing for television: a play about the sophisticated chattering classes I was coming to know increasingly well in London, then a play about the decidedly unsophisticated, blunt-spoken and down-to-earth world I came from.

This play too went down well with audiences and critics, and brought me another commission from the same company and the same producer. This time I was invited to write a trilogy; or, as

Lew Grade, the great showman who ran the company, had a habit of calling it, a "trilology".

A year earlier the company had put out three half-hour plays about a girl of twenty and her relationships with three different men. As the men were played by Sean Connery, Michael Caine and Paul Scofield, this was an immensely prestigious production and a great success. The writer was Alun Owen, a much-admired Welsh writer in his mid-forties who had recently written the Beatles' first film, *A Hard Day's Night*. It was a great vote of confidence in me that I was offered the opportunity of repeating this success.

But I quite dismally failed to do so. Why? I'm still not sure. There were no terms or conditions attached, no demands or restraints, no subjects I was encouraged to consider or advised to avoid. I was offered a clean slate, a blank canvas, to do with what I chose. And I couldn't think of a damn thing.

Of course I tried. In fact I struggled. I made more false starts than I could count. But nothing would come alive. I grew accustomed to the look of patient disappointment on my producer's face as I pitched him yet another idea that went nowhere.

The technical term for what I was experiencing is, of course, writer's block. But that isn't particularly useful because nobody quite knows what it means. Wikipedia's definition is as good as any: "A condition ... in which an author loses the ability to produce new work".

But why does it happen? The answers to that are probably as numerous as there are writers: we all screw up in our own way. Like depression, it will disappear in its own sweet time and not before, and whether you get up in the middle of the night and write thousands of words, get drunk, stoned, or scribble in waterproof ink while hanging upside down in the shower, it will all be drivel until the muse consents to return.

Of course "muse" is an even more difficult term to define. It has something to do with a spark of ignition that triggers a chain of events culminating in a finished piece of work. If that sounds rather dry and clinical, it's because it isn't easy to write about a complex organic process, which "ignition" is. I know that the spark that led to the writing of my first stage play at Oxford was a generalised sense of excitement about theatre, the whole business of illusion and reality, the paradox of unearthing truth through the use of pretence and artifice.

In *Public Face* it had started in a growing fascination with these complex, clever people I was spending time with. Although intellectually brilliant, they seemed often emotionally stunted and capable of astonishing small-mindedness. Their vast reservoirs of learning seemed to bring them little wisdom, self-knowledge or understanding of others.

Similarly with *The Innocent Ceremony*, I'd seen all my life how a very real type of intuitive intelligence could exist in people with little or no formal education, and how those who possessed it could connect with others across wide divisions of class, gender, age or anything else.

I don't pretend that any of these perceptions of mine were particularly profound or original, but they served to get me going, to set in motion some process that for want of a better word we call "creative". Whether I wanted to write because I felt the need to tell these stories, or whether I just wanted to write and so had to find stories to tell, is hard to say. What I know for sure, however, is that you can't write a word when the cupboard is bare, your mind is a blank, and the spark hasn't sparked. You can't just bang any old rubbish together and make it work. No matter how clever or experienced you are, it won't. And you can't make the spark happen just because you need it.

At least, I've never met any writer who could.

CHAPTER 28

My new girlfriend, Jackie, who I'd met in Rome, was a lovely blonde who drove a yellow E-Type Jaguar and worked for a property billionaire in Park Lane. She had invited me to join herself, her boss and his wife and a couple of friends on a Caribbean cruise aboard a luxury schooner with more crew than passengers. It promised an agreeable few weeks of sun, sea and fringe benefits during the gloomy weeks of February '69, by the end of which I would have turned twenty-six.

The problem was I'd been offered a job in Berlin by the producer of our Roman epic. Like the idiotically insecure writer I was and probably still am, I took the job.

The Cold War was still at its height, and West Berlin was isolated not only deep within communist East Germany but within the Soviet sector of Berlin itself. Flights from the West had to cover East German territory at a height that was alarmingly close to tree level, twisting and turning to follow a narrow air corridor, and at a speed that felt dangerously close to stalling. I peered out at the grey, drab, frozen fields, half covered in dirty-looking snow. Here and there a figure moved, sometimes a van or tractor bumped along a rutted track. Nobody was having any fun down there. I sat back and thought of Jackie and that schooner in the Caribbean, and ordered another drink.

The production manager from Romania, he of the pink face and pop-eyes, met me off the plane and drove me into the city, where I was installed in a drab modern hotel room overlooking the main drag, the Kurfürstendamm. A typewriter was provided along with a stack of blank paper, and a copy of the script I was to work on. The novel *Passion Flower Hotel* had been a "success de scandale" a few years earlier, about a posh girls' school in Switzerland operating a secret brothel to cater for the boys' school across the lake. It was actually a very wittily written farce by a Scotsman called Roger Longrigg under the pseudonym of Rosalind Erskine. It was just asking to be made into a film, but for some reason, perhaps because they weren't being paid enough, the writers who had worked on it so far had failed to bring it up to speed. I wasn't being paid a fortune, but enough to give it my best shot for a few weeks.

Adaptation is a great deal easier than actual writing. It takes skill, but doesn't need that spark of ignition or "muse" that will produce something original. All screenwriters spend a good deal of time adapting novels or re-writing scripts written by others, often far more than on original work; but any who claim it's as hard as original work are either not telling the truth or have never done any original work.

So there I was in the walled city of West Berlin in the depths of winter, knowing nobody except my producer, who took me to dinner with his wife a couple of times, but otherwise with nothing to do when not working but explore the place. And it rewarded exploration.

Inevitably the most dramatic thing to see was the Wall itself. The East Germans, with Soviet backing, had started to build it in 1961 to stop the haemorrhaging of their citizens to the west. Almost ninety miles long and twelve feet high, it ring-fenced the city in grey, forbidding concrete blocks. Long stretches of it on the western side had been colourfully decorated by graffiti artists; any effort to do the same on the eastern side, or indeed any attempt even to approach the wall, risked summary execution by one of the guards in the watch towers placed at regular intervals along their side of the wall.

It came as a shock to walk down an ordinary street and suddenly come up against this monstrosity. It was somehow surreal, and contributed to the sense of faintly hysterical defiance hanging over this outpost of Western freedom and consumerism. Just how great the difference was between the two Berlins was something I would find out a night or two later.

Bertolt Brecht's famous Berliner Ensemble Theatre, which he'd created in 1949, was situated in East Berlin. Despite my misgivings about Brecht, I was keen to see his company in action. I discovered that although East Berlin was effectively a prison to its citizens, visits to the east by West Berliners, and Western tourists from elsewhere, could be arranged. I was able to buy a ticket to the theatre from an agency in the western sector, then presented myself around six in the evening at Checkpoint Charlie, the border control point made famous by countless spy thrillers, to apply for a temporary visa at a cost of five Deutsche Marks. Normally this should have been a routine process over in minutes; I, however, managed to complicate things.

In the first place it probably wasn't a brilliant idea to be carrying in my pocket a copy of Arthur Koestler's novel, *Darkness at Noon*, his famous denunciation of communist terror. It wasn't, however, the book that upset the border officials as they checked me over for contraband or anything else of a suspicious nature. They had probably never heard of the book anyway. What worried them was the thing I was using as a bookmark.

A few days earlier in Soho I had been handed a little card advertising a new disco; some kid on a corner was giving one to anybody who looked young enough to be interested. On the back of the card was a printed street map pinpointing the club's location. It was this that was causing frowns and muttered comments between the two officers in front of me. A third was called over, obviously their superior. He looked at the card, looked at me, took a step forward, and said something. In German.

My schoolboy A-level German having long since evaporated through lack of use, I couldn't find the words I needed to reassure him that this innocent little card was just an advert for a discotheque, and had nothing to do with any plans for a mass escape from the east, and the map on it did not represent secret tunnels beneath the city or anything else remotely sinister. So, in the absence of a better idea, I tried to convey my meaning by executing a few nifty dance steps accompanied by a boisterous few bars of Petula Clark's "Downtown".

The frowns before me grew darker, tinged now with shock at this affront to their personal dignity and lack of respect for the authority of the great state they represented. I curtailed my audition piece and adopted a more measured approach. It took some time, but eventually I was handed back my copy of Koestler's anti-communist tract and waved on my way. All the same, they retained the bookmark to be on the safe side.

I had been delayed for over half an hour, but I still had time to make curtain up. I had been given clear instructions by the concierge of my hotel about the route I should follow to reach the theatre. It was a short walk, ten or fifteen minutes at most. What I had not been prepared for was the bleakness of the scene before me as I entered the eastern sector of Berlin. In contrast to the bright lights and busy street life of the west, the wide street that stretched out before me was dark and deserted.

At least I thought it was deserted, until I began to discern shadowy figures huddled in the doorways of the empty buildings on both sides of me. Nobody had warned me about the possibility of being mugged by roaming gangs of the living dead, which was what they looked like at first glance. Obviously I should have realised there was a risk. However, suppressing the instinct to turn and sprint back the way I'd come, I pressed on.

The further I went with nobody making even the slightest menacing move in my direction, the more I came to see that I had mis-read the situation. No one was in fact looking at me. I was of no interest whatever to them. What they were doing, men and women of all ages, from kids to grandparents, was watching a fixed point in the sky on the far side of the wall. I turned to follow their gaze.

In great red letters, uncensored world news was being displayed on a crawl-screen on top of the Axel Springer newspaper building. I was told later that the East Berliners came out to view this sign at considerable risk to themselves. It was against the law to view this "disinformation" from the west, and routine police raids took place in these crumbling streets arresting a handful of offenders and sending the rest scurrying into the night.

But no one was scurrying anywhere that night, and I continued on my way to the Berliner Ensemble and entered its stately, though dimly lit, portals. The play I saw was a translation of Seán O'Casey's *The Silver Tassie*. It was wonderfully performed, though with – dare one say it? – a certain Germanic mechanicalness that left me somewhat cold. A few nights later I returned, without suspicious bookmarks or anything similar to detain me at the border, to see Brecht's *Mother Courage*. Once again I was impressed, but not moved. It wasn't because I didn't speak German. I knew the texts of both plays well enough to follow the action, but it was all somehow just too practised and well drilled to convey real emotion. But it was an experience I wouldn't have missed.

Aside from this, little of note happened in Berlin. As already mentioned, I turned twenty-six while there, in recognition of which the pop-eyed, pink-faced production manager and his sidekick took me out to a night club. Seated on stools at the bar were a number of astonishingly glamorous and statuesque young women. Hookers, I assumed, but when "Popeye" assured me that everything had been arranged in advance and I only had to take my pick in order to round off the evening agreeably, I thought what the hell. Taking a seat next to the one I found most attractive, and who spoke fluent English in a low sexy voice, I embarked on the kind of polite, inconsequential conversation that one does while knowing exactly where both parties are going to wind up very soon.

Sure enough, after a few sentences she began gently drawing my hand up her smooth thigh towards what lay at the top – which was not at all what I had expected. I looked over in dismay to where my hosts were sitting doubled up with knee-slapping laughter. They had brought me to Berlin's most famous transvestite bar, where you really and quite genuinely couldn't tell the difference – until too late. Or almost.

I exited into the night, pursued by my companions, still massively amused by their little joke, and promising to make it up to me. They knew this other place with *real* girls...

CHAPTER 29

The traffic moved down London's chic Bond Street at a stately pace. It was a beautiful spring morning in 1970, with the women in bright summer colours and the men in light jackets or no jackets at all. Cars with removable tops had removed them, their drivers and companions basking in the sun and beaming contentedly upon the world from behind designer shades.

One car slowing to a gentle stop at a red light on the corner of Conduit Street was an open Rolls-Royce Corniche. Seated in the back with ostentatious poise, smoking a cigarette through his usual black and gold holder as he turned the pages of a script, was Laurence Harvey.

Playing the movie star was still, I could see, by far his best performance, and nothing he had done in the eighteen months since I'd last seen him had changed that. Our German-financed Roman epic had come out successfully (in a dubbed version) in Germany, but had yet to make a mark on the wider world. The script I had worked on in Rome for him had, as I had anticipated, gone nowhere. Meanwhile he had played a small "guest star" role (with a very bad American accent) in a Paul Newman movie, and performed an embarrassing striptease while reciting "To be or not to be" in a laboured Peter Sellers comedy. Apart from that he had hosted a British television tribute to Noël Coward, of which one critic had written, "Laurence Harvey performed and sang, enunciating throughout as though being paid by the syllable."

215

It was no good: the critics would never take him to their hearts. Nonetheless, he remained a star in the minds of the public, which was evident from the way people were nudging one another and pointing him out. Larry himself pretended a lofty indifference to the interest his appearance was creating, while, I knew, soaking it up like a sponge. As the lights changed to green he took a drag on his cigarette, glanced up for a moment, and caught sight of me. He waved me over, but the car was already moving and it was impossible to stop in mid-traffic. With one hand to his ear and the other twirling in the air, he signalled that we should talk on the phone.

Later that day I got a call from Sandy, the secretary who'd been with us in Romania. She said Larry wanted to invite me to a drinks party at the house he had just finished renovating in Hampstead, and where he and Paulene Stone were living with their new baby, Domino, and Paulene's three-year-old daughter from a previous marriage.

I took a moment to catch up on the story so far. In effect Larry was leading two lives. Just after I had last seen him he had married Joan Cohn, seventeen years his senior, and had been playing husband and host in her mansion in Beverly Hills. Now, apparently, he was setting up a new family life in London with Paulene, fifteen years his junior, and their baby. Admirable though his talent for surviving such complications seemed to be, I couldn't help noticing when I met him face to face that the strain was beginning to show. He was even thinner, his cheeks hollow, and his whole attitude one of bone-deep weariness. He droned on to a small group of us he was showing over the house about how the rich tones of some wood surfaces in his new kitchen were achieved by a process of drawing out all the poisons and impurities that had lurked deep in the tree fibres for aeons – "Rather like me" as he plaintively put it.

Ringo Starr stood next to me, listening with a wry smile. Next to him were the actor John Standing and his wife who I'd first met at Dirk Bogarde's house. Larry had signed up for a summer season at the Chichester Festival Theatre, hoping to win back a little professional credibility by appearing with John in Shaw's *Arms and the Man*, directed by John's stepfather, Sir John Clements. Luck still refused to smile on him, however: during rehearsals he broke a bone in his knee and had to play the whole run limping and leaning on a stick. Nonetheless, he and Paulene made the cover of *Vanity Fair* that summer, which, though he pretended to shrug it off, pleased him no end.

As I was leaving the drinks party that night, Larry handed me an envelope in which was a movie script he said he'd like me to read. He'd done the same thing several times in Romania, and I'd realised how uncertain he was in many ways about his own judgment, and how much he missed his old mentor Jimmy Woolf.

I read his script the following morning. I could see why he was considering it: in a cheap, low-budget way it was a reprise of his role as the brainwashed war hero in *The Manchurian Candidate*, only this time played out as an empty chase movie somewhere in middle Europe. I rang him up and told him I found the whole thing painfully thin and lacking the slightest credibility. I have no idea whether he took my advice and turned the project down; I do know the picture was never made.

Unfortunately the same cannot be said of *He and She*. This was a small film he'd just made in Italy and recklessly financed himself. His co-star was Sylva Koscina, who he'd worked with on our Roman epic. It was the story of an intense, destructive relationship between two symbolically nameless characters, and Larry had convinced himself that it said something timeless and profound about the eternal battle of the sexes. No distributor had so far shown any interest in picking it up, and Larry was desperately trying to find someone to champion it. He arranged a private screening in Soho one morning for a handful of friends

217

and people in the business. The writer Wolf Mankowitz was there, having been a close friend of Larry's since *Expresso Bongo*, one of Larry's early successes in the late fifties. We all sat through the new film in shocked disbelief at its awfulness: stilted dialogue, unremitting solemnity, ending in "He" deliberately allowing himself to be run down and killed by "She" in a shiny sports car. It was Larry's all-time most wooden performance, matched only by her robotically plastic one.

As the lights went up I, like everyone else there, slid down in my seat to avoid being the first one faced with having to make a comment. The silence was deafening, stretching out embarrassingly until Wolf Mankowitz broke the tension with a heartfelt, "Fuckin' women!"

As though we'd all been holding our breath, we now began to murmur about what the film was trying to say. Was "She" the winner because she killed him? Or was "He" the winner because he forced her finally to free him from his obsession with her? It was an academic argument that managed to avoid any discussion of the actual film itself.

But Larry knew that nobody was ever going to pay to see this movie. And he was never going to see his money again.

•

The following year, in the early summer of 1971, Larry, inexplicably, chose to appear in the West End in a dreary melodrama called *Child's Play*. Set in a Catholic boys' school in New England, it combined enmities between staff members with hints of demonic possession. It had been a modest hit on Broadway but had little chance of connecting with an English audience. Predictably, it got poor reviews, and Larry himself got painfully bad ones. I was out of town for the opening, but went round to see him in his dressing room a few days later. The actor David Kossoff and his wife were there, and Larry poured us champagne and made a sad little speech about how he stood by his author, and was pleased to say that advance bookings were still good enough to guarantee a run of several months at least. "I can still pull 'em in," he said, as though to reassure himself more than to impress us.

In 1972 he made his last major film, *Night Watch*, with his good friend Elizabeth Taylor, who may have had more than a little to do with his getting the role. The film was financed by the billionaire George Barrie, owner of Fabergé and creator of Brut cologne for men. Barrie had started life as a musician, and now wrote or co-wrote the music for most of the films he invested in. Nonetheless, *Night Watch* was not a success.

But Barrie had taken a liking to Larry, and financed, much more modestly, his next – and last – film. *Welcome To Arrow Beach* was a grisly little piece about modern-day cannibals in Malibu, and not only starred but was directed by Larry himself. It got a brief and limited release, dreadful reviews, and sank without trace.

But by then Larry was past caring. He was dying up in his house in Hampstead, lovingly cared for by Paulene to the end. On 25 November 1973, both of London's mass-circulation newspapers, the *Evening Standard* and the *Evening News*, carried almost identical front-page headlines that elbowed all other news aside. "LAURENCE HARVEY DEAD AT 45", and "LAURENCE HARVEY DIES".

That coverage would have bucked him up no end.

CHAPTER 30

"I know you. You're just going to blow it all on restaurants and having a good time."

"But it's a crazy price. It can't be worth that much."

"It's a good investment, and it's time you bought something."

Prim, still a good friend although we hadn't been together for a couple of years, had decided to take charge of my financial future. Coming from a well-off background, she was shrewd about such things. I had to buy a flat, and she wasn't putting up with any ifs or buts about it. She'd even scouted out several possibilities, including a duplex on the top two floors of a terraced house in up-and-coming Primrose Hill. This was the one, she said, after hauling me off to view a dozen or so others in different parts of town. I knew she was right, but I'd already "blown" more money than Prim imagined, and was barely able to scrape together enough to buy the place. It left me too broke to furnish it except for the essentials – a bed, a desk and a chair, along with the couple of packing cases of accumulated junk I'd been hauling around various rented premises up till then.

My third television play, *The Undoing*, had been recorded in August 1969 and went out a few months later. It was, I knew, competent, moderately entertaining, and uninspired.

After that, as already mentioned, I hit the wall of writer's block. Lunch, usually avoided when I was working, began to occupy increasing stretches of the afternoon, sometimes running on into the evening. A favourite hang-out around this time was a pub in Islington called "The Prince of Wales". That was where I met the great Irish actor, Cyril Cusack. For whatever reason, probably because a lot of Irish actors lived in Islington, which at that time was still a working-class and very un-gentrified part of London, it had become something of an Irish actors' pub. Another familiar face there was Patrick Magee, star of countless films, usually horror, which subsidised his true vocation as a magnificent classical actor, often with the Royal Shakespeare Company. Pat was also one of the foremost interpreters of Samuel Beckett, who had written *Krapp's Last Tape* specifically for him. It gave me a lot of pleasure when, a year or two later, Cyril and Pat Magee appeared together in my adaptation for television of the classic short story "The Monkey's Paw".

Cyril remains one of the few actors I have known to whom the word "great" is not misapplied. When I met him I knew his work only from films, of which he made over a hundred, often in supporting and character roles rather than leads. But whenever he was on screen he dominated it, not by a towering show of force as Orson did. He was a slightly built man of barely medium height, but who drew your attention like a magnet, even when he was doing or saying practically nothing. In his autobiography, Alec Guinness described his admiration of Cyril as "just this side of idolatry". Unlike me, Guinness had seen many of Cyril's stage performances as a leading man in Ireland, London and America, where Cyril had led a company of his own for a time. Guinness described his extraordinary gift of holding the audience's attention as the ability to "create his own centre-stage wherever he was, even with his back to the audience".

He was, in truth, the consummate actor, but he never talked about it. Perhaps because he had been on stage since the age of eight, touring Ireland with his mother and stepfather and their theatre company, he had absorbed his remarkable skills into his bones, where they lay too deep for analysis, even by himself. Some nights, after the pubs had closed, we would wander the hundred yards or so up Vincent Terrace to the elegant but somewhat ramshackle house he'd bought a few years ago with what he considered his excessive earnings from the film of *The Taming of the Shrew* with Burton and Taylor, and my old friend Michael York. Cyril had, as usual, stolen every scene he was in, and the director, Franco Zeffirelli, had used a close-up of his mischievously grinning face as the closing shot of the film.

Cyril's principal home remained in Dublin, and the house in Vincent Terrace served as his base in London, so he rented out the main part of it and occupied only the basement flat, occasionally with his daughter Sinead, then just twenty-one and starting out as an actress. Sometimes I'd go in with him, and if Sinead had left anything in the fridge I might cook up some bacon and eggs or whatever else I found for supper.

Other nights Cyril, who was a devout Catholic, would head off unsteadily for the local church, proclaiming, "Y'know, it's a wonderful thing, t'owld drunk can just walk into the house of God at any time and have a conversation with his Maker – you don't know what you're missin'."

He could be a mean drunk on occasion. "What the fuck do you know, you stupid little twat!" was sometimes his response to the mildest of comments after a certain point in the evening, though his underlying good nature would usually resurface shortly afterwards and all unkind words would be forgotten.

Prodigious drinker though he was, and despite which he remained sprightly and in good health till his death at eighty-three over twenty years later, there was a deeper, quieter and more solitary side to him that served him well both mentally and physically. This was the side that wrote at least two plays and a number of fine poems over the years. He presented me with a collection of his poems that had just been published in 1970, quietly certain that I would be impressed by them – and I was.

One night in the pub we were joined by another fine Irish actor, Jim Norton, at that time in his early thirties. Jim was about to start rehearsals for a play by David Storey called *The Contractor* at the Royal Court Theatre. It was an ensemble piece about a group of workmen who spend the first act erecting a lavish marquee for a wedding party, and the second dismantling it after the event. With a cast of twelve the dialogue was fragmentary and difficult to learn, and Jim said he was having problems with it. Without a second's hesitation, Cyril offered to read the whole play with him if that would help, adding, "With so many characters, I'm sure David will be glad to help us out – won't you?"

The frustrated actor in me inflating with self-importance at such an invitation, which I considered highly flattering, I immediately agreed. In the early evening of the following day, the three of us gathered in Cyril's basement with playscripts open on our knees. Drink was not taken because this was serious business – and, besides, there would be time enough for that afterwards.

Cyril divided up the parts between himself and me, and we got started. I thought I was doing rather well, more than holding my own with both of them, until after a few pages Cyril leant gently towards me and murmured, "David, you can bring it down a bit. Just read the lines – don't act."

I did my best to obey, rigorously not acting and just reading the lines, as Cyril had said I should, and as he was doing.

The only puzzling thing was that in his case, although neither his voice nor intonation seemed to change in the slightest degree, each character he read came alive as a separate and believable individual – whereas all mine sounded the same.

I found myself remembering the old adage that the thing about great actors is that you never catch them acting. Certainly no one ever caught Cyril acting.

Then again, I recalled having read somewhere a remark he once made: "The actor has a constant problem of personal identity. If you asked me for my New Year resolution, it would be to find out who I am."

Perhaps that was his secret. You never caught Cyril acting, because he was acting all the time.

•

Cyril's marriage to the mother of his five children had broken down some years before I knew him. Being Catholic, divorce was out of the question. Nonetheless, his mistress of the past few years had presented him only recently with a sixth child, another daughter. Cyril needed more living space, which meant getting rid of the tenants in his house in Islington and expanding out of the confines of his basement flat.

This struck me as the perfect opportunity to unburden myself of the running costs of my recently acquired property in Primrose Hill. Cyril's tenants were a young couple from Lausanne in Switzerland. He, Jacques, was an osteopath trying, not very successfully, to set up a practice in London. His wife was a designer, bubbling with life and very pretty and speaking hilariously bad English. Her name was Laurence.

Although this was an arrangement that would ultimately lead to considerable upheavals in all our lives, for the time being it was purely business. My flat, being all but unfurnished, was perfect for them, since they had their own furniture. I let them have the place at a rock-bottom rent, just enough to cover my outgoings, on the understanding that I could stay in the spare room from time to time. My demands on that level, however, were slight, as I was by then living mostly in the unlikely suburban surroundings of Cheam.

Oh! Calcutta! had opened on 27 July 1970, at the Roundhouse in Chalk Farm. Rita had been in charge of the bar when I had been invited to a preview of the show a few weeks earlier. The moment I set eyes on her I had fallen desperately in lust. After about a week of relentless persistence, I was getting nowhere. Then I had a brainwave. I volunteered to help out in the bar for no pay during the interval stampede for drinks, and afterwards to serve light snacks and more drinks till the place closed about midnight. On my second night a couple of my contemporaries from Blackburn Grammar School, now working somewhere in London, turned up to see the show. It was impossible to miss the touch of schadenfreude in their reaction when they found their former head boy, a glittering future clearly behind him, in such humble circumstances. Accepting their thinly veiled condescension with good grace, I served them their drinks and said how nice it was to see them and hoped they were enjoying the show.

That night, Rita offered me a lift home.

Her home. In Cheam.

We lived together for the best part of a year, during which time I struggled with a stage play that had been commisioned by London's leading theatre producer Michael Codron, after seeing *Public Face* on television. Within two weeks of delivering a finished draft, a major star had been cast in the lead.

CHAPTER 31

Alastair Sim was a comic genius. His greatest gift, though, strangely, he refused to acknowledge it and claimed only to be "an actor", was for physical comedy. Already seventy-one years of age when I met him and despite never having been an athlete, he still possessed a degree of physical coordination that was as extraordinary as it could be irresistibly funny. As his wife Naomi put it, "Ali only has to think of a piece of business and he can immediately do it."

That "business" invariably exploited his tall, angular frame. As a physical comic he was in a direct line from Buster Keaton to Jacques Tati, both of whom he worshipped. He could creep about like a lugubrious Nosferatu, executing high tip-toeing steps, only to spin around, coat tails flying and eyes wide with panic as he sensed some (usually non-existent) threat behind him.

He executed elegantly convoluted pratfalls, where the big laugh lay in his character's panicky efforts to maintain his dignity while ending up in a heap on the floor.

Exits were a speciality. Bawled out, usually by some formidable matron, he would swivel this way and that like a large bendy toy, snatching up his hat and coat before lurching for the door in a series of balletic stumbles, wrenching it open and disappearing, only to stick his head back round it for one last baleful gaze at his tormentor.

Michael Codron told me that Mr Sim wanted to meet me and talk about the play, which was called *Siege*. One mellow October morning in 1971 I took the Tube up to Hampstead, walked down Church Row, lined on both sides with exquisite Georgian houses, and round the corner into the slightly more austere Frognal Gardens. Number 8 was one half of a large Edwardian semi long since converted into flats. The ground-floor flat was Alastair's London base, in addition to which I knew he had a house in Oxfordshire.

The door was opened by Naomi, a diminutive woman with a twinkling smile and quick bird-like movements. She took me through to a morning room overlooking a small garden at the rear. It was simply, even rather basically furnished. A spongeable oil cloth covered a plain kitchen table, on which stood the remains of breakfast – a box of Scott's Porage Oats and a toast rack.

Alastair was enthusiastic about the play. It was not, he said, the sort of thing he was usually offered. He felt it was a real acting role and not something tailored to the view that people too often had of him.

"Everyone's got about five words for describing Alastair," Naomi said with a chuckle as she poured fresh coffee. "There's always 'pawky'…"

"Oh, God," he said with a resigned laugh, "I always get 'pawky'."

"And 'puckish'," Naomi added.

"'Jowl-wobbling double-takes'," Alastair continued, not to be outdone.

"'Pouchy-faced'."

"Don't forget 'baleful'!"

"And 'lugubrious'!"

They were competing now.

"D'you know what some critic once wrote?" Naomi said, throwing her head back with laughter. "'Alastair Sim's eyes looked like two fried eggs on a plate!'"

The meeting went well and Alastair agreed to do the play. That left two parts (it was a three-hander) to cast. Michael Bryant signed on to play one of them, which pleased Alastair greatly. They were friends having recently appeared together in a film called *The Ruling Class* with Peter O'Toole.

The casting of the third role was, I thought, a stroke of brilliance by the producer. Stanley Holloway had not appeared on stage since his monumental success on Broadway and London in *My Fair Lady*, with Rex Harrison and Julie Andrews. In 1964 he had been nominated for an Oscar after repeating his role in the film. He was, at eighty-two, not just a national treasure but an international one.

He also represented just about everything Alastair hated.

Stanley adored being a star and bathed in the attention it brought him. Always generous with his time and unfailingly courteous, he gave interviews whenever asked and signed autographs for anybody who wanted one. Alastair, on the other hand, never gave interviews and was positively vitriolic about what he considered the degenerate practice of collecting autographs.

America had taken Stanley to its heart in a big way. He'd had his own television series there, was a regular guest on *The Dean Martin Show* and many others, and had co-starred with John Wayne and Kirk Douglas in the movie *In Harm's Way*. He counted Frank Sinatra and Groucho Marx among his friends.

Alastair, by contrast, regarded America with a puritanical disdain. As a left-wing socialist, he saw it as the home of capitalism and therefore the source of all evil. He told me once that he'd refused to accept residual payments from the American earnings of some of his films, though just how true this was I take leave to doubt. As a Scot Alastair was very conscious of the value of money. Though frugal in his lifestyle, aside from a love of Havana cigars, he was well known for negotiating the toughest terms possible whenever he worked.

Stanley was worried about the power of the unions and the efforts of the far left to take over the country. He let his views be known one day in a casual conversation with me and our director, Robert Kidd, causing Alastair to mutter "Bloody right-wing old fool" as he hunched over his script in the corner of the rehearsal room to get away from him. I doubt if the two of them exchanged more than a dozen words off stage throughout the whole of their time together.

The rehearsal room itself was another bone of contention with Alastair. We were using the basement of St James's Church in Piccadilly. Alastair entered on the first morning with his coat collar turned up and a tweed hat jammed on his head, lips curled in distaste and eyes darting around like an arsonist in search of the best place to set a fire. Alastair did not approve of religion, Christianity in particular. He made me a gift a few days later of a terse volume entitled *The Misery of Christianity*, itemising the church's multitudinous abominations since its foundation.

All this was balanced against an evangelical worship of youth. The young were to him mankind's only hope. One day they would rise up with a new consciousness and transform the world. Nobody over thirty would have the vote. Alcohol would be replaced by mind-expanding drugs – though, to be fair, he had no objection to a glass or two of wine and enjoyed nothing more than a good lunch or dinner with friends. But he believed fiercely that one day a younger generation would unleash some innate power in human consciousness that had lain dormant for millenia. In one sweep society would be transformed and Utopia established.

All of which was fair enough, though my faith in his vision was clouded by his uncritical acceptance of the paranormal, and in particular the powers of the young Uri Geller, then at the height of his spoon-bending fame.

Nevertheless, Alastair had a genuine interest in physics, something we shared, and was well read on the subject. At the mere mention of "black holes" or "curved space" his face would light up with a gleeful enthusiasm.

Curiously, for all his vaunted radicalism Alastair held very traditional views on certain things, in particular the sanctity of marriage and the importance of family values. For some reason he chose to give me a lecture on the subject one morning as we walked along Piccadilly towards the Garrick Club – another bastion of tradition that he loved dearly and where he had invited me to lunch. He had met my girlfriend and liked her very much, and suddenly he started talking about the importance of choosing the right partner in life, and once having made your choice of sticking with it through thick and thin. Divorce was out of the question. "A little bedding on the side is one thing; that does no harm. But divorce no, no – it's the worst thing you can do."

It was delivered not so much as a piece of advice to his young companion, more as something he felt the need to get off his chest. He wanted me to know that those were his views. The subject was then dropped as abruptly as it had been broached, and we talked of other things as we headed for the Garrick, where Naomi awaited us.

•

How a play with such a cast could turn into a monumental flop must cast a poor reflection on its author. However, in fairness I don't feel I can take all the discredit. Just before we opened in February 1972, Edward Heath's Tory government had become locked in a dispute with the miners' union which led to power cuts and a three-day working week. As a result the management installed a small generator outside the stage door which had to be cranked into life whenever the lights went out, which happened most nights during our previews, and, crucially, on our opening night. A single overhead bulb, illuminating the stage just enough to prevent the actors from falling over the furniture and bumping into each other, was a poor substitute for what was supposed to be a dazzling summer afternoon.

On top of which we were in just about the worst theatre imaginable for a play that was essentially a small-scale chamber piece. The Cambridge was a barn of a place with nearly fifteen hundred seats, more hospitable to musicals and other large-scale entertainments. Alastair had enjoyed a huge success there four years earlier with Pinero's *The Magistrate*, which had come in from Chichester with a cast of around twenty. What we needed was something smaller like the Criterion, with a little over five hundred seats, or The Fortune with just over four hundred. But they were unavailable. The fact is that when you're looking for a West End theatre for your play you have to take what there is, however unsuitable.

The reviews were, as we say politely in the business, mixed. Herbert Kretzmer, himself a noted dramatist and lyricist (*Les Misérables*), gave the play a rave in the *Daily Express*. *The Sunday Times* was good, as were one or two of the other main broadsheets. But it was not enough. Even with much-loved performers like Alastair and Stanley involved, people were not persuaded to venture out of their homes on a winter night to face power cuts and transport delays and all the rest of the general gloom that lay over the country at that time. The notice of closure went up within days.

My parents had come to the opening, of course, bringing a couple of their posher friends from the Rotary Club of Chorley who were anxious to meet the young man from "up here" who was apparently getting on so well "down there". Along with my sister and brother-in-law, they had all been thrilled to go backstage and meet the stars, who were gracious and welcoming and touchingly generous about me.

My old Oxford friend, Michael Gearin-Tosh, had chivvied one or two people he knew to come along, including Iris Murdoch and her husband John Bayley, and their close friend John Simopoulos, who was senior philosophy don at St Catherine's. John rarely went to the theatre, and had done so on this occasion only with reluctance. But he had found himself surprisingly engaged by the play, and asked me afterwards if I was aware of how many levels it worked on. I said I hoped I was, and I had certainly intended that it should.

Another unexpected fan was someone I had never heard of until I got a letter a few days after he'd seen the play. Sir Ellis Waterhouse, then in his mid-sixties, was a world-renowned art historian and former editor of the art-world bible, *The Burlington Magazine*. He had held fellowships and chairs at several universities, including Princeton and Oxford, and was therefore an acquaintance of Michael's, but he had come to see the play off his own bat after reading something about it in the press. He was so intrigued by and anxious to discuss it further ("a most remarkable piece") that he insisted I spend the weekend with him and his family at their house outside Oxford.

•

I didn't see Stanley again after the play closed. We parted warmly, and I wrote him a genuinely heartfelt letter saying what a privilege it had been to work with such a legend. He sent me a charming and witty reply, thanking me for giving him his "break" in straight theatre. He died ten years later at the age of ninety-two, a real gentleman and one of the most loved individuals in the business.

Michael Bryant remained a friend, and played the lead only a year later in one of my most successful television plays.

Alastair and Naomi also remained friends. Laurence and I

weekended at their modest but comfortable house in the country, and they came to dinner with us several times. He appeared in half a dozen more movies before he died in August 1976, and in three more West End plays. We went to see them all, always dining with them after the show at their (and our) favourite restaurant, Bianchi's in Soho. I am quoted in Mark Simpson's biography of Alastair as finding him "a shagged-out old man, totally exhausted" when I went round to his dressing room at the Savoy Theatre after a performance of *The Clandestine Marriage*. I regret not having taken care to sound more gracious when I spoke to Mr Simpson on the telephone, but the point I was making concerned Alastair's remarkable powers of recovery. By one in the morning he had to be gently dissuaded by Naomi from ordering yet another bottle of wine and carrying on far into the night. His enthusiasm and energy remained undimmed despite the diagnosis of mouth cancer he had received barely three months earlier.

Only a few days after his death Naomi told me on the phone, sounding as cheerful as ever, that he was still very much around and making his presence felt. Things were being moved about, disappearing, reappearing, and so forth. The atheist's ghost, apparently, was on the prowl. Normally I would have suspected this was a form of denial on her part, possibly masking a serious depression and requiring attention. But "normally" didn't apply to either Naomi or Alastair. One of the first things they ever told me was how they'd met when Alastair was twenty seven and Naomi only twelve. They had appeared together in an amateur production of a play in Edinburgh and had fallen in love with each other at once. Over the following six years Alastair had more or less adopted Naomi and her widowed mother, even bringing them down to live with him in London when he decided to become a professional actor. They had married when Naomi turned eighteen.

A little weird? Who's to say? All I know is I never met a happier and more devoted couple. Plus they had produced an enchanting daughter, Merlith. Married to a doctor, she struck me as a paragon of sanity and good sense in contrast to her eccentric parents. They were as touchingly proud of her as she obviously was of them.

CHAPTER 32

In the months leading up to *Siege* my relationship with Rita was coming to an end and my days in Cheam were numbered. I was increasingly using the spare room in my flat, as per my arrangement with Jacques and Laurence. When I'd first met them with Cyril Cusack I had been immediately taken by Laurence's dazzling smile and the air of chic, simple elegance she had about her. But I reminded myself that she was married, presumably happily, to the good-looking young man at her side. So that was the end of it.

Except it wasn't. It turned out that the marriage was, in fact, under considerable stress. She and Jacques had been teenage sweethearts, and by the time they married in their twenties the best of their relationship was already behind them. He had tried various careers, including journalism and training as a television cameraman, but had shown little inclination to persist in any of them. What brought him finally to study osteopathy I have no idea, unless, as a childhood friend of theirs who grew up to be a surgeon suggested, it offered the cachet of white-coat authority without the rigours of real medical training.

Whereas Jacques spoke English fluently, having gone to an American school in Lausanne, Laurence spoke hardly a word. Nevertheless, in London she was the breadwinner of the couple, working long hours designing and installing window and point-of-sale displays in Harrods and elsewhere for companies like Lancome and Guerlain.

Jacques, having more time on his hands than was good for a young man, had started playing around behind his wife's back. Perhaps unwisely, he boasted to me about this: not that I took any direct advantage of this inside knowledge, but inevitably it changed the way I looked at them as a couple. One night I took them along to meet some friends of mine in a restaurant. Among them was a woman with whom I'd had a mild flirtation some time back: "mild" because she was married, not very happily, to a minor city banker and had two pre-teen sons. That was not an apple-cart I had any intention of overturning and getting buried under. Jacques, however, felt differently, and within twenty-four hours of meeting, he and Jennifer had embarked on a raging affair.

Laurence, who already harboured more than a few doubts about her husband's general reliability, immediately had a shrewd idea of what was going on. Rather than creating a scene, which she was more than capable of doing, she coolly invited Jacques to confess to the affair and they would both, well, decide where to go from there.

Jacques, however, remained adamant in his denials. He refused to discuss Jennifer and how deeply in love with her he was – except with me. Laurence was pretty sure I was in on Jacques's secret, but didn't embarrass me by insisting I tell her what I knew.

Complications multiplied when Jacques began using me as an alibi. When he was spending an evening with Jennifer he would tell Laurence that he was at some innocent all-male event with me. When, having synchronised our watches, we both arrived back at the flat at the same time so as to maintain the illusion of a boys' night out, she would politely enquire if we had enjoyed ourselves, and leave the matter there.

Things came to a head when Jacques informed me he desperately wanted a weekend away with Jennifer. He asked whether I could possibly arrange a weekend somewhere for myself, while pretending to Laurence that he and I were together. My answer was no I bloody well couldn't. We reached a compromise: he would tell Laurence that he had been invited down to Plymouth to visit a nuclear submarine on which an acquaintance of mine was second in command (true), having met this person some time ago at an all-male dinner with me in Oxford (untrue).

Laurence, wholly undeceived, merely shrugged, but asked no questions and therefore avoided forcing me to tell her any lies. She and I went out to a movie and a very enjoyable dinner that Saturday, but that was as far as it went.

However, the next time Jacques asked me to cover for another weekend away (I forget where I was supposed to pretend he was this time), Laurence and I looked at each other on the Saturday morning and thought, sod it!

And went to Paris.

•

Jacques did his best to play shocked and indignant ("She's my *wife!*") when I informed him that Laurence and I were having an affair, but quickly realised that he had very little claim to the moral high ground in this situation. He and Jennifer did what they had both wanted to do for some time, moving out of their respective marital homes and into a flat in South Kensington. Two divorces followed rapidly and without complications. Laurence attended her hearing in a stylish fedora lent to her for the occasion by Jeremy Brett, who had taken an enormous liking to her, as had all my friends.

But finally, as the dust settled, the realisation gradually bore in on me that my life had changed profoundly in a way I had failed to see coming. I had walked, eyes wide open but seeing nothing, into a state of what could only be called domesticity. For the first time in my life a woman was living with me on my territory instead of the other way around, as had always been the case until then. How, just supposing I wanted to, did I get out of this? I could hardly leave my own home. It was a sobering moment.

Not a bad one. But sobering.

Jacques and Jennifer married almost at once, and we never saw either of them again. We heard the marriage had fallen apart and they had divorced not much more than a couple of years later.

Laurence and I remained together, though it would be a full eight years before we married. There would be fights, sometimes physical, broken crockery and at least one very large smashed window; neither of us was good at backing down from confrontations. There were separations and reconciliations. But she, with the precedent of her first marriage as a warning, had no desire to make the same mistake twice; and I still required a great deal of talking down from the chilly heights of my commitment phobia. Neither of us intended falling into the trap so poignantly described in Congreve's *The Old Bachelor*: "Thus grief still treads upon the heels of pleasure: Married in haste, we may repent at leisure."

As far as was possible, we got our repenting over beforehand.

CHAPTER 33

Although *Siege* had been a disappointment, it had attracted enough attention to bring in fresh offers to write for films and television. A play I'd been working on called *When The Music Stops* went immediately into production with a cast headed by the young Edward Fox and was broadcast in October 1972.

The day after it went out I got a call from Peter Willes, the autocratic head of Drama at Yorkshire Television, to say that David Mercer had watched it and wanted to know whether it might have been written by "a lad who was up at Oxford a few years back".

I had met David Mercer when Peter Hay, my Hungarian friend who was well connected in political and theatre circles, had persuaded him to come up and talk to our drama group in Merton College. Mercer at that time was a radical left-wing voice in television drama, turning out major works such as his trilogy *The Generations*", followed by *A Suitable Case for Treatment* and "In Two Minds". In appearance he bore a marked resemblance to Bertolt Brecht: trim black goatee beard, short forward-combed hair, and a heavy corduroy jacket. He was reserved, courteous, and thoughtful in all he said. Peter and I were invited for a drink a couple of weeks later at Mercer's flat in the less fashionable end of Hamsptead south of the Finchley Road, where he was living with a gorgeous young actress called Kika Markham, who later married the ultra-red Corin Redgrave.

In the decade since then, Mercer had established himself as not just a TV writer but a major stage playwright and screenwriter as well. I'd seen just about everything he'd written. His work was intelligent and often very funny. He didn't preach; while writing from within a perspective that denounced capitalism and was contemptuous of bourgeois society, his characters, like Mercer himself, harboured complex misgivings about their socialist alternatives. They struggled with self-doubt and submitted themselves and each other to brutal questioning. To ease the pain, most of them drank a great deal – also like Mercer himself.

I was immensely flattered to hear that he'd been impressed by my play. I was also mildly surprised, as there had been nothing remotely political about it. However, to quote a leading critic, Mercer himself had written as much about "social alienation expressed in terms of psychological alienation" as he had on purely political themes. That was obviously where we had connected: my play was about a young man setting out to make a career for himself in television while struggling to reconcile his driving ambition with a corrosive sense of the emptiness of it all, and of himself.

Mercer wanted to meet up, and I was bidden to Peter Willes's elegant flat in Cumberland Place, just off Marble Arch, for dinner the following Sunday. There were just the three of us. The evening started with Peter serving large gin and tonics to Mercer and me, while sticking to mineral water himself.

I couldn't help thinking what an odd couple of northerners Mercer and I were, he from Yorkshire, I from Lancashire. Although there was an age gap of fifteen years between us, we shared not dissimilar working-class roots, though from that point on we had taken very different, well, routes. He had failed to get into grammar school, taken various jobs, joined the navy before studying at Newcastle University, been married and divorced twice, led a bohemian life in Paris trying to be a painter, had a nervous breakdown and spent years in psychoanalysis. His accent, manner and general demeanour had remained resolutely northern: a Yorkshireman to the bone.

There was I, on the other hand, with my acquired accent and smooth manners, impersonating a "gentleman" or some Shaftesbury Avenue facsimile thereof, and actually on speaking terms with several Tories. By David Mercer's standards I should have been nothing but a self-seeking class traitor and a snob.

In fact, we got along incredibly well. We talked a little about writing, then moved on to gossip and scandal, egged on by Willes who was a formidabme source of it. We had such a good time that these Sunday nights became a fixture for a while. Every two or three months Mercer and I would arrive at Peter Willes's flat promptly at seven-thirty on a Sunday evening, have a few drinks, dine at the same Italian restaurant round the corner, drink some more, talk, then bid a fond goodnight to our still sober host (Peter never drank on these occasions), and stagger off along the Edgware Road in search of taxis.

It all ended one warm summer evening when I arrived at Peter's flat at the appointed time as usual, to be told that Mercer wouldn't be coming because he was in bed with some infection, so I would be having dinner with Peter alone. Which was fine – except that Peter was as drunk as a skunk.

Peter Willes was not an easy man to deal with at the best of times. Acid-tongued, he could go from seductive charm to screaming tantrum in seconds. While loyal and even indulgent to those he liked, he could make life unbearable for those he didn't. Nobody stayed in his employ for a minute longer than he wanted them there.

But the main thing that made life around Peter Willes something to be negotiated with great care, like walking on eggshells, was the very large elephant that followed him everywhere. It was always in the room, wherever he was. Obviously, by definition, no one spoke of it in his presence, but everyone knew it was there. All the time. And he knew it. He must have.

The first thing anybody was told about Peter Willes, whether before working for him or simply meeting him, was that he was almost certainly a murderer. Nothing was ever proved, and he was never charged. The coroner's jury returned an open verdict, specifically rejecting the alternatives of suicide or accident. The story had made front-page news around the world because the dead man was a well-known actor and playwright called Frank Vosper. Aged thirty-seven, he was returning from New York to Plymouth on the liner *Paris*, sharing a cabin with, as the press reports coyly put it at the time, "his intimate friend Peter Willes", who was then, in 1937, just twenty-five. Somehow the couple had got involved with a girl called Daphne Oxford, who had been crowned "Miss Britain" in 1935, and was currently returning from an engagement as a Broadway showgirl. On the last night of the voyage, following several hours of partying and drinking, there had been a row between the three of them in her state room – something testified to by no less a person than Ernest Hemingway, who was occupying the state room opposite. After this brief interlude of raised voices, Vosper was never seen again. It was subsequently claimed by Willes and Miss Oxford that he must have either fallen out of, or jumped through, an improbably small porthole while they weren't looking. "There was absolutely no question of any love-making," Miss Oxford protested to the press. And nobody doubted her.

Although the shadow of the scandal never went away, Peter Willes nonetheless managed to carve out a successful career for himself. First of all he had a more than honourable war, serving in the tank corps and almost getting his legs shot off, forever thereafter walking with a pronounced limp and leaning on a stick. He was a handsome man with a proud bearing, something of a dandy, and had fitted in well with the elegant establishment of post-war West End theatre. When ITV was launched in the mid-fifties, he was recruited by the largest production company, Associated-Rediffusion, to bring his experience and wide range of contacts to the creation of original drama. He had a freedom back then that today's executives can only dream of, producing everything from cop shows to classics, and plays by "arty" avant-garde writers like Harold Pinter and David Mercer – and, indeed, newcomers like me.

How long Peter had been an alcoholic I have no idea. I would learn later that the evening I found him knocking back the gin wasn't the first time he had fallen off the wagon. Unsure how to handle the situation, I accepted a couple of gins myself, then accompanied him to our usual restaurant. Conversation over dinner was easy enough, with no great confessions or insights or anything out of the ordinary: just the usual flow of gossip and chatter.

Because the alcohol had worsened his habitual unsteadiness, threatening proper coordination between his stick and feet, I thought it best to see him home. I had intended to leave him at his door, but he insisted I come in for a nightcap.

I should probably have anticipated what would happen next. We were barely inside the flat before he made a lunge. Instinctively I ducked it, and, his balance being what it was, he hit the floor. I managed to haul him to his feet and help him to the sofa. But he wouldn't stay put. Levering himself to his feet, his stick out of reach now, he started towards me again with an alarming swaying motion, then veered off to the drinks table to pour himself another gin.

It seemed like a good moment to disappear, so I started edging towards the door. But he called after me. Wasn't I just at least a little bit... that way inclined?

"No, Peter. Sorry."

"Are you really... quite sure..?"

"Absolutely."

He'd started towards me again as he spoke, and again he fell. This time I caught him, but his drink went everywhere and the cut-glass tumbler exploded on the floor. There was nothing for it but to get him to bed.

I had no intention of undressing him, but I did manage to manoeuvre him to more or less the centre of his large bed so as to minimise the chance of his rolling over and falling off. Then, ignoring the drowsy mutterings coming from him, I placed his stick within his reach, turned down the lights, and left.

When I got home Laurence said I was still red-faced and palpitating. "You won't believe what just happened," I exclaimed. But she found it only too easy to believe, and was annoyingly amused.

The next day I had a meeting at YTV's London headquarters with Pat Sandys, the company's script editor, a calm and intelligent woman who was one of the few people capable of dealing with Peter in even his most tempestuous moods. The first thing I noticed on arriving was that Peter wasn't in his office, which didn't surprise me, but I made no comment about his absence and nor did anyone else. Pat (the mother, incidentally, of the actress Samantha Bond) knew I'd had dinner with him the previous night, but asked no questions. This, I came to realise, was the second elephant in any room with Peter Willes: his alcoholism. From time to time he would go on a bender, after which the company would quietly ship him off to a clinic where he would dry out and recuperate, then return to work. He was too valuable an asset for them to lose, so coping with these occasional vagaries was a small price to pay.

Sure enough, when he reappeared three weeks later he was his old self and behaved as if nothing had happened. Whether he remembered anything of that last evening of ours I had no idea, but we picked up exactly where we'd left off before it and continued working together with no problem. He even came to dinner at the flat a few times and invited Laurence and me out in return. Charm itself.

Sadly, I never saw David Mercer again. He married an Israeli woman and went to live in Haifi, where they had a daughter. He died of a heart attack in 1980 at only fifty-two. The last major thing he wrote was a film called *Providence*, directed by Alain Resnais. It was a complex multilayered piece about a tormented, alcoholic, dying writer played by John Gielgud. Dirk Bogarde played his son.

CHAPTER 34

Over the five years from 1972 until 1977 I wrote a handful of movie scripts and over fifty plays, adaptations and episodes of series for television.

The adaptations, obviously, were the easiest, and I found myself knocking off six in quick succession from classic short stories for a series called *Orson Welles Great Mysteries*. Sadly, this did not lead to a reunion with Orson; while the shows were all filmed in London by Anglia Television, he shot his top-and-tail introductions in Los Angeles, directed by Peter Bogdanovich. These were big budget productions by television standards, pre-sold all over the world and with international stars. The casts of my own shows included Christopher Lee, Jane Seymour, Irene Worth, José Ferrer, and, as already mentioned, Cyril Cusack and Patrick Magee.

Episodic television was a new experience. As a craft it occupies a halfway point between adaptation and original writing. You're given the main characters, their background, all the essentials of their lives, and told to come up with a new twist on the formula. When one of Peter Willes's producers at YTV suggested I write an hour-long episode of a show called *Hadleigh*, I said I wasn't sure I could do it, but I'd give it a try.

James Hadleigh was a gentleman landowner played by the charming Gerald Harper, and the series revolved around his business interests, his love life, and whatever human drama he got involved in week by week. Pulling in a staggering nineteen or twenty million viewers per episode, as top shows did in those days of just three TV channels, it was entering its third series. I ended up writing four episodes. The following year, for the fourth series, I was given the job of sketching out all thirteen episodes, six of which I wrote myself. One of them was a "special", filmed entirely on location in Hong Kong. I was sent out there for a month to come up with a story and write the script. Ensconced in the colony's finest hotel, the Peninsula, on comfortable expenses, I managed to mix a good deal of pleasure with work. It also gave me a chance to visit my sister Margery, who had recently moved out there with her second husband, formerly a chief superintendent in the Blackburn police force, now a member of the Independent Commission Against Corruption.

Between these two seasons of *Hadleigh* I wrote six episodes of YTV's other top series, *Justice*, starring Margaret Lockwood as a brilliant and uncommonly good-looking QC. We needed a legal adviser on the series, and I proposed my friend Michael Beloff for the job. He was a fast-rising star at the bar by then, but the money was good and very acceptable to a young married man with two small children to raise. It was also a way to pay him back, at least in part, for his kindness in throwing me a lifeline to *The Observer* ten years earlier.

Commissions came in from just about every major independent company, and also the BBC, for whom I wrote an episode of *Colditz*, several episodes of a new series called *Oil Strike North*, and a one-off play about spies called *Nanny's Boy*, which remains one of the best stories I've ever come up with.

I found myself developing a useful sideline in tightly plotted thrillers with twist-in-the-tail endings. It happened because I found myself at one point with a couple of commissions to write original plays of my own choice. For any writer that is an ideal situation, and between '72 and '77 I did in fact write a half dozen totally personal and original plays of the kind with which I'd broken into television a few years earlier. But "personal and original" takes time, care, and "something to say". You can't just knock them off.

You can't just "knock of" worthwhile thrillers either, but they do tend to yield more readily to "mere" craft. I'd loved the famous Francis Durbridge serials when I was a boy, first of all *Paul Temple* on radio, then *The Scarf, Portrait of Alison, The World of Tim Frazer* among others on television. Those were the days before video recorders, so each cliff-hanging episode had to be watched live as it went out, and on those nights pubs and restaurants across the country would empty and streets would clear of traffic.

The first "thriller" I wrote, *The Professional*, starring Michael Bryant from *Siege*, proved hugely popular. A few weeks later I wrote another called *Love Me To Death* that knocked the BBC's *Match of the Day* off its top spot in the Saturday night ratings, a rare event. There were several more over time, collectively described by Alan Coren in his column in *The Times* as "hokum well hoked".

Because my name was appearing on the nation's TV screens with almost metronomic regularity by now, I found myself considerably more persona grata up in Lancashire than I had been for some time. Visits to the parents, often accompanied by Laurence (and no nonsense about separate rooms, though we were still unmarried) triggered invitations from all sides. "David 'ere's on 'ob-nobin' terms with 'ousehold names these days" was the introduction I got from a prominent local solicitor at a drinks party he and his wife had thrown for us. The fact that nearly everyone there had seen a play of mine starring Kenneth More only the previous week had them almost touching the hem of my garment, and the revelation that I would soon be rehearsing another one starring the sainted Felicity Kendal was enough to have the smelling salts sent for.

Dad was, frankly, a bit puffed out with pride to have his son lionised by these local worthies; Mum too, though she was always ill at ease on social occasions. However much she wanted it, she could never truly convince herself that she was "one of them". I could see this just as I had always seen it. As a child it used to infuriate me that she felt the need to apologise for herself in front of her "betters", putting on a deferential smile, an over-careful speaking voice, executing a kind of mental curtsey to them. I have to admit rather shamefully, this indignation was not so much on her behalf as my own. By diminishing herself she diminished me, and I was damned if I was going to accept that. But that was a chip on my shoulder that would always be there, increasingly disguised by decent tailoring and fancy manners though it was.

At least I was glad that I was no longer considered an embarrassment to the parents. Partly to make up for all the past disappointments and anxieties I had caused them, but also to rub their noses in the fact that I was making good money these days, I bought them their first colour television. Their friends were duly impressed. You didn't argue with brass up north.

•

Laurence gave up designing sales displays and dressing windows a few months after we got together and returned to her true passion of painting and sculpting. Now that she was no longer in a marriage where French was spoken all the time, her English came on apace, though not always in directions one might ideally have wished. In the relatively bohemian world of show business in which she now found herself, curse words and obscenities were habitually and liberally sprayed around without any intention of causing offence, or any serious risk of doing so. However, most of us in that world understood very well the difference between the kind of language we might use among ourselves on the studio floor, in rehearsal rooms or at theatrical parties, and what was more appropriate in the conventionally respectable outside world. Laurence, for all her quickness at picking up the language as she heard it spoken, was a little slow at mastering this distinction.

Consequently, formal gatherings at which we found ourselves from time to time were liable to be mildly jolted by exclamations such as "Sheet a breek!" in response to some unexpected piece of information just imparted to her. "Sheet and dee-rees-yon!" was another one she would roll out in response to some absurdity she felt required comment, always with a poised and perfect elegance.

At other times, when a task she may have embarked on turned out to be more difficult or boring than she'd bargained for, a muttered "Ferk zees for a game of mar-bells" might drift lightly but distinctly through the air.

A discussion about some new film or play might bring forth the considered verdict that "It ees quite interesting, but does not grab you by zee balls".

My personal favourite was delivered at a drinks party given by a rather upmarket journalist I vaguely knew. During one of those brief lulls in the general conversation that can occur from time to time, Laurence's unmistakable laugh reached me from the far side of the room, followed by, "'Oo is zees focking eed-yot, anyway?"

I looked over nervously, to see her extended forefinger prodding the purple shirt front of an Anglican bishop – who, to his credit, appeared charmed and highly amused by his exotic companion, and their conversation continued happily as the general chatter mercifully closed over them once more.

Naturally, I did my best to alert her to these hidden traps in the path to mastering a new language – I had my own problems in French – but there are always nuances and slang that remain to trip you up for a long time.

"I just 'ad zees meeting wiz a gallery and it went – what was zat word you said last week? – it went bum-gangsters!"

"No, darling, the word you want is 'gangbusters'."

"Ah, yes."

On one occasion, however, she managed to cause significant offence without any misuse of language whatsoever. At a small dinner party given by an American diplomat, I was enchanted to find myself sitting next to the actress Patricia Neal. On the far side of the table Laurence was seated next to her husband, the writer Roald Dahl, a man who I'd heard from various sources took himself very seriously. Having not the faintest idea who he was, and attempting to make polite conversation, Laurence asked him what he did for a living. His long face darkened and froze into a rigid Nordic fury, after which he refused to address a single word to anyone for the rest of the evening. I was afraid Patricia Neal might actually die from fighting to suppress the helpless laughter the incident had provoked in her; she'd had a bad stroke ten years earlier and fully recovered, but I was worried for a while.

CHAPTER 35

"Do you know how I look?" was the beguilingly modest question Maximilian Schell put to me over the phone when he said he would meet me at Munich Airport. Indeed I did know how he looked: he was an international star, with an Oscar to prove it.

Max had already directed one film based on a Turgenev story in 1967, now he was working on an original script called *Der Fussganger* (*The Pedestrian*), and wanted some help getting it into shape. I spent two pleasant weeks script doctoring, meaning well paid but without credit. The film was a huge success domestically, and was Oscar-nominated in 1973 for best foreign film.

Shortly afterwards I got a call from Claude Chabrol, who, along with Jean-Luc Godard, François Truffaut and Éric Rohmer, had been a leader of the French "New Wave" of film-making that began in the late 1950s. As a critic for the influential Cahiers du Cinema he had been one of the first to elevate the role of film director to that of "auteur", and to reappraise the films of Hitchcock as high art rather than mere entertainment. By the mid-seventies, having been an auteur himself for fifteen years by then, he was on a career high following a string of films that had been not only critical hits around the world but, by the standards of "art" movies, financially successful.

I was thrilled at the prospect of working with him on an adaptation of the Patricia Highsmith novel *Ripley's Game*. A few days later I sent him a brief outline about how I thought we should approach the story in movie terms. He responded with gleeful approval, and an invitation to lunch in Paris.

Two days later I rang the doorbell of his apartment in one of the more fashionable avenues not far from the Arc de Triomphe. Claude was a famous gourmet, a well-known figure in the world's best restaurants, and known to be a brilliant cook himself.

He opened his front door and flung out his arms as though to give me a hug, but held back and converted the gesture into a warm handshake; I was English after all. We went through to a large high-ceilinged living room filled with antiques, pictures and polished floors. As he poured champagne we were joined by his companion, Aurore Paquiss. I knew he was still married to the beautiful gazelle-like actress Stéphane Audran with whom he had made several films, but they were separated and would eventually divorce.

Claude himself, in his early forties at the time, was short-ish, round-ish, with a broad smiling face and a pair of large horn-rimmed spectacles that gave him the look of a friendly owl bursting with curiosity and enthusiasm. From the moment we met we talked movies. He was obviously pleased that I knew his essay on Hitchcock, and we discussed enthusiastically the lengthy series of in-depth interviews with Hitchcock published only recently by his friend Françios Truffaut.

We talked about Claude's other heroes and influences, particularly Lubitsch and Lang – and, of course, Orson Welles. He was fascinated that I knew Orson because they had worked together a couple of years earlier. Claude had directed him in a film called *Ten Days' Wonder* along with Anthony Perkins and the French actors Marlène Joubert and Michel Piccoli. I had seen it, and, as Claude was the first to admit, it had not been a wholly successful venture. Perkins and Orson seemed awkward and out of place, and the French actors were ill at ease working in English.

Claude admitted he had been apprehensive about working with Orson, who had initially tested him with suggestions about how he himself might have shot the scenes they were working on; but, as Claude told it, he managed to dazzle the great man with the speed and inventiveness of his set-ups, after which Orson became sweetness itself. No doubt this benevolence was encouraged by long lunch breaks and late dinners at the best restaurants in the Alsace, where they were shooting; Claude never denied, indeed was rather proud of, the fact that he always chose his film locations according to the quality of local restaurants. On this score alone, he and Orson were a marriage made in heaven. Only on one occasion, said Claude, did Orson disgrace himself by getting so drunk that he was unable to work for two days. But he was suitably contrite and there were no further problems.

The lunch that Claude had prepared was simple but magnificent, as were the wines, the coffee and cognac, and the cigar that followed it. We parted in late afternoon with the warmest of embraces, Englishness forgotten, promising to see each other again soon. As we shared the same vision of the film we were to make, I said it would take me no more than a month to have a first draft ready. Claude, eager to get started, was already talking about some very fancy casting – not to mention possible locations and their accompanying epicurean potential.

Unfortunately – how often that word crops up in stories about the film business – it turned out that Claude, never a master of detail, had failed to renew his option on the Highsmith book by the required date. Although, since our meeting, he had been furiously trying to do so on any terms possible, he had been beaten to the post by another producer who had been after the rights for years. It was eventually made as a film called *The American Friend*, directed by Wim Wenders and starring Dennis Hopper and Bruno Ganz. It was far from the film Claude and I had wanted to make, and I didn't much like it. I preferred the 2002 remake starring my friend John Malkovich and directed by Liliana Cavani; unfortunately, it had not occurred to her to ask me to write the screenplay.

I saw Claude many more times over the years, and it was always an enjoyable encounter. Once in the mid-eighties Laurence and I were in San Francisco and we bumped into him strolling along the street cheerfully enjoying the sun. "I am 'aving a wonderful time 'ere," he told us, waving his arms to embrace the whole city. "They make a festival of my films, and all I 'ave to do is accept the adoration and answer a few questions, then they take me for the best dinner in town, and on top of it all I get paid!"

Two stories about Claude that give a glimpse of his very particular charm. In one, he was talking to a friend of mine about a new film called *Who Is Killing the Great Chefs of Europe?*, a clever comedy-thriller that had been directed by the Canadian Ted Kotcheff. Claude had been offered it first, but had turned it down.

"What was the matter?" my friend asked. "You didn't like the script?"

"No, the script was fine." Claude gave a dismissive wave of his hand. Then his mouth turned down with remembered distaste. "It was the *recipes!*"

The other is a remark he made in defence of his fashionably left-wing views while leading a comfortable bourgeois life and making films about the middle classes.

"Okay, so I'm a communist. That doesn't mean I have to make films about tractor factories."

•

Another disappointment was a film that did get made eventually, though less well than it should have been. Some time in 1974 I was given a book by James Herbert called *The Survivor*. Herbert was a highly successful writer of schlock-horror which I had little taste for, but underneath the multiple layers of blood and gore was a more than serviceable ghost story. The premise was that shortly after take-off from Heathrow a Boeing 747 crashes in an open field. All three hundred or so passengers and crew are killed, with the miraculous exception of the pilot. Over the next few days, the salvage teams clearing the wreckage become plagued by strange and increasingly sinister incidents, and some deaths – all in the open space where the plane has come down. There was a twist in the tail which, though fairly unpredictable, was neatly done. I immediately saw it as a movie.

The first draft wrote itself in twelve days. The young producer, formerly in the record business and trying his luck in films for the first time, was surprised by my speed but thrilled with the result. Three weeks later, when I was back working on one of my television shows, my agent rang to say that my second cheque still hadn't arrived, and the young producer wasn't answering his phone.

It didn't entirely surprise me; he'd struck me as a touch flakey. But two days after that I got a call from a friend who was head of the Paramount office in London. It turned out that the young producer was in Hollywood and my script was the hottest thing on the studio lot. I was shown an internal memo saying this script was a "must make" as soon as possible. *The Omen* had just been a huge hit, as was *The Exorcist* not long before. Scary was box office.

My second cheque arrived, giving the young producer full rights to make a deal on my script. I got on with my television work, trying not to give off the air of a man about to have a big Hollywood movie to his credit. Then I heard from my friend in Paramount that the studio had dropped the project. The young producer, apparently, had overplayed his hand and demanded too rich a deal for himself. When the studio balked he had flounced off, confident he could get what he wanted elsewhere. This pattern was repeated, several times, until the young producer eventually left town, taking my script, and was never heard of again.

It was a big disappointment. However, when I arrived in Hollywood some three years later I found I had an open door to Paramount's legendary (though mad as a hatter) head of production, Don Simpson, who remembered the script well and put me to work on several projects at the studio.

There was still no trace of the young producer when the script, having changed hands several times by then, eventually got made in Australia in 1981. It starred Jenny Agutter, Robert Powell and Joseph Cotton.

By coincidence I was already in Sydney working on another film (with James Mason) when *The Survivor* started shooting. It turned out to be a not bad film, though made on a much lower budget than it would have been in Hollywood. It was directed by the actor David Hemmings, increasingly keen to move his career from before the camera to behind it. In fact he was a very capable director, staging a spectacular plane crash with little money and great ingenuity. But his grasp of story was less sure, and he dealt with the ending very heavy-handedly, not helped by some dialogue re-writes that he'd scribbled himself during shooting. I made my views very plain to him on the terrace of the Carlton Hotel at the Cannes Festival the following year. He merely sat there looking glum and rather crestfallen throughout my mini-tirade, which left me feeling bad afterwards, as I'd always liked him. He was definitely a little crazy, but genuinely gifted as an actor, director, and – interestingly – amateur magician. And remarkably unassuming about all of it. I had liked him a lot; he was good company. But we never spoke again after that day in Cannes.

To my surprise, a few months later I received an ornate diploma from Spain informing me that I had been awarded first prize for my screenplay by the "Sitges Festival Internacional de Cinema Fantástico y de Terror". I had it framed, but never actually hung it up: a fair compromise, I felt, in view of the everything.

•

The Fifth Musketeer was a rare instance of a movie leaping straight from page to screen without a pause for breath in between. It is tempting to suggest that a pause or two might have been a good idea, but that wouldn't really be true. It was always going to be what it was – a rollicking swashbuckler with one or two laughs.

The director, Ken Annakin, had a solid list of credits going back thirty years, including some big budget hits such as *Battle of the Bulge* with Henry Fonda and Robert Ryan, and *Those Magnificent Men in Their Flying Machines* with almost everyone. The producer, Ted Richmond, was an old Hollywood hand whose credits went back even further and who had worked with some of the biggest stars around, including Robert Mitchum, Steve McQueen, Dustin Hoffman, not to mention Elvis Presley and a talking mule called Francis back in the fifties. Always immaculately dressed and groomed, he gave off a world-weary air of "been there, done that", and wasn't impressed by any of it, especially actors. "Sex appeal? Yul Brynner? Couldn't get laid in a whore house!"

The film was being made for two, arguably three, reasons. One was that the studio had money frozen in Austria, and all they could do with it was make a film there. The other two were Sylvia Kristel's tits. Although most reference books and websites date the film from 1979, it was actually shot in 1975. Silvia Kristel was hot off the soft porn mega-hit, *Emanuelle*, and was anxious to broaden her range a little, though contractually agreeing to bring a little of what she was most famous for to the party.

For whatever reason, Ted and Ken had decided on a remake

of the 1939 film version of *The Man in the Iron Mask*, originally directed by the great James Whale, who had been responsible for the Boris Karloff *Frankenstein* amongst other landmark movies. I was given the original script and asked if I could bring it up to date, keeping it a period costume picture, but with a new twist or two. I did my best, and was gratified that it "cast up" sufficiently to include Rex Harrison, Olivia de Havilland, Lloyd Bridges, Cornel Wilde and Ursula Andress amongst its stars.

CHAPTER 36

The high point of my time in British television was *Alternative 3*.

"The biggest hoax in television drama was David Ambrose's *Alternative 3*, shown by Anglia Television on the ITV network on 20 June 1977."

That was the verdict of *The Guinness Book of TV Facts and Feats* in 1984. They continue: "It was science fiction in the guise of an investigative documentary about the disappearance of a number of prominent scientists; the explanation was that the United States and USSR were colonising Mars because the earth was dying slowly in man-made pollution."

Inevitably it was described as "reminiscent of the scare caused in the USA by Orson Welles's radio spoof, *War of the Worlds*, in 1938. Many viewers took it at face value. Within seconds of the show finishing at 10 pm the switchboards of newspapers, government departments and even police stations were jammed. The show made headlines everywhere the following morning; the *Daily Mail* even devoted its front-page cartoon to it. The director, Christopher Miles, and I were photographed having lunch at Bianchi's in Soho while discussing with journalists the power of the media to mislead and deceive. It sold around the world and became Anglia Television's most successful export to date. Even today if you Google it you will get around two billion results, many from conspiracy theorists who still insist it was all true despite my repeated public assurances to the contrary. At least four books have been written about it, and a DVD of it was released to celebrate the thirtieth anniversary of its first broadcast.

Sir John Woolf, co-founder and director of Anglia Television, was a great showman, and had partnered his brother James (Laurence Harvey's early mentor) to produce such classic movies as *The African Queen, Room at the Top, Day of the Jackal* and *Oliver*. I doubt if any other producer in television would have had the nerve to go through with a show like this. Certainly, all his junior executives were chewing their fingernails with anxiety about the panic we were likely to provoke. When they were proved right, John Woolf called the director Christopher Miles and myself into his office and presented us with large bonus cheques – not simply on account of the money his company stood to make through world sales (as writer I owned the copyright and was in for a bit of it anyway) but because he said he hadn't had so much fun in years.

In all truth I had not been consciously influenced by the thought of Orson's famous radio show. I'd listened to a CD of it a couple of times, finding it clever but not particularly memorable, though I could see why it had the impact it did at the time. *Alternative 3* came about quite unexpectedly.

In the late summer of 1976 I had an open commission from Anglia Television to write a play of my own choice; the problem was it turned out to be one of those times when I didn't have a fresh idea in my head. In desperation I started to work on a vague notion I'd been playing with about people who went missing and were never heard of again. I even called the Home Office to get some idea of the numbers involved annually, which was surprisingly high. The trouble was I still had no idea where the story was going: no second act, let alone a third.

One day over lunch at a pavement café just round the corner from my flat in Primrose Hill, I explained the problem to my friend Christopher Miles. We had known each other for about four years, ever since I'd written a screenplay called *Sun Trap* for him which we had never managed to get set up. Suddenly, as I talked about the problems I was having with my current script, the idea came to me. Make it much bigger than I had so far been imagining it. Make it about a vast and sinister conspiracy. Something inconceivably huge.

Suppose, for example, there turned out to be a pattern to these disappearances. Suppose they represented a cross section of society, from scientists to artists, from philosophers to plumbers, all the kind of people who would be needed for...

For what?

How about a hand-picked group being sent out to create a human colony somewhere in space?

But why all the secrecy? Why were people just disappearing quietly instead of announcing proudly the great adventure they were embarking on? The obvious answer was to avoid panic. Massive panic. The best reason for which, it was again pretty obvious, would be the knowledge that planet Earth was doomed.

But how? And why? I decided I would work that out later, eventually coming up with the greenhouse effect and global warming after a good deal of reading and talking to scientific advisers. Such ideas were largely unknown and certainly not widely discussed at that time. Nor were they issues I had any intention of championing or campaigning about. They simply provided the central hook on which I could hang my story – Hitchcock's famous "McGuffin", meaning the plans the spies are after, the secret code or list of names, something of no intrinsic value or interest but which gives rise to the action.

The remaining question was where was this survival colony being set up? The moon? Too obvious, and too close. And yet there was so much known activity going on up there with a steady stream of American and Soviet landings since 1969 that it couldn't be ignored.

What if, I wondered, the Americans and Russians weren't competing in the space race as we all assumed, but in fact secretly cooperating? What if they were building a gigantic spaceship, a kind of Noah's Ark, on the far side of the moon, the side invisible from Earth? The moon's low gravity would enable an immense ship to be launched from there, something far greater than could be launched from Earth.

But where would it be going? The answer was kind of unavoidable. Invasions from Mars and Little Green Men were part of common folklore by now. H.G. Wells's *The War of the Worlds* which had provided the basis for Orson's broadcast in 1938 had been written in 1898, and I couldn't begin to count the number of stories and movies on the theme since then.

So why not reverse it? Instead of Mars invading Earth, let Earth invade Mars.

But how do you invade Mars on a television budget? The answer, of course, was by fragmenting it, telling the story like pieces of a puzzle coming together.

Like a documentary.

"Now you're cooking with gas," Christopher said as the idea took shape. He wanted to direct the show, and I couldn't have been more pleased. Nor could John Woolf. Christopher was "a film director", which was considered a step up from television in those days. We began to accumulate a little clout.

Our first stipulation was that it be done on film. Taped studio drama was still the norm at the time, the film made for televison a rarity. But John Woolf saw our point and gave us the green light.

There was a huge amount of material in public domain covering the space program and moon landings, and NASA gave us a whole lot more when we asked. We cut it together, here and there dubbing in actors' voices that viewers would assume were coming from NASA control or inside one or other of those space suits we could see out there.

We staged interviews and intercut them with newsreels, and sometimes we faked our own newsreels. Christopher caused consternation in the film lab by insisting they degrade a length of perfectly good footage until it looked like something hastily snatched on a tourist's old 8-mil camera.

The whole thing was to be presented as a special edition, hastily assembled, of a regular program called *Science Report*. It was a title that most people could probably persuade themselves they'd heard of. Christopher even managed to get some spacy-sounding music composed by Brian Eno. To make it convincing, however, we needed a credible anchorman, or woman, someone to host the show and pull together all the threads, rumours and "sensational new evidence" we claimed to have uncovered. We talked to several high-profile journalists, including Jonathan Dimbleby, but they all thought it was shaky ground for people like them to get onto. I've no doubt they were right. In the end we cast Tim Brinton, not a journalist but a former news presenter on both BBC and ITV. His familiarity to viewers was just what we needed. At the time he was cutting down on his television work because he was trying to become a Tory MP. What on earth can have possessed him to lend his authority to this farrago of deceit I cannot imagine. Both Christopher and I tried gently to warn him that his involvement could impact badly on his political career, but he insisted it was just an acting job and he had the right to earn a living despite his political ambitions. Two years later he was elected MP for Gravesend, and went on to have an influential career in parliament for nearly ten years.

Nevertheless, the first paragraph of his obituary in *The Daily Telegraph* in 2009 read: "Brinton was best known at Westminster for his tough line on immigration and trades union reform. But his legacy is a spoof science documentary, Alternative 3 (1977), which became a cult classic and still finds a ready market on DVD."

I only realised quite what a cult classic it had become when Richard Linklater's film *Slacker*, shot in Texas fifteen years after the show was broadcast and itself something of a cult, featured a character who insisted at great length that every word of *Alternative 3* was true.

A year or two before that a young man had arrived on a bicycle at our door in Hampstead, saying he had come from California to find me. He had to know if *Alternative 3* was true or not. We invited him in for tea, and he proved to be polite and sweet natured and not at all the raving nutter I was afraid he might have turned out to be. I assured him I'd made it all up, and he seemed both disappointed and reassured in equal parts. What I didn't tell him was he could have spared himself the trip to find me: I was working mostly in Los Angeles by then, and had just flown back the day before.

It was in Los Angeles that the single weirdest incident arising from the show took place. One day in November 1980 I got a call from a Japanese television producer wanting to interview me about *Alternative 3*. I knew the show had been huge in Japan and was still playing on cable all year round. When the producer called he said he and his camera team had to go to Las Vegas to film some story there, but would be returning to LA on Saturday morning and would like to film me in the afternoon. I said that would be impossible because I was going to be out on a film location; could we make it Sunday instead? They agreed.

Casually, because I had just made my first trip to Vegas only two weeks earlier, I asked where they would be staying. The producer said the MGM Grand, making some remark about it being rather expensive for four of them. I told him that the group I'd been with, also four of us, had stayed at the Riviera which was offering reduced rates to attract new customers. Hearing this, he said at once that he would switch their reservations.

The night they should have been at the Grand, 21 November, a fire broke out killing eighty-five people and badly injuring several hundred. The worst of the fire had been in the part of the hotel where they would have been staying. By casually recommending the Riviera as I had done, I had saved their lives.

That wasn't all. When they arrived to interview me on the Sunday morning they were in a strangely excited, almost hysterical mood. I could understand they might still be a little agitated after their narrow escape on Friday, but as I tried to make out what they were telling me (only the producer spoke English, and not too fluently at that) I realised that something even more remarkable had happened. The flight they would have been on if I had not delayed them by a day had crashed. In the space of twenty-four hours I had twice saved them from death, so now there was absolutely no convincing them that I was not a seer, a shaman, a man with mystical powers to predict and even shape the future. I spent over an hour protesting, on film, that all of it was just a remarkable coincidence, and that *Alternative 3* had come entirely from my imagination and had no basis in reality. They refused to believe me, and I had no way of convincing them.

And so the cult lived on, and apparently still does. It has been described as "the most dangerous TV programme ever made", but for me it was a lucky break. A Hollywood agent who'd been in London and seen it said he would like to represent me out there. All I had to do was get on a plane and he would introduce me around. He was sure I would get plenty of work.

So I went.

CHAPTER 37

"I wonder what the poor people are doing?"

My young friend Peter stretched out his considerable length on a sun lounger amidst the brilliant colours and manicured lawns of the Beverly Hills estate we had just driven over to. It was a Sunday morning, the drowsy stillness broken only by the distant "thwock" of a tennis game in progress. The pool by which we sat sipping champagne was pure Hockney, glittering lazily with diamond-sharp ripples, and the house beyond was as sprawling and luxurious as anything I'd ever seen in the movies.

"This," I kept telling myself, "is Hollywood. It actually feels like I hoped it would."

All the same, Peter's remark had threatened to prod the dormant puritan in me to some feeble protest. But then the infectious grin on his face as he enjoyed his own bad taste put it quickly back to sleep.

I had been exploring and enjoying some of the many aspects of Hollywood for the past few months, but this promised to be one of the most interesting so far. I'd had an introduction to Peter through Ken Annakin, who had directed my *Fifth Musketeer* picture two years earlier. Ken had worked with Peter recently on a project about the Tour de France that had never got off the ground, but had described him as one of the nicest people he'd ever met in "this town", as Hollywood people invariably described their workplace. He was, said Ken, someone I should definitely look up. I did, and we hit it off immediately.

Only twenty-three, he had an openness and an absurdist sense of humour that made him hugely enjoyable and often hilarious company. I had been working on a couple of TV movies as well as developing story concepts for *Star Trek* with its legendary creator, Gene Roddenberry, but in my free time I'd been helping Peter look for a project to develop with his father's production company. Now we thought we'd found one.

The tennis game at the far end of the garden came to an end, and I watched as two middle-aged couples in gleaming whites came off the court and picked up towels to dab at their perspiring faces. A butler emerged from the house to serve them cold drinks.

"Come on," Peter said, levering himself to his feet, "let's go say 'Hi'."

I followed him. One couple, our hosts who had invited us to lunch, I didn't know. I did know they were seriously rich. The square-built man giving us a friendly wave had inherited a retail chain which he had cannily expanded into a variety of invest-ments and holdings, creating the kind of wealth that endowed charities and arts foundations and inhabited a world of private jets and luxury yachts.

The other couple were Peter's parents. I didn't know his mother, a strikingly good-looking woman who greeted me with a ready smile, but I did know his father. At least I felt as though I did. He was seated now in a canvas chair with one ankle perched on the opposite knee, an athlete reclining after a hard workout. He gave me a shrewdly appraising look, curious to meet this young Englishman his son had told him about.

At the same time, fleetingly, I saw something in his eyes, a kind of one-step-removed watchfulness, something I suspect he did reflexively when meeting people more than just casually. He was observing my reaction to meeting him.

So, maintaining what I hoped was a cool but respectful

demeanour, avoiding any hint of toadying or untoward excitement, I shook hands with Kirk Douglas.

•

In his autobiography published in 1988, Kirk writes: "Around 1979, my son Peter brought me *The Final Countdown*, a script outline he owned about a modern ship that gets caught in a time warp and goes back into World War One. But Peter shrewdly knew that we had to pick a moment in history that everyone would recognise, and came up with Pearl Harbour. Imagine the USS *Nimitz*, a nuclear-powered aircraft carrier, going back in time to just a few days before Pearl Harbour."

Broadly true, though the details were as follows. Peter was a computer wizard and a serious techy generally. He had come across the original script after it had been doing the rounds of studios and production companies for years and getting nowhere. He immediately saw its possibilities. Above all he was fired up with the prospect of shooting a movie on a modern carrier and featuring its state-of-the-art hardware in all its glorious detail.

My end of things was the story, which, in the script as it stood, went nowhere. Once the carrier found itself in World War One, not much happened and the whole thing tailed off anticlimactically. On that Sunday morning in Beverly Hills we did not yet have a solution to the problem, but Kirk, responding to Peter's enthusiasm, was willing to put up the money to option the script through his production company, Bryna, which had made pictures such as *Paths of Glory*, *Seven Days in May* and *Spartacus*.

A few days later Kirk, Peter and I met in a small office on the MGM lot. It was mid-morning and Kirk was in a cheery mood, greeting me with a handshake and a cod English accent. "David! How veddy veddy nice to see you again."

It was a good-natured bit of teasing which, happily, did not become a habit. Despite my friendship with Peter, I'd been a little wary of meeting his father. Although I'd known and worked with some formidable people, Kirk Douglas was an authentic, Golden-Age-of-Hollywood megastar. He had the reputation of being a difficult and sometimes volatile man. He was no more than five feet seven or eight, but at sixty-two he was fit, solid as a rock, with the arms and shoulders of the wrestler he had been in his youth: not a man to tangle with. But I soon found myself accepted as a family friend, invited for lunch or dinner at the house in Rexford Drive and for weekends in Palm Springs. Later, when my agent had to draw up a contract for me with Kirk's company, he came out of the meeting with a faintly surprised smile on his face. "That was easy," he said, "Kirk likes you."

But that morning at MGM everything was in its early stages. So far there was no discussion of Kirk actually appearing in the film; he was there simply as chief executive of Bryna Productions, and the three of us were chewing over the kind of picture we wanted to make. Peter had already made a preliminary approach to the US Navy and was optimistic about getting their cooperation. As a result of this we had the interest of an independent financing company, the two heads of which were due to come and see us in half an hour.

As we waited, Peter enthused about the high drama of life on board a carrier, zooming back and forth across the floor in a series of remarkable impressions, with full sound effects, of F-14 fighters taking off and landing on the flight deck. Kirk and I sat watching. At least, I sat. Kirk had perched on a sofa with his legs bent back beneath him at an eye-wateringly painful-looking angle. Catching my look, he explained it was an exercise to keep his joints flexible. I could imagine.

As we talked, it became clear that Kirk and I shared a concern that we had no third act and precious little second act to our story. Then I had an idea.

"Suppose," I said, "that instead of going back to World War One, we go back to World War Two – on the night before Pearl Harbour."

Kirk thought about this, and a light went on. "Peter... Peter... listen to what David is saying," he said. But Peter had heard. The aerobatics came to an abrupt end and he sat down with the look of a man confronting the obvious. That was the way to go. Everything, the whole of the rest of the story, flowed from that. And that was why the Writers' Guild of America, which decides all writing credits on movies, awarded me a "story by" credit as well as first place on the "screenplay by" credit.

•

It is often said that the best way for friends to fall out is to do business together. Peter and I tested that proposition to breaking point over the next few months.

The first problem was that, initially at least, I wasn't being paid. I was, however, being paid elsewhere, and quite handsomely. I was still developing a couple of ideas with Gene Roddenberry, plus I'd been commissioned to write two television movies for different networks, and I was developing a script at Paramount, where my earlier script *The Survivor* had been so well received. Peter would have liked me to work full time on his project, but reluctantly acknowledged this was impossible. However, since we spent so much of our spare time together it was a constant preoccupation – amidst, it has to be said, an equally constant round of parties, fashionable clubs and swanky restaurants, and other hilarious goings-on. Life in Los Angeles with a scion of Hollywood royalty can be, I readily admit, a lot of fun.

But there came a point where I simply didn't have time to do another revision of another draft of *The Final Countdown*, so I persuaded Peter to hire an English writer I knew who had just arrived from England and needed work. Gerry Davis had written for *Dr Who* and co-created the highly successful BBC TV series *Doomwatch* in the early seventies. I thought he'd be a good match for our project, but I turned out to be wrong. He was a competent writer, but Peter and he never saw eye to eye. On anything. Although I was thirteen years older than Peter, we were close enough in age to enjoy a lot of the same things and to share a sense of humour. Gerry was thirteen years older than me, which put him in a completely different generation from Peter; nor did he have much of a sense of humour. I thought the draft he wrote was very useful, though it didn't take us all the way. Peter, however, hated it, fired him, and threw out his draft, although ultimately Gerry was awarded a screen credit for his work on the screenplay.

Without saying anything to me, Peter then wrote a whole new version of the screenplay himself over a long weekend. He biked it over to my apartment, making it clear that this was the film he wanted to make. It was a "fait accompli". My name remained on it, but most of what I'd done so far was mangled or cut out. The thing even had a new title, *The Aberrant*. Not catchy, I thought.

In a heated phone conversation I told Peter it was no longer a film I wanted anything to do with. I insisted he take my name off the new script, and I quit. After I'd hung up I resigned myself to the fact that this must surely be the end of our friendship, which I regretted. But I couldn't see what else I could have done.

Next morning I got a phone call from Kirk. He sounded pained. "David, what happened between you and Peter?"

I explained as best I could. He seemed sympathetic, though without conceding any criticism of Peter. "Look," he said, "the two of you need to get together and talk this through."

Kirk Douglas the peacemaker. An original piece of casting, I thought; but, as it turned out, effective. Peter called shortly afterwards. We were both a little muted to begin with: both, I suspect, a little shamefaced at having behaved like prima-donnas. Then, after some verbal footshuffling, Peter said something that really touched me. "I want you to know," he said, "that our friendship's more important than the movie."

In a company town, where *nothing* could *ever* be more important than *The Movie*, this was a remarkable thing to say. At that moment our disagreement was over, and I was back on board for the duration. We decided lunch would be a good idea.

Peter came over with his dog, a big shambling black labrador called Shaft. Laurence and I were living in a classic old Hollywood apartment building just off Sunset Boulevard and not far from the Chateau Marmont. The interior was largely art deco, like a set out of every black-and-white movie I'd ever seen. I half-expected Barbara Stanwyck or Gene Tierney to walk in at any moment, shadows from the venetian blinds falling across them at an angle. Sliding glass doors led out to a large terrace, protected from the sun by a yellow-and-white-striped canopy. We decided to leave Shaft with a large bowl of water and free run of the place; he was a well-brought-up dog and could be trusted not to tear up the furniture. Usually, as I knew, he simply went to sleep when he was alone.

Some two hours later, or possibly more – it was a long and convivial lunch – Peter and I wound our way unsteadily back to the apartment. As we took a shortcut through a nearby parking lot, Peter stopped abruptly, listening to something. A dog was barking not very far way. To me it was just a dog; to him it was unmistakably Shaft. It was a relaxed bark, not the sound of an animal in pain or unduly alarmed, but it was persistent. There had to be some reason for it. We hurried on.

The sight that met us when we reached my building stopped us both in our tracks. Shaft had either jumped or fallen from the balcony, and was now precariously perched on the sun blind of the apartment below. Beneath him was a sheer drop of about seventy feet to solid concrete.

As soon as he saw us he began wagging his tale vigorously and paddling back and forth on the dangerously thin fabric beneath his feet. At any moment the blind could have ripped under his weight, or he could have lost his balance and slipped off it to his death, or least terrible injury.

Peter and I tore into the building, up to my apartment, and ran to the edge of the balcony. We were relieved to find Shaft still there, looking up at us with a wide canine grin, tongue lolling out to one side, waiting for us to come up with a solution. Seeing us at a loss, he started gathering himself in an attempt to spring up to where we were. He couldn't possibly have reached us and would certainly have fallen back and either slipped off the blind or taken it with him to disaster. "No!" Peter shouted, holding out both hands in warning. "Stay! Good boy, stay!"

Shaft obeyed, plonking his rear end down heavily, which brought forth an ominous creaking from the canopy. Either the fabric was beginning to tear, or some part of the framework that held it in place was threatening to give way.

What could we do? It would have taken a fire truck and a ladder to get him down safely, and time was against us. There was only one thing for it. Despite our advanced postprandial condition, neither of us at our sharpest or most coordinated, we would have to haul him up ourselves.

"Hold on to my legs, David!"

Peter pitched himself over the edge of the balcony and began inching down while I clung on to him. He was slim but muscular and over six feet tall, and quite heavy. I wondered what would happen when the weight of the dog was added to his.

"Come on, Shaft. Come on, boy. Don't struggle, just let me..."

Suddenly I felt the extra weight, and knew I couldn't hold them both. He began to slip from my grasp.

"Hey, David, hold on there!"

I got a better grip below his knees, and began to haul. But it was too much. The balance tipped and I found myself being pulled down by the two of them.

"What'ya doing? What'ya doing?"

"What d'you think I'm doing? I'm trying to..."

There was one last chance. I managed to wedge my knees under the concrete lip of the balcony's edge, and that gave me purchase. Just enough. I hauled Peter up far enough for him to risk holding on to Shaft with one arm while reaching up with the other to help pull himself to safety. Somehow they both got over the balcony's edge, and the three of us collapsed on the astro turf.

Shaft, thirsty after his ordeal, sloppily emptied his water bowl, then came over to lick his master's face, and then mine. We started to laugh. It was all we could do. Thinking about what might have happened was too awful. It was, I suppose, what could be called a bonding experience.

Certainly the dog thought so.

CHAPTER 38

Over the following weeks and months, Peter did a brilliant job of persuading the Department of the Navy to let him shoot our picture on the USS *Nimitz*, the biggest warship in the world. I was marginally involved in the latter stages of this process only to answer questions from a group of four-star admirals who wanted certain assurances about the script. Above all there was to be no reference to the fact that the carrier was powered by two nuclear reactors, a demand which at that time was understandable. The previous year Peter's older brother Michael had produced *The China Syndrome* about a meltdown in a nuclear power plant in California. That was fiction: scary, well researched, but fiction. Only days after the film opened there had been a real-life meltdown in a nuclear plant on Three Mile Island in Pennsylvania, triggering widespread panic. Nuclear power in general was a hotly debated issue at that time, one in which the Douglas family already found itself involved. The last thing the navy needed was another Douglas adding, as it were, fuel to the fire.

Aside from that, their only concern was that there should be nothing in the film that might bring the navy into disrepute or ridicule. There wasn't, so that was fine. They gave us their blessing, even hoping that the publicity might help in their enlistment drive. And on top of it all, they were going to get to meet Kirk Douglas. These hard-headed, no-nonsense, top-brass military chiefs were,

281

I realised, as star-struck as any bunch of kids at the prospect of rubbing shoulders with Hollywood glamour.

Kirk had decided by this time to play the captain of the *Nimitz*, which meant I now found myself talking script with him as well as Peter. Each of them seemed to have a new idea every time we met. After our adventure with Shaft, Peter had decided we needed a dog in the story. I said he was nuts; then, annoyingly, thought of a way to do it. Which, it has to be said, is typical of writers. Alongside all the variations on "How many whatevers does it take to change a light bulb?", there was a version that went: "How many writers does it take to change a light bulb?" Answer: "Are you sure it needs changing?"

Writers resist change because, however simple a new idea may sound, it invariably impacts on the script in unforeseen ways. You find yourself unpicking much of what has been done while figuring out how to keep what is essential. Kirk had a genuine respect for writers; nevertheless, he was relentless in his endless search for improvement. He explained his philosophy to me one morning when we met yet again to go over various scenes with a fine-tooth comb.

"It's like in the gym. You work out, you push yourself to the limit, then you go further. You gotta give it both knees. You start doing stuff you didn't know you could do, then you push yourself on up to a whole other level. Then you start again…"

As he spoke he was reaching for imaginary wall bars and weights to give a physical dimension to his words. I don't know what had brought it on; perhaps I'd demurred over some re-write or other, but I don't think so. It wasn't an aggressive or hectoring lecture. If it had been I would have noticed; later I would see him back our very large and heavy director up against a wall, lift him off his feet and hold him there until he was satisfied he'd got his point across. In my case, I think he just wanted to be sure we shared the same work ethic. I did my best to convince him.

"Of course, Kirk... I agree... absolutely... well, that's what I always... right... the only way..."

Reassured, he relaxed somewhat. He never wanted things doing his way for just arbitrary reasons, though sometimes for interestingly trivial ones. One day he said, "Can we cut this line 'Follow me'? I've done so many westerns where I've been leading a bunch of guys off somewhere, and I don't say anything, I just... I'll show you what I do."

He got to his feet, took a couple of steps away, then looked back and gestured with his head for me to follow.

"Okay," I said, "got it." The line went.

Another line that had to go was "This is it" as a crisis approached. "People don't say 'this is it' in real life. That's only in movies."

Fair enough.

•

A few weeks later Kirk and I were both in London for different reasons. For me it was still home, though I was now spending most of the year in Hollywood, often though not always accompanied by Laurence. Kirk was making a science-fiction film called *Saturn 3* at Shepperton Studios. He asked me to go out there so we could talk some more about our film which was due to start shooting as soon as he'd wrapped up this one.

Kirk sent his driver to pick me up in central London. The driver and car, a large BMW, were employed by the production to be at the star's disposal throughout the shoot. We chatted during the hour or so's drive. I asked him how he got on with Kirk, and he said fine, he was good to work for. I made some remark about what great shape Kirk was in for his age and what energy he had. The driver agreed, but adding he was inclined to flake out around ten in the evening and take to his bed. I smiled at this. Kirk had a notorious habit of bringing his and Anne's dinner parties to an end by disappearing for a few minutes and reappearing in his pyjamas – a hint to his guests that it might be time to begin thinking about leaving. I had seen him do it in Palm Springs.

When I arrived on set at Shepperton, Kirk had just finished his last shot of the day. I immediately got the impression that all was not well on the production. Kirk was unsmiling, wearing a tunic that was supposed to be space station issue but could equally well have suited a Roman soldier. His hair was glued into a state of careful dishevelment, and he had a crimson daub on his temple that was supposed to be blood. His co-star Farrah Fawcett was standing nearby, so Kirk, observing the social niceties as always, introduced us. But when he presented her as "Mrs Majors", the frost between them was unmistakable: she had separated from Lee Majors only recently and had announced publicly that she no longer wished to be known as Farrah Fawcett-Majors.

From there I accompanied him to make-up, where he cheered up slightly. He obviously liked the efficient middle-aged and very English women who draped a sheet over him before removing his pancake and fake blood, then washed and dried his hair. I was brought a cup of tea and a plate of biscuits while all this went on, then we walked over to his dressing room. As he was getting out of his costume and into a tracksuit, there was a knock at the door. A balding man in a neat suit and tie put his head around.

"Come in, Stanley," Kirk said.

This was Stanley Donen, the director. *The* Stanley Donen, who had made at least two of my all-time favourite movies, *Singin' in the Rain* and *Charade*. Not to mention *Two for the Road, Indiscreet, Funny Face, Seven Brides for Seven Brothers*, and too many more to list.

"I just wanted be sure that we're... you know, okay... after..."

Obviously there had been some incident, some flare-up of tempers on the set earlier in the day.

"Oh, sure!" Kirk waved his concerns away as though the whole thing was forgotten. "You still need a ride back to town?"

"If that's okay."

"Sure it is. Come and meet David."

This was not only a thrill for me, it was a chance to show off a little: Stanley Donen's wife, Yvette Mimieux, had just signed on to co-star with a whole list of legendary names in a TV movie of mine.

"No kidding," Stanley said, seeming pleased to hear this. "Have the two of you met?"

"Not yet," I said.

"Well, you're about to. She's here, so we'll be riding back together."

I never found out what had happened to Stanley's car and why he and Yvette needed a ride, but I was glad they did. Kirk sat in the front with his driver, Stanley and I in the back with Yvette squeezed in between us. It was a surreal experience to find myself travelling through the drab outer suburbs of London in this little Hollywood bubble. Nearing the outskirts of the city we slowed to a crawl, stopping at red lights alongside trucks and motorbikes and family cars. I watched as people glanced casually in Kirk's direction, then took a second, harder look, telling themselves it simply wasn't possible this could be who they thought it was just inches away in rush-hour traffic. Then the lights changed, and they were left wondering.

Kirk and I were dropped off at the Berkeley Hotel in Knightsbridge where he was staying. We had as yet barely spoken about the script, but his car would be returning to take us to dinner after dropping Yvette and Stanley off where they were living nearby. I followed Kirk as he strode quickly across the pavement and into the hotel, head down to avoid being recognised. Nevertheless, passers-by stopped and stared. "Was that..? Did you see who..?"

His room was a simple one, spacious enough, but not a luxury suite, or any kind of suite. In one corner was a collection of bar-bells and other weights that he obviously used every day.

"Help yourself to a drink," he said, nodding towards the mini-bar as he pulled off his tracksuit and headed into the bathroom.

"Thanks, I'll wait till dinner," I said with uncharacteristic restraint, knowing Kirk hardly drank at all and thinking I'd better keep a clear head.

"Italian all right for you?" he called through the half-open door.

"Great."

"Let's go to Mimmo's. You like Mimmo's?"

"Love it. Been going for years."

It was a slight exaggeration, but I'd been a few times. Mimmo d'Ischia was an Italian restaurant just south of Eaton Square in Belgravia, very popular with visiting movie stars, showbiz folk in general, and minor royalty. The walls were covered with photo-graphs of the owner posing alongside his celebrity clientele.

Kirk emerged from the bathroom in his jockey shorts and briskly pulled on a pair of trousers, shirt and jacket, all light-weight and suitable for a warm summer evening. He picked up the phone and dialled from a list of numbers he kept by it. "Could I have a table for two in about half an hour? For Kirk Douglas." He repeated the name with emphasis to make sure there were no misunderstandings. "*Kirk. Douglas.* Thank you."

As we emerged from the hotel, descending five or six steps to where his car was waiting, I noticed how he kept his gaze straight ahead to discourage interruptions and approaches. Nevertheless, one rather large middle-aged man spotted him and lunged forward.

"Mr Douglas, sir, I would like to shake your hand."

Kirk took the outstretched hand willingly enough but avoided eye contact or any break in his stride. It was something I'd seen stars do many times: never stop, otherwise you're trapped.

"A privilege, sir," came the voice from behind us as we piled into the car and the driver shut the door. The windows in the back, where I had sat earlier with Stanley and Yvette, were of dark glass so nobody could see in, unlike those in front where Kirk had been on full view. He was quiet and abstracted suddenly.

"It was great meeting Stanley and Yvette," I said by way of making conversation.

"Yeah, nice people," he responded vaguely.

"And a terrific director," I said. "How's the movie going?"

Kirk gave a non-committal grunt, confirming my earlier suspicion that all was not well. I would learn later that the whole production had been a nightmare. Kirk had come on board only at the last minute when there were already problems, including budget cut-backs. As Anne told me once, Kirk suffered from a slight Messiah complex which made him think that if he just put enough effort into a troubled project he could make it come right. It didn't always, and this was one of those times. First they'd had to replace the director, who had conceived the original story but had never directed before and apparently wasn't cutting it. Stanley Donen had been the producer hired by Lew Grade to supervise the production, but found himself with no choice but to step in and take over.

Martin Amis, who had (somewhat improbably, I thought) written the screenplay, would later incorporate the whole disastrous episode into his novel *Money*. It included a vicious caricature of Kirk as an ageing movie star "obsessed with his own virility". I have to admit that when people took against Kirk, they really hated him. But I also have to say that although I've heard people bad-mouth him for any number of reasons, I never once in all the time I knew him heard Kirk do the same about anybody.

We arrived at Mimmo's to a warm welcome and were shown to our table. The place was busy. People glanced our way, but this was a cool crowd, too sophisticated to be impressed by movie stars, or at least to show they were. Kirk ordered a beer; I had a glass of white wine. He still seemed preoccupied, and I was beginning to wonder what the point of our meeting was. So, like nature, abhorring a vacuum, I weighed in with another conversational gambit.

"I heard someone a while back describing the difference between working with you and working with Michael," I said.

"Hm?"

"They said if Kirk's having trouble getting his point across he'll grab you by the lapels and shake you till your teeth rattle. Michael, on the other hand, will just lob powder-puffs at you non-stop, till you go down on your knees and promise him anything if only he'll stop."

Kirk looked stony. Oops, I thought, that's pissed him off. But then he cracked a grin and chuckled. "Who said that?"

"I don't know. Just heard it somewhere."

"Probably right."

He relaxed, as though whatever had been on his mind had lifted somewhat. Our food arrived and we started to talk about the script. He had some questions about the logic of time travel. A traditional time-travel story usually involves someone travelling into the past, doing something while there, then returning to the present to confront the dramatic consequences of this action. The classic of the genre is Ray Bradbury's "A Sound of Thunder", where a time traveller visits the pre-historic past, breaks the rules by stepping off the floating pathway to which visitors are confined, and accidentally crushes a butterfly. When he returns to the present, he finds the world radically changed very much for the worse – by the "butterfly effect".

Our story was a bit more of a brain twister. It required acceptance of the idea (if anyone chose to think about it) that a man could exist in the past even before setting out from the present to go there. A few critics of the film would object later that there was a lack of logic in this premise, while generally admitting that it didn't spoil their enjoyment of the story. However, I have always maintained that such criticisms were based on an oversimplified notion of time travel. Being fairly up to speed on current thinking in theoretical physics, I was aware of all the counterintuitive paradoxes and ambiguities involved. To my mind our story made perfect sense.

Kirk nodded thoughtfully as I continued to expound ideas about the participatory universe, quantum indeterminacy and parallel worlds, until he sat back and held up a hand.

"Wait, whoa, David, slow down. Look, I'm a meat and potatoes man," he said, abandoning for a moment his spaghetti vongole. "You gotta keep it simple. If I can understand something, you can be pretty sure most people will. If I can't, the odds are I won't be alone. Now start again."

In the end he agreed that the idea was sound, and would at worst be the cause of "an ice-box moment". This was a term originated by Hitchcock to describe the experience some hours or even days after watching a movie when, just as you're opening the fridge door to get a piece of last night's cold chicken, you suddenly find yourself wondering, "Wait a minute, how did that bit of the movie work?"

We started talking casting. Kirk said he'd met Donald Sutherland, who was also in London shooting a film. "D'you know him?"

I said I didn't.

"He's a very bright guy, I'd really like him to play Lasky."

Warren Lasky was one of three key roles in the movie.

"Great idea," I said.

"I've sent him the script."

"And..?"

"He wants to talk to you."

Donald Sutherland and I met for dinner in Soho a couple of

nights later. There is a particular kind of body language that anyone who has worked in Hollywood knows. It has been perfected by most stars and some executives as a way of saying, "You have my full attention for reasons of courtesy, but I've already made my mind up, and the answer is no."

Sutherland was deploying this body language with every inch of his angular six-foot-four-inch frame. The fact was that he had commitments for the best part of two years, and it was extremely unlikely that he would be able to fit in with our timetable. He gave me a lift home in his chauffeur-driven Bentley, came in for a drink, and we parted cordially. A few days later Martin Sheen signed up for the role.

The other main roles went to Katharine Ross, Charles Durning and James Farentino. The director was Don Taylor, a competent craftsman who had just had a big success with *Omen II*. He was also, though we didn't know it at the time, a functioning alcoholic. Alcohol is banned on all US Navy ships, unless the admiral himself chooses to produce a bottle for distinguished guests in the privacy of his quarters; otherwise, even guests in their own quarters are supposed to remain dry. Which is why, when Peter and I followed our director up the gangplank of the *Nimitz* for our first few days of shooting at sea, we were alarmed to hear a suspicious clinking sound coming from his large suitcase. An hour or so later, when the three of us were invited to the admiral's quarters for an official welcome, Don showed up already several drinks ahead. Topped up with a couple more, courtesy of the admiral, he became alarmingly expansive, and made a very unfortunate remark.

"I just wanna tell you all," he began, raising his glass to the handful of top brass gathered around us, "how much we appreciate the terrific cooperation we're getting from the navy on this picture. I know there are some do's and don't's we're supposed to

290

obey while we're here, and we'll do our best. But in the end, you know what, we're gonna make the picture we want to make the way we wanna make it – and fuck the navy!"

With that he downed his drink, blissfully unaware of the blood-drained horror on Peter's face, or the suddenly fixed smiles of our hosts and the worried looks passing between them.

Peter spent the rest of the day tearing his hair out, smoothing things over with the navy, and yelling at his associate producer for having let this happen – though, as I tried to point out, it was hard to know what he could have done to avoid it. He also made sure that our director understood he had made a faux-fucking-pas of a high order.

From then on, whenever he was on board ship, Don at least had the decency to conceal his vodka in aftershave and hair-lotion bottles. And it has to be said that, despite his personal problems, he did a good job. As already mentioned, Kirk lost his temper with him only once, and that was because he felt he was shooting a scene lazily instead of "giving it both knees".

Aside from the question of whose idea it was to locate the action around Pearl Harbour instead of in World War One, the only other point on which I take issue with Kirk's autobiography concerns his claim that "... in spite of the *Nimitz* and the jets and the special effects (not special or effective enough), the picture did not do well".

He is right about the rather cut-price special effects, though they worked well enough to serve the story; and some of the fantastic flying sequences – all real – more than made up for it. He was also right in that the picture did only average business on its release in the USA and Great Britain. But it did huge business overseas, especially in France, Germany and, interestingly, Japan.

Not only that: in the years since Kirk wrote his memoir the picture has become a much-loved sci-fi classic. It has been issued and re-issued in a series of increasingly fancy DVDs, and plays constantly on television around the world. On the industry bible, imdb.com, it is selected as one of the most memorable films of just about everyone involved in it. I was, and still am, affectionately proud of it.

CHAPTER 39

Whereas *The Final Countdown* was an independent production made with no executive interference – the financial backers and distributors in effect just accepted the film that we wanted to make – *Disaster on the Coastliner*, an all-star made-for-TV movie, was a pure product of the Hollywood machine.

I had originally been commissioned by the network (ABC) to write something called *Murder on the Metroliner*. Everybody likes mysteries set on trains, and I was delighted to be writing one. The Metroliner was a high-speed train running between New York's Penn Station and Washington DC. I began my research by riding it both ways and talking to some of the people who worked on it. On my return journey I found myself in the same carriage as a couple who bickered quietly but interminably. I recognised him as the actor Gig Young, a handsome but ravaged alcoholic in the twilight of his career; she was an attractive young blonde. The following day they were found dead in their Manhattan apartment. He had shot her, then put a bullet through his own head. He was sixty-four, she thirty-one. They had been married for just three weeks. It was his fifth marriage.

Naturally, being a writer, I wondered if I could use the story. In the end I didn't; instead, I came up with a murder mystery that took place entirely on the moving train. I wrote a detailed outline and handed it to the production company who were contracted to make the movie, and to the network who were the final arbiters of everything, including whether the production would ultimately get the "green light" or not.

At this point I found myself embarked on something called "the development process".

This is a process that over ninety percent of scripts written in Hollywood, whether for TV or feature films, do not survive. It isn't a particularly rigorous process; in fact in many ways it is the opposite of rigorous. It is, however, relentless and destructive.

It is administered by teams of people called "development executives" who are employed by studios, networks, and production companies. Sometimes they call themselves "creative executives", though most of them know what an oxymoron that is and stick, sensibly, with the former title. Their job, essentially, is to take anything that has been written, or sometimes even just thought of, and suggest other ways of doing it. Not necessarily better ways, just other ways.

Their suggestions come in the form of "notes", often many pages long, neatly typed out by their secretaries, or "assistants" as they prefer to be called. These notes are not merely offered for the writer's consideration: they are there to be acted upon. If the writer refuses to do so for any reason, whether concerns over character consistency, narrative coherence, or a desire to protect the integrity of the original idea, or even just sheer weariness after multiple drafts, then that writer is simply fired and another writer brought in.

It is something of which no writer in Hollywood is proud, but the fact is that many of them (myself included) make a substantial part of their income from re-writing the work of other writers to satisfy various executive whims. By and large, the more re-writes of this kind a script undergoes, the further it declines in quality. This is known in the business as "Development Hell", and can go on for months or even years.

Eventually it becomes obvious to everyone, including the executives responsible, that "this just isn't working out". At which point the script goes into "turnaround", a zombie-like state somewhere between dead and undead. Anyone wishing to buy a script in turnaround is welcome to do so, but a frequent obstacle to such a rescue is that so much money has been lavished on re-writes, renewed options and whatever else, that the price tag is now impossibly high.

This had already happened to me with two projects, one for television, the other a feature film, so I was determined this time to hang on for grim death and do whatever it took to stay the course. The experience was something akin to what I can only imagine riding a rodeo bronco to be.

First, my story was picked over by the production company's development people, and then picked over again by the network's people, and their eventual verdict was that it was fine, but needed "something more".

This was quite usual. Everything always needs "something more", though there is rarely any clue in the executive notes, which are generally vague, abstract and often self-contradictory, as to what that "something more" might be. Nevertheless, I persevered through several drafts, determined to keep my project on the rails (excuse the pun) for as long as possible. But I could see the jaws of Development Hell yawning ahead. I had to think of something fast.

What I thought of was a classic, over-the-top, high-concept ploy, something I just knew the network would be hard pressed to ignore.

"Okay," I said at our next meeting, "you want to give a little more 'Oomph!' to this story? Let's make it about *two* trains, not just one. We've got one Metroliner travelling north, and another travelling south, and they're on a collision course."

That did it. "Tell me more," said the head of ABC Films, leaning forward with clasped hands on his desk. "How would it work?"

"Let's say it's sabotage," I said. "A disaffected railroad employee, a man with a grudge, sabotages the whole signalling and track-switching system..."

"Can that be done?"

"There's always a way," I said, on a roll now. "I'll talk to some people. I'm sure I can make it credible."

"Okay, go on."

"Then this guy gives the company – what? – two, three hours to meet his demands. Otherwise... kapow!"

Now everybody started throwing in ideas about how to increase the stakes and heighten the suspense. Let's have the President of the United States travelling on one of the trains. Too much? Okay, how about his wife? Maybe too like that movie where President Henry Fonda has to incinerate New York while his wife's there. Okay, how about the Vice President?

In the end we settled for the Vice President's wife. "We're gonna make this movie!" said the network chief, fully enthused by now. And they did.

But not without a few more near-surreal corporate idiocies along the way.

"Look," I said to our producer a few days later, "why don't we stop pretending we're going to shoot this on the east coast? You know perfectly well that's going to turn out to be too expensive, and the network's going to want to switch it to the west coast. Why don't I just write it for two trains between Los Angeles and San Francisco?"

"There are no direct trains between LA and San Francisco, never mind high-speed ones."

So I set my script on the east coast Metroliner. A few days after I'd delivered it, I got a call from the producer. "You were right," he said, "the network wants to re-locate everything to the west coast."

"But you told me there were no high-speed direct trains between..."

"We'll have to invent one. How long will it take you?"

It took no time at all, just a simple matter of changing place names and a few other references. Everybody was happy.

But there was a footnote yet to come. During pre-production it became clear that the only stretches of track that were both suitable for our main action sequences and also available for long enough were on the east coast.

Naturally, I assumed we would simply switch back to the east coast version of the script. But no, that was too logical. Executive decisions had been made and could not now be reversed. The network wound up paying to have west coast-type billboards and other bits of decor constructed alongside the east coast track to "cheat" for the west coast. Connecticut cop cars and a couple of police helicopters were re-painted to look like California ones. The actors were flown over, at considerable cost, to shoot their action scenes, then flown back to Hollywood to complete their studio work. All other location scenes were shot in and around Los Angeles and San Francisco.

The cast was led by William Shatner, *Star Trek*'s Captain Kirk, which was a nice coincidence for me, having met him with Gene Roddenberry. He played a charming con man who turns hero under pressure, and won rave reviews for a performance that had some critics comparing him to Cary Grant. Yvette Mimieux played his intended victim who eventually falls in love with him. Lloyd Bridges, who had been in my *Fifth Musketeer* movie, played a senior Secret Service agent. E.G. Marshall was a railroad executive, and Raymond Burr, who I'd watched as "Perry Mason" and "Ironside" from childhood, played the railroad chairman. There they were, these distant images from my childhood.

The director was Dick Sarafian, who'd made a movie called

Vanishing Point some years earlier, hailed as "an existential car-chase movie". He kept the action going without a slack moment, and the film stands up today and is still shown on television around the world.

CHAPTER 40

Bobby Littman was a dandyish Englishman, an agent with a small but glittering client list. He wasn't my agent, but we knew each other and met up from time to time. He told me a story over lunch in Beverly Hills one day soon after my arrival. It was, he said, a morality tale, and revealed a great deal about the sort of place Hollywood was and how it worked.

"There was this woman executive at one of the major studios who I'd met a few times and done several very successful deals with. I liked her, she was attractive, and after a while I began to think maybe I'd like to see a little more of her outside of business. So I sent her an expensive bouquet of flowers with a note saying I hoped she wouldn't find this inappropriate, but would she like to have dinner with me one night.

"She rang back and thanked me, said the flowers were lovely and looked marvellous in her office, and she'd be delighted to have dinner with me. Quite soon we'd started an affair. It went on for several months. Very pleasant, very enjoyable. Then one day she got fired. She went out of town and I didn't see her for a while. Eventually I heard she'd got a new job with some production company, but it wasn't anything that brought us into contact any more. Then one day I ran into her on Rodeo Drive, and d'you know" – he paused, making sure I was paying attention before he delivered his punch line – "I couldn't remember her name."

My own agent, Gary Salt, described a "perfect Hollywood

moment" he'd just witnessed one afternoon on the Columbia lot. He'd been at a meeting in an office a couple of floors up from ground level. The office had a small balcony that he'd stepped out onto for a moment. From there he saw two men emerging from the commissary below, chatting and joking like old friends who'd been having lunch together. As they walked they began to separate, heading for their cars on opposite sides of the space below. Because of this they had to raise their voices to continue their conversation, and Gary was able to hear what they were saying.

"This was great! It was really good seeing you."

"You too. Let's do it again soon."

"Right, I'll call you."

"I'll look forward to it."

"I'll definitely be in touch."

Then, as he opened his car door, one of them paused and called over, "What was your name again?"

Two examples of the brutal pragmatism of Hollywood friendships. Your only value to others is the extent to which you can further their career – and vice-versa. Executives are courted, flattered and grovelled to by writers and producers in the hope of cosying up to a development deal. Few things are as cringe-making as listening to a group of new-ish and still hopeful writers extolling the virtues of some executive vice-president ("He is *sooo* nice!", "She is *sooo* clever!") in the hope that their fawning obsequiousness will get back to its subject and dispose him or her to listen with increased indulgence at the writer's next pitch meeting with them.

It is little wonder that writers in Hollywood grow bitter and burn out with time. I had looked up my old friend from Rome, Millard Kaufman. In his early sixties by now, he was finding work thin on the ground despite having a distinguished career and two Oscar nominations behind him. When I asked him what he was currently working on, he used a word I couldn't quite make out at first. But it was a word I would increasingly hear other ageing writers use. In fact, though it came out as a single word, it was actually a compound of five.

"This-piece-a-shit-fer." As in, "I'm working on this piece of shit for…"

Add on the name of whatever star, director or producer you're developing or re-writing a script for, with little hope of seeing it, or at least your contribution to it, survive into production. Everything was "this-piece-a-shit-fer…"

It was a defence mechanism against the disappointment of being pushed aside by age, changing fashion, and the arrival of younger interlopers – like me. Generously, Millard and most other writers of his generation that I met didn't seem to resent us new-comers. They accepted their displacement as the natural order of things. Many of them tried to revive earlier careers they'd had in the theatre; quite a few tried a whole new career in novel writing. Few succeeded. Millard, I knew, had written several novels that were turned down by just about everyone before he got his first one published at the age of ninety. He died two years later just before his second one was due to come out.

His example as much as any other persuaded me not to put down roots in "this town". Los Angeles, anyway, is a city built on sand with a fault line running through it. Earthquakes of varying seismic levels are a common experience which most people who live there try to block out of their minds. But the fact is that it's neither liter-ally nor metaphorically an ideal place for roots of any kind.

Perhaps to convince myself as much as anyone else that I was an independent spirit and not someone living in fear of displeas-ing the powers that be, I did something fairly unusual right at the beginning of my time in Hollywood. Having been to several meetings at one of the studios to discuss whether or not I was the ideal writer for some project they were developing, I announced that I would be flying back to England on the following Thursday, therefore I would be unavailable for further meetings and would be glad if they could make their minds up before that deadline.

Leaving town when you have a deal in the works is just something nobody does. Meetings are sacred. They are the staff of life. People fill their days with meetings from breakfast to dinner. It is not for nothing that the writer William Goldman once suggested the creation of two new Oscar categories, one for "Best Meeting of the Year", and another slightly lesser one, the equivalent of best supporting actor, for "Best Meeting Based on Material from an Earlier Meeting".

So there I was with my plane ticket bought, and a steely determination not to bend to the will of the studio executives who simply didn't believe that I meant what I said about leaving Thursday. Not surprisingly, because they didn't take me seriously and talked vaguely about another meeting to finalise everything the following week, they were aghast when my agent told them I'd left for Europe; and, equally unsurprisingly, they scratched my name from the project.

But when I did it again with a different studio a few months later, things took a surprising turn.

"He's gone? What d'you mean he's gone? Why didn't somebody stop him? Why didn't somebody tell me he was leaving? Get him back, damn it!"

It cost them a return ticket, first class, from London to LA, and a week at the Beverly Hills Hotel. The reason for such extravagance was nothing to do with my being the only writer capable of doing the job; I could have given them the names of at least a dozen writers who could have done just as good a job, and who lived only twenty minutes from the studio. But no, I had shown a level of independence they weren't accustomed to. Anyone with that kind of confidence, they reckoned, had to know something they didn't, and they'd better buy into it.

Executives, in truth, are very insecure people. The only thing they can be sure of in their lives is that sooner or later they are going to be fired. They will then find themselves on the street looking for a job: if possible another executive job, but more likely a step down to independent production, which can sometimes mean little more than hanging a sign on the door of your spare room at home and getting a new phone line installed. At worst, a former VP at a major studio can find him or herself on a short-term consultancy contract with the Film Board of Turkey or New South Wales or one of the Baltic states. Executive bone yards are many and sometimes far afield.

But it is hard to have sympathy for them. Their sole ambition while in power is to hang on to their job. In theory they are supposed to be encouraging and nurturing creative talent: in reality they are desperately trying to avoid making mistakes, and the best way to do that is to avoid taking risks. An executive who champions a film that flops will be out of a job inside weeks. An executive who sits on the fence and avoids commitment of any kind will survive longer. There is an old and horribly true joke about an agent who gets a script from a writer client one Friday morning, reads it at once, and realises it is brilliant. He owes a big favour to an executive at one of the major studios, so he calls him up and says, "I have, sitting on my desk, the greatest script I've ever read. I'm not letting anyone else see it, and I'm going to bike it over to you right now. Read it over the weekend and call me."

Monday goes by without any call from the executive. So do Tuesday and Wednesday. Finally, on Thursday, the agent calls the executive and says, "What happened? You didn't call me. Did you get the script okay?"

"Oh, sure, I got the script."

"And you read it?"

"Yeah, I read it."

"So what do you think?"

To which the executive replies, "How do I know what I think? Nobody else has read it yet."

CHAPTER 41

One of the good things about working in Hollywood when I did was that many of the icons of my youth were still alive and I got to meet them, sometimes even to work with them. Aside from Kirk and various others already mentioned, I made movies or mini-series with legends like Richard Widmark and David Niven.

My first agent in LA, Paul Kohner, was something of a legend himself. Hungarian by birth, and still going strong in his seventies, he had specialised in representing the cream of European talent, starting with Garbo, Dietrich, Lubitsch, von Stroheim, Ingmar Bergman, and many more. Every Friday afternoon he hosted a poker game in his office. One day he took me through to meet his regulars; I shook hands with John Huston, Billy Wilder, William Wyler, George Burns and Walter Matthau. At least they are the ones I remember. I think Jack Lemmon might have been there too; if not, I certainly met him with Paul on another occasion in a curious little restaurant called Dominick's.

Dominick's was one of the most exclusive haunts in Hollywood, and outwardly one of the most unprepossessing. It was a simple cabin set back a couple of yards from the sidewalk on Beverly Boulevard in West Hollywood, bang opposite the great square mass of the Cedars-Sinai Medical Centre. To anyone walking past, it looked like nothing more than a dingy bar. To the cognoscenti who parked their (very expensive) cars around the back and entered through the kitchen, it was the "in" place of all "in" places.

It had started life in the fifties as a hang-out for Sinatra and the Rat Pack, and was owned by a family of three. Dominick himself was a burly Italian-American who ran the place from behind the bar as his personal fiefdom. His word was law as to who was allowed in and who not. Jovial enough if he liked you, I was warned he wasn't a man to get on the wrong side of: he kept a pump-action shotgun beneath the bar.

His wife Peggy was mistress of the kitchen. A neat, grey-haired woman with large round glasses that gave her eyes a curious staring quality, she grilled the best chicken and the best steaks and home-made burgers in town. That was it, the whole menu. The wine list was equally short and of equally high quality, with excellent Burgundies and Bordeaux at surprisingly reasonable prices.

Peggy's sister Addy was the waitress, also wearing glasses and with a goofy manner that reminded me of the actress Jean Stapleton. But underneath that goofiness was a shrewd woman who knew exactly who was who and who they knew.

The drill was you entered through the kitchen, pausing to make an obligatory fuss of Peggy, who would accept the homage of a kiss on the cheek without pausing in her work, and then went through into the restaurant itself. This was small and softly lit by little lamps on the tables and walls. There were hardly more than a dozen tables in all, some of them partitioned into separate booths that did nothing to lessen the sense of crowded intimacy in the room.

Having been introduced to the place by Kirk and Peter Douglas, then also by Merrill Heatter, creator of *Hollywood Squares* and a bunch of other successful game shows, and with whom I was developing a movie at the time, I was very quickly persona grata with Dominick and could get a table under my own name whenever I wanted. I have to admit to being seriously awestruck at dining cheek by jowl with Fred Astaire and Groucho Marx and their wives; with Dean Martin and a couple of friends; and at bumping into Johnny Carson at the bar one night, who was exceedingly gracious about my spilling his drink.

One night when I was dining alone with Peter, a tall figure on his way to a nearby table stopped and leant over us. "Hey," said the figure, "I hope you guys are going to have some work for an old man one of these days."

It was Gregory Peck.

•

Laurence and I were married by the early eighties and living in a beautiful Georgian house in Hampstead, paid for by Hollywood. It had an artist's studio at the end of the garden where she worked on her paintings and sculptures.

When I was in LA for any length of time, which I increasingly was, she would come with me and we would rent a place to live. At different times we had a large house just off Mulholland Drive, a house in Malibu Colony, flanked on one side by Larry Hagman (JR from *Dallas*) and on the other by the comedian Don Rickles. Our first place had been an apartment in a fine old West Hollywood building called Colonial House, which had originally been part of the Garden of Allah complex where the likes of F. Scott Fitzgerald, Robert Benchley, Dorothy Parker and other east-coasters in town for the money, the booze and the sex had thrown wild parties throughout the thirties and forties. Our neighbour in the apartment below was Bette Davis. My sole encounter with her was short but memorable.

There was a pool behind the building in which I used to swim for half an hour or more every evening around dusk. The reason for the timing was threefold: first, I was working most of the day; secondly, swimming during the day meant getting a tan, and a tan was the sure sign of an out-of-work loser in Hollywood; thirdly, I liked to have the pool to myself, and nobody else used it after sundown.

One evening after I'd finished my laps and was standing in the shallow end, about to climb out, I heard a voice which nobody who had ever been to the movies could fail to recognise.

"How many's that, then? A hundred?"

I looked up. Silhouetted against the lights in her apartment, was Bette Davis leaning over her balcony with a drink in her hand.

Quick as a flash, though not quite as wittily as I might have wished, I replied, "No, I only managed eighty laps tonight. I've got to go out."

Then she said something that has remained with me ever since, because I can't believe she said it to many men in her life, if any.

"You scare me," she said. "Every night, up and down, up and down. You scare me."

Whereupon she turned and tottered off, the ice clinking in her glass, to get a refill.

•

Another meaningless but memorable encounter took place in the parking lot of the Chateau Marmont, where we sometimes stayed on shorter visits. The Chateau didn't have a restaurant in those days, but all the suites were spacious and had their own kitchens, so you could cook your own dinner and have friends over if you wanted. The parking lot was underneath the building and you turned into it directly off Sunset Boulevard. One late afternoon I had parked my car, taken a large bag of groceries and several bottles of wine from the trunk, and was headed for the elevator to go up to my floor.

On the way was a door that I was having some trouble holding open long enough to get through without dropping everything.

Suddenly a gardener appeared, Mexican I thought, if only because of the rather loud red and green herbaceous design on his short-sleeved shirt. With great kindness he held the door open and fixed it back so I could get through safely.

Feeling I should acknowledge his effort with more than mere thanks, I managed to fish a couple of dollars from my pocket and hand it over. I hadn't taken more than a few steps when a thought hit me like a sledgehammer. That was no Mexican gardener, that was...

I turned, to see Robert De Niro, his face split with a grin from ear to ear, proudly slipping my two bucks into the breast pocket of his colourful shirt.

•

The only other movie star who ever held a door open for me was Robert Redford on the Columbia lot one day. I hadn't recognised him at first: he was much shorter, despite Cuban heels, and more slightly built than he appeared on screen. But when I realised who it was, I gave a simple nod of thanks, receiving a polite nod of acknowledgment in return, and passed through the door ahead of him. There exists, I had learnt, a certain protocol regarding stars and doors: stars always wait for you to go first. If you find yourself in an elevator with one, no matter how major, they will always wait for you to leave before making a move themselves. If you hold back, they will make a courteous little gesture and murmur, "Go ahead, please."

I don't know why this is so. It's tempting to think it's some atavistic defence against the risk of getting a knife in the back, something that must have happened more than once in their careers.

But I suspect that is too fanciful.

Perhaps it's a kind of false humility. Stars are people with whom no one disagrees. Their every whim is catered for, they are bowed and scraped to from morning till night. So every now and then, when finding themselves before an open door with a "civilian" waiting to go through it, they get the chance to play humble. Some kind of compensatory mechanism, perhaps. A ritual to appease the gods who might otherwise punish them for the sin of hubris.

In other words, a superstition.

CHAPTER 42

My old friend Michael York and his wife Pat had been living in Hollywood for some years by the time I got there. Laurence and I saw them fairly often, but one night when she wasn't in town they invited me to join them for dinner at Morton's along with Joan Collins and her husband, and another woman friend. Morton's, one of the hottest dining spots in Hollywood, was owned by Peter Morton, married by then (small world) to Larry Harvey's widow Paulene. I was placed next to La Collins, at that time in the full flush of her *Dynasty* fame, and found myself on the receiving end of what I can only call "the full treatment". This was Joan's technique for dealing with the male of the species, evolved over many years and doubtless foolproof, if a little startling.

The first step involved fixing the male in question with a full-on, wide-eyed gaze and batting her eyelids several times to simulate a kind of child-like wonderment. Thereafter every exchange in the conversation above the utterly banal would be accompanied by an enthusiastic "Gosh!" or "My goodness!", or even on one occasion, "Oh, listen everyone, listen to what David just said."

Joan had been telling me about a novel she had recently published called *Prime Time*. It was her first, and she wished to emphasise that she had written it all herself. We were talking about constructing stories, and I'd mentioned the old adage that if a thousand men can write a first act, maybe a hundred can write a second, and if you're lucky you might find one who can write a third. This was the thought Joan wished to share with the table – and which Michael promptly topped with, "And as Chekhov said, only God can write a fourth."

It had seemed to me at the beginning of the evening that Joan's performance, the fluttering eyelids and the hundred-watt gaze, was almost certainly an elephant trap for male vanity. I had been doing my best to side-step it and avoid embarrassment, but as I watched her take out her compact and check her make-up for the fourth time during dinner, I began to realise there were no hidden depths of any kind waiting for the unwary to fall into. Joan was, and is, an old-fashioned star in the Joan Crawford tradition, always "on", always impeccably turned out and ready to perform for her fans. Very different from so many younger actresses who make a point of looking like bag ladies in public and pretend to despise their own glamour and wealth. Joan liked to dazzle; it was what she did best.

Eva Marie Saint, too, dazzled, but in a different way. Laurence and I dined with her one night in the mid-eighties at a small dinner party in Westwood given by the writer David Shaw and his wife. This was the woman who had won an Oscar for *On the Waterfront* opposite Marlon Brando, and played femme fatale to Cary Grant's on-the-run hero in *North by Northwest*. Now she sat opposite me in her mid-sixties and practically unchanged. A little older, of course, but with barely any make-up and showing no signs of the plastic surgery that most stars indulge in, male and female alike, in a vain attempt to hold back the years. She was simply a beautiful older woman, low key and unassuming, and a charming companion.

Around this same time I spent another evening at Morton's, this time with just Kirk and his great friend Jack Valenti. Jack had been special assistant to Lyndon Johnson during his first three years in the White House, then had become president of the

Motion Picture Association of America in 1966. He remained in the post, perhaps the single most powerful in the movie business, for almost forty years.

The dinner came about for a couple of reasons, one of which was a shared love of good cigars. Not long before I'd been at the Douglases' house on Rexford Drive for a casual dinner with Kirk, Anne and Peter. Although they didn't smoke, Anne said I was welcome to do so if I wished. I said I never smoked cigarettes, but sometimes liked a cigar after dinner, whereupon Kirk ran off to the kitchen and returned with a box wrapped in tinfoil. "I keep these in the fridge for when Jack Valenti comes over," he said, offering me one. It was in perfect condition: a fridge, Kirk had found, was as good as a humidor for keeping them.

As it happened, I'd read Jack Valenti's book *A Very Human President* about his years with LBJ and found it interesting, so Kirk said he would get us together some time. A week or two later the three of us met up for a drink at Rexford Drive before heading off to dinner at Morton's. As we left the house for Kirk's waiting car and driver, I dropped one of the minor bricks that have always been a habit of mine. I casually inquired, "Do you still drive, Kirk?"

I realised at once that the way I'd put the question implied that I thought of him as an old man (I was thirty-four, he was sixty-one) who probably needed help to cross the road, not to mention to pull on his trousers and tie his shoes. Kirk, still proud of his physical fitness, and with good reason, turned to me with a slow-burning look of surprise. I quailed slightly as he squared up his shoulders and buttoned his immaculately cut jacket across a board-hard stomach and said, "Hey, what is this..?"

But a grin spread across his face, and Jack was highly amused. Peter had warned me about Jack Valenti's love of fancy words. It wasn't that he used them in general conversation, just that he liked to collect them and test people on them. I got past "jejune", "inspissated" and one or two others without a problem, but he got me on "callipygian", a term of Greek derivation for beautiful buttocks.

During dinner, a procession of the Great and the Good of Hollywood who happened to be at Morton's that night came over to pay their ritual respects. They were mostly senior studio people and producers, along with a couple of TV stars, one of whom was Henry Winkler, then at the height of his fame as "The Fonz". Both Kirk and Jack accepted these tributes as a seigneurial right, and disposed of them with a brisk graciousness. Since entering, neither of them had so much as glanced across the room to see if anyone they knew was in tonight, let alone gone table hopping to greet them. When you're big enough in Hollywood, Hollywood comes to you.

Marvin Davis was big. Six feet four, over three hundred pounds, and supposedly a multibillionaire from oil and real estate holdings. "Supposedly" because after his death in 2004 this vast wealth was exposed as something of a myth, and lawsuits began flying between family members over what remained of it, if anything. But in 1981 he had bought Twentieth Century Fox, and although he knew nothing about the film business, this made him "a player".

Above all he loved the glamour of it all and the company of stars. So when one weekend down in Palm Springs Kirk said, "Marvin and Barbara want us to go over and see a movie after dinner", I knew who he was talking about. I had the impression that for Kirk and Anne accepting the invitation was more of a chore and social obligation than anything else. The Davises were famous for their lavish parties, especially their Christmas parties, but intimate dinners with them were less readily sought after by members of the Hollywood A-list they were so keen to be part of. So going over to watch a movie *after* dinner was a perfect compromise which would cut down on unnecessary conversation.

What I hadn't anticipated was how far away they lived. Peter took the wheel of a large station wagon, and Kirk, Anne, Peter's girlfriend at the time, and I piled in together. We drove for at least an hour before reaching the Davises' spread, just one of their many lavish homes, and got out gratefully stretching our limbs.

A butler opened the door and we filed in, led by Kirk, with me bringing up the rear. The Davises stood lined up in the hall to greet us. Marvin wore a tailored red jacket in contrast with Kirk's loose tracksuit; Barbara was smartly dressed and made up, with carefully lacquered hair, making Anne's easy-going sweater and slacks look all the more sophisticated; and with them were a preppy-looking young couple, one of whom I recognised as their daughter Patty. I had been working on a project at Fox soon after Marvin bought the studio, and Patty had appeared at a couple of script meetings, explaining sweetly that she was sitting in as a way of learning about the business and hoped I didn't mind. I didn't. I really didn't. Nor did the Fox executives who worked for her dad. They minded even less than I did.

It would be Patty who, after Marvin's death, would kick off the name-calling and lawsuit-filing by claiming that her father and other family members had defrauded her out of a $300m trust fund. But that night all was sweetness and light. Happy families.

My impression of the room we went through to was overwhelmingly of gilt, rich fabrics, and furniture chosen more for decoration than comfort. Along one side of the room was a table covered with every imaginable kind of dessert, cheese, soft drink or wine. I had a glass of champagne and a piece of chocolate cake. Everybody had something. Then, with a minimum of delay, drinks and plates still in hand, we trooped through to the screening room.

The film was some dreary comedy of such banality that everyone sat through it in total silence. At the end the Douglas party was immediately on its feet, thanking its hosts for their hospitality, and heading for the door. No further drinks, no further conversation. We drove home bored, half-asleep (except, fortunately, for Peter at the wheel) and went to bed. The evening had been the most perfect demonstration of social interaction devoid of all content. A masterpiece, I felt, in its class.

CHAPTER 43

Like Michael York, Jeremy Brett had settled in Los Angeles by the time Laurence and I got there. He was living with an actor called Paul Shenar in a wisteria-covered house not far below the Hollywood sign. He had also recently married a television producer, Joan Wilson, who lived mostly in New York. Not surprisingly the immigration authorities were looking suspiciously at this marriage, which was Jeremy's sole claim to US residency and therefore his only chance of pursuing a career in America.

Such suspicions were hardly surprising, but I'm quite sure there was more to the marriage than a mere cynical arrangement. Although often described by others as bisexual, Jeremy always described himself as homosexual. Perversely, this didn't prevent him from falling in love with women from time to time. As a young man he had been briefly married to the actress Anna Massey, by whom he had a son he was devoted to. Despite several long relationships with men, and intervening periods of intense homosexual promiscuity, he had many women friends and could become deeply involved with them. How often this led to sex I don't know. But I felt he genuinely adored his wife Joan, and she him, though whether there was a physical side to the marriage I rather doubted; at least, he continued living with Paul Shenar throughout it. Nonetheless, when Joan died after nearly ten years he suffered a severe breakdown.

By this time, 1985, he was back in England and becoming hugely famous (and wealthy) as the latest incarnation of Sherlock Holmes.

Ironically it was in LA in 1980 that he had his first encounter with the character. Laurence and I went to see him play Watson to Charlton Heston's Holmes in *Crucifer of Blood* at the Ahmanson Theatre, where the Oscar ceremonies are held. It was a pretty good show, though I couldn't forget Orson Welles's acid remark that nobody ventured on stage in Hollywood except mad men and Charlton Heston.

We met Heston backstage with Jeremy. He was famously well mannered, a courteous man. I constantly marvelled at the low esteem in which he was held by so many of his fellow actors. It wasn't just that he could be wooden, or that he lacked the self-awareness to get a better wig than the tatty rug that perched on his head like a dead crow; it was because he represented everything that the predominantly liberal-leaning Hollywood despised in their Republican opponents. And of course he was President of the National Rifle Association, which to many on the left of centre meant he was in league with the Devil, regardless of the fact that he had marched with Martin Luther King and Marlon Brando for civil rights in the early sixties.

Jason Robards could perform something like a stand-up routine on Charlton Heston, whom he referred to disparagingly as "Chuckles". I spent an evening with Jason at Peter Douglas's apartment. The only others present were Peter's girlfriend and Jonathan Pryce, who would become a lifelong friend. Jason and Jonathan were working together in a picture Peter was producing called *Something Wicked This Way Comes*.

"Chuckles is so vain that when he had to play a scene as an old man with a bald head, he refused to admit he was really bald and made them fix a bald wig over his wig!"

That was just for starters.

"One day on *Ben Hur* he was totally naked except for this itty-bitty loin cloth, standing there with his arms folded and his feet planted like he thought he was some kind of Greek god. Then somebody noticed he had a testicle protruding from out one side his loin cloth. Ugliest damn sight you ever saw. Everybody saw it, and you know what? Nobody told him. Chuckles spent the whole afternoon struttin' around, showing off his physique, with this testicle sticking out."

The stories flowed in that gruff Robards voice, always on the edge of a cackle of laughter. I knew he was a recovering alcoholic who hadn't had a drink in ten years, and was impressed by how easily he relaxed into the postprandial glow bestowed upon the rest of us by a couple of bottles with dinner. I hope he found us as amusing as we did him; at least we were a good audience.

Peter and I remained close friends throughout my time in Hollywood, despite not making another picture together. We tried to get a couple of things off the ground, but without success, which came as neither a surprise nor a disappointment. Most things in Hollywood don't get off the ground. Compared with the mountain range of projects ("prah-jects" as I came to pronounce the word with increasing sourness over the years) that the industry has in various stages of development, the actual output of pictures is a mole-hill. There is a myth in the outside world that film producers are forceful individuals who make things happen. The truth is that most of them would be hard pressed to produce water out of a tap. The cost of making a movie that has any chance of being seen widely enough to make a profit is so high that producers are heavily dependent on the accountant-run major studios to put up the money and guarantee distribution. Not surprisingly the law of lowest common denominator comes into play, provoking one industry insider to observe that "the average Hollywood product these days is any one of nine bankable stars outrunning a fireball".

True enough to be embarrassing.

Inevitably, defenders of the industry point to the list of small independent films for which producers and directors have mortgaged their homes and risked every last cent they possessed to get made, and which have gone on to become breakout smash hits and make fortunes. It's all true. But for every one of those pictures there are dozens of others no one has heard of, their brave makers having lost everything and never worked again. To quote William Goldman again, the golden rule in Hollywood is: NOBODY KNOWS ANYTHING. As proof of which I came across a couple of readers' reports that were gathering dust in the back office of a major producer I was working with in the mid-eighties. Readers' reports are mostly written by freelancers outside the studio, giving executives a brief summary of the story and the reader's evaluation of it. Depending on this, the executive will pick out the scripts that sound worth reading personally. With these curling and dust-covered readers' reports, the script they described wouldn't have been so much as opened.

"The writers haven't paid much attention to reason in this little fantasy... It's all primary colors, a comic strip. After a while it has a kind of mad appeal, but it's also very hokey, and even within its semi-fantasy parameters logic is ignored... I have to say: Not recommended."

The second report was no more encouraging. "This script seems to embody a completely adolescent viewpoint. It is sweet and coy and essentially silly. The story and characters are competently set up... (but) the premise is the cliché of clichés, which wouldn't be so terrible if the authors had reworked it in some devastatingly fresh manner. I didn't find that fresh approach here... Frankly, I don't feel that the expense involved in developing or making such a film could be justified on this old war horse of a premise."

By the time I read these two insightful commentaries, *Back to the Future* had been made by another producer at another studio, gone on to spawn two sequels and a TV series, and had earned more than a billion dollars.

CHAPTER 44

"The camera loves her. She's a star."

"Not yet she isn't. And she's past thirty."

"She's great-looking, she's smart, and she can act. With the right role she can be huge."

"She's never carried a picture."

"She doesn't have to carry this one. It's her and the guy."

"What d'you think, Ed?"

"Well, I dunno..."

I was sitting with producer Ed Pressman and director John Frankenheimer in Le Dome on Sunset Boulevard, one of the "in" places for industry power-lunches. The subject of our discussion was Sharon Stone, seated two tables away with her agent. We had been talking casting for a script of mine when she walked in, quite by chance. I said she would be perfect for the female lead. They were unconvinced.

It was the kind of conversation that made me understand why big stars behave as badly as they sometimes do – because they remember the times before they were big stars, when their futures were being tossed around as casually as Sharon Stone's was that day at our table.

The fact is that aside from looks and talent, actors need luck, an awful lot of it, to make it to the top. Frankenheimer had talked vaguely about a young actress called Julia Roberts for the role. Not only was she ten years younger than Sharon Stone, but he had found her "very promising" in a recent picture called *Steel Magnolias*, where she had received sixth billing, three down from Daryl Hannah. But Julia Roberts, by the time of our conversation, was busy shooting a picture called *Pretty Woman*.

It is interesting to speculate, if some other actress had got that role in *Pretty Woman*, whether that actress would have become a mega-star instead of Julia Roberts?

And if Julia Roberts hadn't got that particular breakthrough role, would she eventually have got another that would have made her as big a star as she is? Or would she have gone on taking third billing to the Daryl Hannahs of the world – until people started saying she was too old now to make it as a star?

Nobody knows – including the stars themselves.

I had met Sharon Stone briefly a few years earlier when she was going out with an HBO executive I knew. I'd never heard of her at the time, and she struck me as nothing special, just another middlingly attractive young woman in a town full of them. Her career, mostly in television, was also middling at best.

But in 1990 I'd seen her in the Arnold Schwarzenegger film, *Total Recall*. She didn't have much screen time, but she had been stunning: a face the camera loved and that didn't have a bad angle, a presence that held your attention, and an intelligence that was unmistakable. Despite their misgivings, Pressman and Frankenheimer eventually signed her up for our picture.

Year of the Gun, based on a novel by Michael Mewshaw, was set in Rome in 1978 and revolved around the kidnapping and murder of former prime minister Aldo Moro by the Red Brigades. An American journalist (Andrew McCarthy) and a photographer (Sharon Stone) find themselves involved in a way they have neither intended nor fully understand. It was a good story, with layers of intrigue and deception constantly unfolding.

I had considerable respect for John Frankenheimer. He was at his best a masterly film-maker, as evidenced by *The Manchurian Candidate*, *Seven Days in May*, *The Birdman of Alcatraz* and many more. All the same, I didn't like him very much.

He had been extremely complimentary about my screenplay and was very keen to make the picture, which was to be shot entirely on location in Rome. Because I knew the city well, he had insisted I accompany him on a couple of pre-production trips to scout locations and audition European actors for key parts. He was a tall, athletic tennis fanatic, with a restless, driven manner and a braying foghorn voice. I don't believe he had a shred of humour in him: I never saw him laugh once, even less make a funny remark. All the same, I felt we had a pretty good relationship, at least professionally.

Which made it all the more astonishing when he turned up one day not long before shooting began with a new script in his hand. It still had my name on it, but sharing the credit with another writer.

Jay Presson Allen was a clever New Yorker who had written several stage plays, most famously an adaptation of Muriel Sparks's *The Prime of Miss Jean Brodie*, and screenplays including *Marnie*, *Prince of the City* and *Cabaret*. A formidable talent.

"Your script's brilliant," Frankenheimer assured me earnestly, "we all admire it, including Jay Presson Allen. But I felt it might be helped by... well, I think you'll find she's brought something to it that... well, that I think amounts to a real collaboration between the two of you."

Annoyed though I was at having this sprung on me, I started to read the new version with interest, but was soon baffled. All Ms Allen had done was insert a few speeches into scenes I didn't think needed them and which slowed down the story; she'd also cut out some visual sequences that moved the story forward more effectively than the dialogue she'd put in its place.

Ed Pressman was a heavyweight independent producer almost exactly my own age (forty-seven by then) who had already made major pictures like *Wall Street*, and who had backed the careers not only of Oliver Stone but people like Brian de Palma, Terrence Malick and Kathryn Bigelow. He was known in the business as "a class act", a man with taste and a nose for talent. When I asked him what was going on, I got a typically Ed reply.

"Well, you know, um... we thought... John... John and... nothing's, it's not... we'll see if... if in fact we... what we... if in the end..."

It wasn't evasiveness, it was just the way he talked. Short and round-ish, with a bald head and rimless glasses perched on a small beaky nose, Ed was, and is, an exceedingly smart man with a soft voice in which he never seems to complete a sentence or quite round off a thought. From his track record, however, one is forced to conclude that what goes on in his head is a great deal more clear and decisive than what comes out of his mouth.

I liked Ed, and was oddly encouraged by our conversation; and besides, the changes were in the end of limited scope; I just couldn't understand why Frankenheimer had wanted them.

Then I realised. It was the reason behind most demands for re-writes: insecurity and a lack of confidence in one's own judgment. After a fifteen-year run of brilliant success, John had hit a bad patch in the mid-seventies. His last big hit had been *French Connection II* in 1975, after which he'd had a half dozen expensive flops and developed a serious drinking problem. As he liked to say, holding out his thumb and forefinger so that barely a sliver of light could pass between them, "I came *this* close to getting cirrhosis", usually adding, "I made several pictures during that time that I don't even remember making."

He'd been sober for the last few years, but felt he was still struggling to get back to where he deserved to be. *Year of the Gun* had looked promising to him, but he was disappointed not to have landed a bigger star than Andrew McCarthy as his leading man, and was having to make do with the as-yet-unproven Sharon Stone as his leading lady. So the addition of a glamorous name to the writing credits boosted his confidence a little.

But of course the writing credits would be decided only by the Writers Guild of America (WGA), whose adjudicators had the final word on the matter. Having already been through a number of these arbitrations, I knew perfectly well that on the strength of her contribution to the script Jay Presson Allen would not be accorded any screen credit. I'm sure she knew this herself and was unperturbed. Nevertheless Frankenheimer was furious when I said to a group of visiting journalists, who had asked me how I'd enjoyed collaborating with Jay Presson Allen, that I had never met the lady, and anyway her name would not be on the finished movie.

"How d'you know that?" Frankenheimer had snarled at me afterwards.

"It's obvious," I said.

"It's not obvious to me."

His angular frame was perched awkwardly on a folding chair as he studied a production schedule in a house where we were shooting for a couple of days. He had called me over, so that I found myself standing like a naughty schoolboy sent for by the headmaster. He didn't look up at me, but I could feel the tension in him.

"Well, it is to me," I said. "I've been through a few of these arbitrations, and I know how much you have to do as second writer to get a credit."

"That's not my experience. Things can go either way."

He was talking rubbish, and I think he knew it. I suggested we put a bet on the outcome, but he declined.

•

Some weeks later, by which time he was editing the picture in Hollywood, I got a surprising call from Frankenheimer at my house in France. He told me he was having trouble cutting the last twenty minutes of the film together, so he was sending me a rough cut of the whole film along with every bit of footage he had shot for the ending. He wanted me to see if I could figure out a way of making it work. He also said that our producer had approved the shooting of one or two extra scenes if that proved necessary.

Touched though I was by his humility in admitting he had a problem, I was also disappointed when I watched the rough cut and saw how this state of affairs had come about. He had made some perverse directorial choices that had thrown certain characters out of focus, particularly the one played by Valeria Golino, and obscured some of the relationships between them. It took me a week to plough through all the footage, by the end of which I'd found a way of cutting it together that was as close to what I'd originally intended as possible, requiring only one new scene between Stone and McCarthy that could be shot easily on a sound stage in Hollywood.

I debated whether to tell Frankenheimer what I thought of the job he'd done, or to stay discreetly silent. In the end I thought to hell with it, why should it always be the writer who defers to the director? Why do writers put up with this far too common notion that the screenplay is a mere "blueprint" that the director will take and bend to his or her own personal vision? Having myself directed both on stage and film, I am firmly in the writers' camp over the question of which function is the more important. There is a story about the writer Robert Riskin, who had written all of Frank Capra's famous movies in the thirties and forties and was sick of hearing critics and public alike swooning over "the Capra touch". One day he strode into Capra's office, flung a hundred blank pages onto his desk, and said, "Okay, genius, give *that* the Capra touch!"

326

Although Frankenheimer had followed my suggestions for the re-cut to the letter, I fully expected him to be seriously put out by my comments on his direction of the picture. However, when I saw him in Hollywood a few weeks later he was positively unctuous. I had by then been awarded sole screen credit by the WGA, as I knew I would, and no further mention of Jay Presson Allen was made. John insisted on setting up a private screening of the finished film for me, even though I said I would have been happy to wait for a scheduled studio screening in a couple of days.

"No, no, I insist. You wrote it, it's your screenplay, you have a right to see it."

It wasn't, finally, a bad film at all. The reviews were generally respectful, one or two of them rather good. It made no money at the time, though later did well on video and DVD, causing it to be described by some critics as "underrated", which as back-handed compliments go is right up there with "cult movie".

I also discovered later that Frankenheimer's passivity in the face of my criticism had been merely skin deep. A friend of mine overheard him droning on in a restaurant about this "arrogant fucking Englishman who thinks he knows everything, swanning around with this elegant French wife..."

"She isn't even French, she's Swiss," put in Frankenheimer's wife, whom I'd never liked either.

"Total fucking snob. Intellectual snob. Social snob. And he's even a fucking wine snob! And d'you know what he had the nerve to say about Jay Presson Allen..."

Ah, to see ourselves as others see us! When Jonathan Pryce made a picture with Frankenheimer a few years later, I warned him not to mention he was a friend of mine; it would not have been a positive recommendation.

One outcome of the whole faintly depressing story was, however, beyond question: nobody would ever again sit around debating whether or not to offer Sharon Stone a part in their movie. She went straight from *Year of the Gun* to *Basic Instinct*, and deserved, at thirty-four, every bit of the mega-star fame she suddenly found herself revelling in.

CHAPTER 45

"Hey, David, great to have you back in town. Guess you must be running out of money, huh?"

Such was Peter Douglas's invariable greeting whenever I returned from a sojourn in Europe. He wasn't a bad judge of character. At one point he even attempted to make a psychological survey of the true Hollywood mentality, or at least to determine if such a thing existed.

Somehow or other he had got hold of a copy of the Minnesota Multiphasic Personality Inventory, a psychological profiling tool normally available only to trained professionals in the mental-health field. I think he'd got it from one of his computer-geek friends, and it required the subject to answer between five and six hundred yes/no questions in a single concentrated session. The answers were then fed into a program which analysed them, and up popped a clear picture of the subject's mental health. At least that was the theory.

Inevitably, I was one of the first he roped in for this exercise, but I know he also got a huge cross section of the business to cooperate, from major stars and executives down to wannabees, one-shot wonders, and downright failures. Having answered all my questions, I forgot about the project until I dropped in on him one afternoon a few weeks later and found him collating his data.

"So what did you find?" I asked. "Any common profile to people who survive in this business? Or those who don't for that matter?"

"Nah, not really. Except a lot of them are really nuts one way and another."

"No kidding," I said, in a tone of voice indicating any other result would have surprised me.

"Really. I mean some of these guys, off the graph."

"And the women?"

"Jesus, them too, some of them."

He was fairly discreet by nature, so I didn't press him on any particular individuals – except myself, of course.

"So how did I come out?"

He tapped a few keys, read the scroll-up on his screen, and said, "You're pretty sane."

I waited for him to enlarge on this, but when he didn't I said, "Is that it?"

"Yeah, pretty much."

"Not a very profound diagnosis, is it?"

"I'm summarising. What d'you want to know?"

"I don't know what I want to know. What can you tell me?"

He tapped away at a few more keys. "You seem pretty normal."

Was he hiding something? Possibly that he didn't know what he was talking about? But no, I thought, he was seriously into this and had been putting in many hours of work on it. I felt sure he was giving me my profile as he saw it, and an alarming feeling of blandness began to creep over me.

"Is that it?"

"Yeah, pretty much."

"Well, could you maybe manage a little more detail?"

He tapped his keyboard a few more times, then said, "Main thing that shows up is nobody better fuck with your freedom."

Still not much of a clinically precise analysis. Indeed, it didn't seem much of anything when he said it. But shortly afterwards, the words began quietly to detonate in my head.

It was obvious. I just hadn't seen it before. It was a mini-epiphany.

That was what had been driving me all my life: the need to avoid being categorised, boxed-in, herded. Which, looked at another way, spells self-centred and totally selfish.

A mixed virtue, if indeed a virtue at all.

But it explained everything.

I had no idea if it was a good thing, or a bad thing: if it made a good writer, or a bad writer.

All I knew, at that moment, was that it had made me one.

•

I took time out from Hollywood in 1986 to direct a two-hour TV film in England. It was from a script of my own based on a true story I'd bought the rights to, about a man recovering from a failed suicide bid. The kicker was that when he woke up he found himself in a hospital ward filled with other men who had also tried to end their lives. Putting them together to relate to one another as best they could was a kind of experimental therapy. If it sounds bleak in summary, in reality the situation produced a good deal of comedy, admittedly some of it rather dark.

My friend Denholm Elliott had agreed to play the lead, but in the end my dates clashed with something he was already committed to. Fortunately I managed to replace him with Anton Rodgers, an actor I had long admired and was delighted to be working with. The rest of the cast included some fine character actors, along with two promising newcomers I believe I can make some claim to having discovered.

Kate Buffery had played only two minor film roles, but I had seen her in a one-act play by David Hare at the National Theatre. The moment she came in to audition I cast her. She was brilliant, not to mention beautiful, as a sympathetic young doctor, and swiftly went on to a highly successful career in television.

Stephen Dillane had done no more than half a day's filming in a minor TV role when my casting director lined him up with about thirty others to audition for the second male lead. I had never heard of him and knew nothing about him, but I sensed a remarkable quality in him when he read for the part of a young footballer who has had his feet shorn off in a car accident. He found everything there was to be found in the part: the bitterness, the despair, the humour, and finally the hope. And, of course, he has since gone on to a highly distinguished career in theatre and film.

One of the main reasons I wanted to direct a movie was simply to show I could do it. Having always been dubious about the mystique surrounding direction, both on film and in the theatre, and suspecting there was more than a little of the emperor's new clothes about the job, I was keen to prove myself right or wrong.

In the event *Comeback* was nominated for the prestigious Prix Italia, and I was offered several further film projects to direct. I regret now that I didn't take up some of these offers, but at the time I felt I had proved my point that directing was not rocket science. However, I had also proved the truth of Billy Wilder's remark that the problem with making movies was that ninety per-cent of your time was spent making the deal, and only ten percent making the movie. Such a division of labour did not appeal to me. All the same, I have continued to direct here and there on stage, and have always found the experience exhilarating.

In 1988 I once again took time off from Hollywood to write two films in Europe. The first was *Taffin*, a low-budget thriller shot in Ireland and starring Pierce Brosnan. The second, *The French Revolution*, was at the time the most expensive picture ever made in Europe. It was released in two parts of three hours each, with an international cast that included Peter Ustinov, Klaus Maria

Brandauer, Sam Neill, Claudia Cardinale, Christopher Lee and Jane Seymour.

A year or two later I took more time out to write a mini-series about the espionage and deception behind the 1944 D-Day landings in Normandy. Based on a book by Larry Collins, variously entitled *Fortitude* or *Fall From Grace* in different territories, it had begun as a French production by TF1, the country's largest television network. Because of the considerable budget and the international nature of the subject, they were looking for an American partner, either a network or a major studio, which was their main reason for approaching me as someone who was "known over there".

Pascale Breugnot was an inventive and very successful television producer in France. Tall and striking, with wiry red hair and an eye-wateringly colourful wardrobe, she was a single mother with a young daughter and a bulldog named Ulysses. I have never worked with a better producer, or even one half as good. The culture clash between her and Hollywood was awesome to observe.

As head of drama for TF1, Pascale was accustomed to having control of all elements of her productions from script to budget and casting. She had never heard of "development" in the Hollywood sense of the term, and so was quite unprepared for what she met when she went over there.

She had asked two young and inexperienced French producers, who were struggling to break into Hollywood, to look around for possible co-production partners. Obviously seeing this as a great opportunity, and armed with an impressive calling card from France's biggest network, they had set up meetings with a long list of independent production companies and studio executives. By the time Pascale, her assistant and I stepped off the plane in Los Angeles, she already had more partners than she knew what to do with. Nevertheless, she optimistically assumed that this would simply make raising the finance easier than if she was on her own, and expected to start moving into production right away.

Instead she found herself deluged in meeting after meeting with stacks of notes and memos about how this or that part of the script should be re-written and the whole story re-thought from the ground up. The fact that she had a deadline to meet if she was going to get the show on the air in time for the fiftieth anniversary of D-Day was dismissed as irrelevant. As one development executive I knew quite well, and had always thought a fool, said to me, "How does she think she can go into production before she's heard what everybody has to say?"

Pascale had in fact heard what everybody had to say, and was baffled by it. "Why do these people think they know something we don't?" she asked me. "We've got a script that's ready to go, and everybody's coming up with mad ideas to change it that don't make any sense. It's crazy."

I explained that this was how "development" worked. All "these people" were paid fat salaries to raise objections to anything that was put in front of them. Give them apples, they'll want oranges. Offer them wine, they'll want beer – or, more likely, mineral water. "They don't give a damn whether your show gets made or not," I told her. "Their worst nightmare is it gets made, and it's a flop, and they wind up carrying the can for not having stopped it. So unless something happens to get them out of your way, your project is going straight into Development Hell and will never be heard of again."

She thought a moment. "Unless something such as what happens?"

"Such as a major director or a major star gets involved and says 'This is something I want to do. Now everybody get out of my face'."

She nodded, understanding. "But we haven't got either of those."
"No."

I didn't add, "Alternatively, a producer with enough balls could just kick them all out of the door and go it alone." I didn't have to, because she had already seen that for herself.

The next day she fired all her partners, bringing a bunch of lawsuits down on her head claiming breach of contract and breach of just about everything you could think of except possibly marriage, and even that wouldn't have surprised me. But Pascale ploughed on, doggedly selling syndication rights to individual broadcasting stations all across the United States. She was doing amazingly well but still had some way to go, when something little short of a miracle happened.

As I was told it later, the head of one of these stations read the script and said, "Sagansky ought to see this."

Jeff Sagansky was at the time head of CBS, one of the big three American networks, and the local station head was a friend of his. With Pascale's permission he gave the script to Sagansky, who read it over the weekend and said, "We should be making this."

In one move we had leapfrogged all obstacles and achieved everything that the intermediaries, ten-percenters and generally irrelevant hangers-on had failed to deliver. The show was in production within weeks. Among the cast were Tara Fitzgerald, James Fox, and my old friend Michael York. At four hours in length, it went out over two nights in the States and most countries in Europe to coincide with the fiftieth anniversary of D-Day. It was universally well received.

And it was the last time Pascale Breugnot worked in Hollywood.

CHAPTER 46

In a city built on sand, rumour is the first thing to take root. I triggered an unexpected proof of this in the mid-eighties.

The oft-repeated mantra that in Beverly Hills death is optional is, of course, an exaggeration. Nevertheless, there is a remarkable level of denial about its inevitability. People convince themselves that if they stay young they cannot die; their weapons for doing so are diet, exercise and plastic surgery.

They are obsessed with their health, living in fear of germs, of secondary smoke, of hidden toxins and whatever new threat may have been discovered since last week. They struggle to convince themselves that if they're careful enough about avoiding poisons and bad karma, they will live, if not forever, at least for a very long time. (Or, as the joke goes, it will just seem long.)

Having listened once too often to someone droning on about their new macrobiotic regime or some alarming-sounding irrigation process, I formulated a response designed to liven up the conversation a little.

"How interesting," was my initial comment, followed by, "So tell me, what do you think about this new ruling by the Surgeon General's office?"

"What ruling is that?"

"The one about cats and dogs – you know?"

"Cats and dogs? I don't believe I do."

"In restaurant kitchens."

"No, I haven't heard this."

"Well, it seems that everyone out here has been living such sanitised and antiseptic lives for so long now that they're losing all natural resistance to commonplace trivial infections."

"Really?"

"Really. So they're passing a law that makes it compulsory for every restaurant in California to have a cat and a dog... well, maybe more than one of each depending on the number of covers they serve... but at least one cat and one dog at total liberty in their kitchen night and day, peeing on the floor, taking a crap wherever they like, sticking their nose into anything they fancy and generally having the run of the place."

"What...?!"

"The idea is to restore a natural immunity to these odd diseases people are starting to catch."

"Where did you hear this?"

"I read it somewhere. Medical section of some magazine."

By this time, more often than not, the jaw of the person I was talking to would be near the floor unless of course they'd seen through the hoax already. A surprising number didn't. I left them shaking their heads and coming to terms with this unthinkably radical idea.

It took less than two weeks for the story to get back to me. Like Chinese whispers, it had gone from person to person, its origins increasingly obscured, until it had become a free-floating piece of information that people found oddly credible.

Of course it could easily have been checked out. But even if it were proved that no such announcement had ever emerged from the Surgeon General's office, it still felt like something that *might* have been true, or it might even *come* true. Or maybe it was in some secret planning stage, but word had leaked out prematurely.

Ultimately, the mere fact that the story was in circulation now meant that, unlikely as it may sound, there must be some truth to it. No smoke without fire, after all.

·

Reflecting this obsession with their physical well-being was an equal concern for their mental health. Perhaps it shouldn't have, but it came as a surprise to me to discover, little by little, that everyone I met in Hollywood, almost without exception, was in therapy. They didn't normally volunteer the information, but if you asked them they would readily admit to being in anything from full-blown analysis to, "Well, I see somebody from time to time."

So universal was the practice that I wondered vaguely whether I should try it myself in a "keep up with the crowd" kind of way. The main thing that put me off the idea was seeing how little good it seemed to be doing them. One evening I was invited to a barbecue at the Malibu beach house of a successful producer I shall call Joanne. It was a pretty high-achieving group of people: a well-known director, a couple of studio executives, a cardiologist, a Beverly Hills dermatologist (they're the real Hollywood royalty), and a couple of showbiz lawyers. As the evening wore pleasantly on and drink was consumed and a joint or two passed around, I became aware of a curious groundswell of frustration and puzzlement amongst them. It took only a few questions to bring their common problem into the open. They didn't understand why, despite their successful careers and comfortable circumstances, they weren't happy.

What, I inquired, did they mean by happiness?

Their answers were fragmented, but what they were trying to say soon became clear. To them, happiness was something they had believed would automatically accompany the kind of lives they had all achieved. Because it hadn't, they felt themselves to be

339

in some way at fault. What were they doing wrong? Why could they not reach the ultimate and simple human goal of happiness?

That was, essentially, what they were all seeing their different shrinks about, whether on a couch, in "group", or merely in some sort of "loose therapy" which I never quite got a clear definition of.

As someone with no qualifications in the field beyond a layman's grasp of psychoanalytic theory, I quickly found myself holding forth on the subject with some authority. First of all, I reminded them of Freud's remark that psychoanalysis claimed only to reduce neurotic misery to common unhappiness. It was not designed to produce a state of mind called "happiness", and made no promise of doing so.

This I thought would have been made clear to them by their therapists, but apparently not. So, accepting another glass of wine and a toke from a fresh joint, I expanded on the subject.

Happiness as a state of mind? A permanent state of mind? That could only be, I ventured to suggest, an American idea since "the pursuit of happiness" was enshrined in its constitution. We Europeans, on the other hand, regarded happiness as a pleasurable and often surprising encounter to be enjoyed while it lasted but not hankered after when it had passed. It was, I suggested, a little like being tickled. Or having a cathartic sneezing fit. Or an orgasm. It could be repeated, but not grasped and wrapped around oneself like a warm blanket to keep one in a state of permanent contentment.

They all got the idea with no difficulty. The only amazing thing was they hadn't got it before. It should, I would have thought, have formed a central part of all their various therapies. Unless, of course, their therapists feared that admitting the impossibility of achieving a state of permanent happiness might pose a threat to their income stream. But perish such a cynical thought.

Over several years, whenever I ran into Joanne or any of the group from that night, they all said how well they remembered our conversation and how it had changed their thinking for the better. I was, I told myself, in the wrong business. Maybe I should hang up a "loose therapy" shingle myself and start doling out advice professionally.

But no, silly idea. One tended to get silly ideas in Hollywood. I made myself there and then a solemn promise and stuck to it. If ever I heard a little voice in my head saying "Maybe I should get therapy", I would, instantly and without hesitation, head for the airport (LAX).

"The road to LAX," Orson once said, "is paved with good intentions."

Sadly, he later admitted, he didn't get out when he should have. Not many people do. But everyone thinks about it.

"I thank this town for giving me enough money to leave it," said one producer I knew after a surprise hit which bought him a huge ranch up in Washington State where he went to live with his horses.

Everyone has their own favourite line to describe how they feel about Hollywood. One of the first I heard when I arrived was, "This is a place where you fall asleep by the pool with a drink at your elbow, and wake up twenty years later."

I created a couple of lines of my own in my story *Hollywood Lies* that I put into the mouths of grizzled old professionals giving advice to some new recruit. One was: "In this town you have to consider yourself lucky to be working with thieves and liars, because the alternative is idiots."

Another, slightly more generous and even a touch sentimental, was: "Kid, this is a phoney business. The stars' teeth, tits and hair are phoney. The sets are phoney. The stories are phoney. The happy endings are double-phoney. But let me tell you one thing that you have to understand if you're going to succeed in this business: you can't fake phoney."

When I did a HARDtalk interview with Tim Sebastian for BBC television, he used that last quote in his introduction, though leaving out the word "tits" so as to avoid, I suppose, offending viewers of a sensitive nature.

I've never met anyone who worked in Hollywood who didn't have a love-hate relationship with the place. The love part is easy to understand: we all love movies. The hate part comes from the obstacles and frustrations we encounter when trying to make them.

But what is it people want from Hollywood? Fame? Fortune?

As Orson again said, nobody goes into the movie business just to get rich. There are easier ways of making money.

One leading agent I knew said it was all about cachet. "It's not about money, it's about class. It's working with the right people, making the right kind of movies. That's what it's all about in Hollywood."

I supposed he knew what he was talking about in terms of "class" and "cachet". After all, his star client was Liberace.

CHAPTER 47

I could tell he'd been brooding over something for a while, until eventually he said, "There's something I don't understand."

"What's that, Dad?"

"If it only takes me a couple of hours to watch one of these films of yours, how come it takes you so damn long to write 'em?"

I hadn't been ready for that, and wasn't sure I had an answer.

"That's a good question, Dad. There's probably more work goes into it than you think."

He grunted, unimpressed. This new-found interest in the details of my profession had come about because of something that had happened the previous night. Laurence and I had returned from Hollywood a few days earlier. She had gone to see her parents in Lausanne, where her father was recovering from a serious operation, and I had taken the train up north. Mum had by then, early 1987, been in a home for nearly ten years and was suffering from dementia. She didn't know me when I visited; she had informed one of her fellow residents the day before that I was "the clergyman".

I was staying with Dad for a few days in the bungalow he had moved into in Leyland, part of a sheltered housing scheme. He was confined to a wheelchair having lost his right leg below the knee due to circulatory problems. I had given Dad's phone number to my agent in Hollywood because there was a deal in the wind that was likely to turn into a firm offer very soon. The phone call had come around seven in the evening, eleven in the morning in Hollywood. Dad was trying to concentrate on the television news – until he heard me talking figures, whereupon he switched the sound off and gave my conversation his full attention.

As is always the case, deals of the kind I was engaged in start with an offer to the writer's agent, which is then discussed between agent and writer, and a counter-offer is made. Then, after a further short negotiation, terms are agreed. What had hit Dad like a lightning bolt was the sum of money he heard me turning down before hanging up.

"You turned down how much?" he exclaimed in disbelief. "You're mad!"

"It's all right," I assured him, "they'll be calling back with a better offer."

There were four more calls in the course of the evening, three involving increased sums of money, and the fourth clarifying my position on profits in the event that there ever were any. I was beginning to worry about Dad's health as this went on: the suspense was killing him, but he made it to the end.

"By the left," he said when it was all over, "is that what you always get paid?"

"Sometimes more," I said, "sometimes less."

"And how many of them d'you write every year?"

"It depends. Two, maybe three."

"By 'eck!"

Then, after a few moments' reflection, he realised there was something wrong with that statement.

"Hang on a minute, I've never heard about you making three films a year."

"Oh, I don't."

"Then what d'you mean saying you write three?"

"I write them, but they don't always make them."

This brought a puzzled frown. "But they pay you for 'em?"

"Oh, yes, they pay me."

He took a few more moments to absorb the implications of this. "You mean they just chuck all that money away?"

"You could say that, yes. They chuck it away."

This was beyond his comprehension. "They must be bloody mad."

"You know what, I rather agree with you."

Another silence followed while he turned the matter over in his mind, feeling the need to say something more but not sure what. Finally he took me by surprise.

"You've done well."

It was a grudging compliment, but a compliment all the same. I felt myself surprisingly touched that he had felt the urge to pay it. But we didn't say any more. And I didn't tell him I was planning to quit. He would not have understood the frustration of seeing your work trashed by executive change-overs, directorial whims, producers' weakness, and sometimes just plain bad luck. It wouldn't have meant anything compared to the money he had just learnt I was making. He wouldn't have understood that if you submit to all of it long enough, just for the money, it will kill you.

So I didn't tell him I was already working on a novel that I hoped would be my lifeboat out of Hollywood, because I knew by then I needed one. I could feel the burnout beginning, and didn't want to wind up writing "this-piece-a-shitfer" like some of those old hands I'd met who'd never got out. I could not imagine a fate worse than that.

Dad didn't live to see my first book published a year or so later, and Mum of course never knew anything about it. It was called *The Man Who Turned into Himself.*

My hope was that, perhaps finally, I was beginning to do just that.

END